ISSUES IN INSTRUCTIONAL SYSTEMS DEVELOPMENT

THE EDUCATIONAL TECHNOLOGY SERIES

Edited by

Harold F. O'Neil, Jr.

U.S. Army Research Institute for
the Behavioral and Social Sciences
Alexandria, Virginia

Harold F. O'Neil, Jr. (Ed.) Learning Strategies

Harold F. O'Neil, Jr. (Ed.) Issues in Instructional Systems Development

Harold F. O'Neil, Jr. (Ed.) Procedures for Instructional Systems Development

In preparation

Harold O'Neil, Jr. and Charles D. Spielberger (Eds.) Cognitive and Affective Learning Strategies

ISSUES IN INSTRUCTIONAL SYSTEMS DEVELOPMENT

Edited by

HAROLD F. O'NEIL, JR.

U.S. Army Research Institute
for the Behavioral and Social Sciences
Alexandria, Virginia

ACADEMIC PRESS   New York   San Francisco   London   1979

A Subsidiary of Harcourt Brace Jovanovich, Publishers

ACADEMIC PRESS, INC.
111 Fifth Avenue, New York, New York 10003

United Kingdom Edition published by
ACADEMIC PRESS, INC. (LONDON) LTD.
24/28 Oval Road, London NW1 7DX

Library of Congress Cataloging in Publication Data
Main entry under title:

Issues in instructional systems development.

(The Educational Technology series)

    Includes bibliographies.
    1. Data processing——Education. 2. System analy—
sis. I. O'Neil, Harold F. , Date
LB2846.I87   370'.2'854   78—20048
ISBN 0—12—526640—5

PRINTED IN THE UNITED STATES OF AMERICA

79 80 81 82   9 8 7 6 5 4 3 2 1

Contents

7 Production of Computer-Based Instructional Materials   133

R. A. AVNER

8 Implementation Issues in Instructional Systems Development: Three Case Studies   181

ROBERT K. BRANSON

List of Contributors

Numbers in parentheses indicate the pages on which the authors' contributions begin.

R. A. AVNER (133), Computer-Based Education Research Laboratory, University of Illinois at Urbana-Champaign, Urbana, Illinois 61801

JOHN W. BRACKETT (101), SofTech, Inc., 460 Totten Pond Road, Waltham, Massachusetts 02154

ROBERT K. BRANSON (181), Center for Educational Technology, Florida State University, Tallahassee, Florida 32306

T. E. COTTERMAN (89), Advanced Systems Division, Air Force Human Resources Laboratory, Wright-Patterson Air Force Base, Dayton, Ohio 45433

WILLIAM P. HARRIS (41), Lincoln Laboratory, Massachusetts Institute of Technology, Lexington, Massachusetts 02173

ROBERT S. LOGAN (1), Telemedia Inc., 310 South Michigan Avenue, Chicago, Illinois 60604

A. F. O'NEAL (69), Courseware, Inc., 10075 Carroll Canyon Road, San Diego, California 92131

H. L. O'NEAL (69), Courseware, Inc., 10075 Carroll Canyon Road, San Diego, California 92131

SUSAN S. TAYLOR (21), Control Data Education Company, Box O, Minneapolis, Minnesota 55440

Preface[1]

A program of research in instructional systems development was initiated by the Defense Advanced Research Projects Agency (DARPA) in 1976.[2] The goal of the program was to develop and evaluate an integrated system to reduce the time and cost to produce high-quality instructional materials. This book records the program's progress to date and suggests further avenues for research.

The need for this program was identified in a field test of a computer-based training system. It was difficult to bring authors who use this system to a level of competence needed to produce good curriculum materials in a reasonable time at an acceptable cost. Similar difficulties have been noted for other systems employing individualized instruction. This problem is especially acute in the Department of Defense because of the high turnover of authoring and instructor personnel.

As in other emerging fields, the instructional systems development literature reveals little agreement on basic terms. However, for the purpose of this book we have adopted an instructional systems development model. This model consists of five phases: analysis, design, development, implementation, and control. Detail on these phases can be found in Chapter 1. In our terminology, an author is an individual who participates in these phases. This book suggests ways to accomplish these phases. However, there exist many research and development issues that must be resolved before we know enough to write procedural guidelines. Thus, the chapters in this book vary both with respect to the number of phases

[1] The views and conclusions contained in this preface and the rest of the volume are those of the respective authors and should not be interpreted as necessarily representing the official policies, either expressed or implied, by the Defense Advanced Research Projects Agency, the U.S. Army Research Institute for the Behavioral and Social Sciences, or the U.S. government.

[2] The editor was a program manager at DARPA from 1975 to 1978.

in the instructional systems development model, the level of detail on procedural aspects, and environments for which they are most appropriate.

In order to provide an intellectual foundation for the instructional systems development program, several critical issues were identified and, where appropriate, research and development was initiated. Initially, a state-of-the-art assessment was commissioned (Chapter 1). Since instructional development is either predominantly school oriented (Chapter 2) or on-the-job oriented (Chapter 3), several complete systems designed to teach instructional systems development were either documented or developed. Then, in order to provide alternative intellectual resources for authors, several support facilities were identified or designed: a management system (Chapter 4); a resource to quickly locate evaluative information on existing research on instructional systems development (Chapter 5); and, finally, a system to identify existing curriculum material (Chapter 6). Finally, several issues that would impact on any subsequent research and development were identified. These were length of time required to produce instructional materials (Chapter 7) and issues in implementation (Chapter 8).

This book summarizes our research to date and presents our collective ideas of where such research should be directed. It is a preliminary progress report on approaches we have developed and a means of sharing ideas concerning ways of accomplishing our goals. We feel that our intellectual community consists of advanced students and researchers in the fields of educational technology, curriculum and instruction, educational psychology, teacher education, and, to some extent, computer science. In addition to our colleagues in these disciplines, we feel that our work will be of interest and use to developers of instructional systems in education, industry, and the military.

This book could not have come into existence without the help and encouragement of many people. In particular, the intellectual and administrative support of Robert Young and Dawn Parnell formerly of the Defense Advanced Research Projects Agency; Robert Seidel, Harold Wagner, and Carol Hargan of the Human Resources Research Organization; and Joseph Zeidner of the U.S. Army Research Institute for the Behavioral and Social Sciences. Finally, I acknowledge my appreciation for the help and moral support I have received from the staff of Academic Press.

Harold F. O'Neil, Jr.

1

A State-of-the-Art Assessment of Instructional Systems Development[1]

ROBERT S. LOGAN

Instructional systems development is defined as a general systems approach with multiple components called phases that, operating among a certain set of constraints, are used to produce an instructional system. The phases are sequential sets of activities called *analysis, design, development, implementation,* and *control.* Thus, the definition follows quite closely the model described in Interservice Procedures for Instructional Systems Development (TRADOC, 1975), which is discussed in several chapters of this book.

In addition to a brief discussion of the systems approach and a fuller discussion of interservice procedures, this chapter considers two questions. First, what tools and procedures are available that facilitate application of instructional systems development? Second, are these tools and procedures indeed useful for the analysis, design, development, implementation, and/or control of instructional materials?

The first question is considered from a more or less objective base derived from an earlier study of authoring tools and procedures (Logan, 1977), now updated. Considerations relating to the second question are admittedly subjective. I have developed and discussed instructional materials for both technical training and language training in civilian and military environments and in sophisticated

[1] Preparation of this paper was supported in part by the Defense Advanced Research Projects Agency under Contract Number MDA 903-76-C-C086 under terms of ARPA Order 3976. Views and conclusions contained in this document are those of the author and should not be interpreted as necessarily representing the official policies, either expressed or implied, of the Defense Advanced Research Projects Agency or of the U.S. government.

Western and developing Eastern cultures; and all the activity has driven me to one very simple point of view: Instructional systems development is a logic set for talking to one another in order to produce a package of learning whose beauty lies in the eye of the beholder.

INSTRUCTIONAL SYSTEMS DEVELOPMENT

The Systems Approach

The ideal of analysis is not new or complex. A problem is examined and criteria for choosing a solution are considered. Cost, feasibility, and effectiveness of possible solutions are weighed. Better alternatives for those obviously wrong are created and examined again. Before Caesar stepped from the muddy north bank of the Rubicon, he surely did such an analysis with infinite care.

During World War II, analysis was codified into a rather formal structure called *operations analysis.* Then as now the quintessential element of analysis was based on subjectivity: We want to know what the expert thinks. The difference between then and now is that now analysis is viewed as an alternative, self-correcting process using explicit models to create precise structures and terminology that form communication links between decision makers. That is, a model provides a context that is both concrete and constant.

Solutions are chosen through either optimization or insensitivity. Optimal solutions are selected according to a fixed set of criteria; we say something is best because it falls on one absolute, favored side of the scale. Insensitive solutions are fuzzy. They may not be clearly the best solutions but they will "work under many different contingencies and even give some sort of reasonably satisfactory performance under a major misestimate of the future [Quade & Boucher, 1975, p. 15]."

The idea of optimal versus insensitive solutions has some impact on the perceived usefulness of authoring tools and procedures. This impact is considered in the second section of this chapter. Briefly, consider two competing authoring tools that may be employed to resolve certain authoring difficulties. One tool may be shown through sophisticated experimental design and statistical computation to be clearly better than the other tool and yet may not be accepted by management because of bad reputation, uncertain hardware support, or lack of time for the proper teaching and maintenance of it. The other tool, albeit statistically less effective, may be adopted because it is readily available or because some key management person *thinks* it is better. The point is this: An adopted tool or procedure has at least a chance of being useful, whereas one that is rejected has no chance of being useful — no matter how effective it is statistically or empirically. The tools and procedures represent an insensitive solution that considers situational and managemental factors in addition to empirical data.

Differences between operations analysis and the systems approach — including its latest evolution, instructional systems development — are mostly matters of terminology and emphasis. Principles, general considerations, and the sequence of process are the same. Whether the system being developed is concerned with instruction, transportation, or waste management has little effect upon the general application of the systems approach to that system. That is, systems analysis approaches an instructional system in the same way it approaches any other system. Those readers who desire more detail on the systems approach should read the classic book by Churchman (1968) and then return to the next section of this review. Those of you familiar with the systems approach should continue with the next section of this review. (These simple directions are called *branching,* an instructional technique used to avoid giving information already known, to reinforce something newly learned, or to correct errors as they occur.)

Interservice Procedures for Instructional Systems Development

All ISD models organize instructional development activities into sequential steps with identifiable phases (Baker, 1970; Butler, 1972; TRADOC, 1975; Wong & Raulerson, 1974). This review is structured around Interservice Procedures for Instructional Systems Development (IPISD), a model chosen because it is supported by a validated workshop and is accepted throughout much of the training community (TRADOC, 1975). It provides an accepted communications link, a concrete and constant context through which decision makers can understand one another.

In the following summary of the steps and phases of IPISD, refer to Figure 1.1 as necessary for perspective and guidance.

Phase I: Analysis

Analyses in this phase of IPISD are based on job information. After a job is analyzed, job tasks are divided into two categories. One category contains tasks not selected for instruction. The other category contains tasks selected for instruction that are called *training requirements.* Performance standards for the training requirements are determined by interview or observation and are verified by a subject matter expert (SME). We want to get expert judgment in here early.

In existing courses of instruction, performance standards may exist prior to analysis. For example, in existing Air Force technical training courses, performance standards are found in documents known as Specialty Training Standards (STS) or Course Training Standards (CTS).

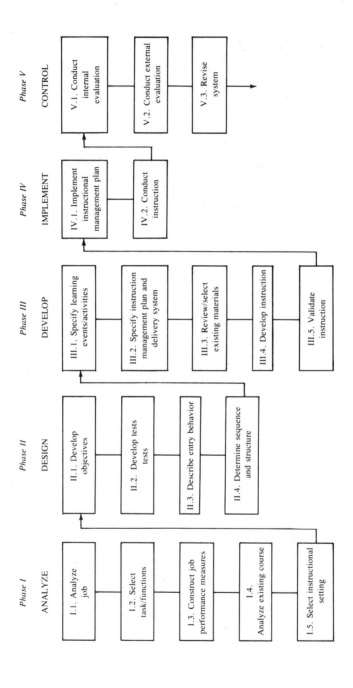

Figure 1.1 Interservice procedures for instructional systems development model.

4

Next, existing course documentation is analyzed to determine whether some of the course was developed originally according to ISD procedures and to define the course more thoroughly. Of the tasks to be trained, we have to know to what level and depth similar tasks are being trained and how the existing training was documented as it was developed.

The training requirements are then analyzed, and the instructional setting most suitable for each requirement is selected. Most instructional development efforts build on prior existence. New or modified instruction seldom requires that existing settings be razed so a new environment can be built. This means that most training settings for new instruction are either used as is or adapted in a minor way, especially when the training is non-computer-based.

Phase II: Design

In the design phase of IPISD, training requirements are converted into terminal learning objectives. In essence, the job situation is transformed into a valid learning situation without, perhaps, the full resources or pressures of the job.

Each terminal learning objective is further analyzed into learning objectives and enabling steps. These less comprehensive objectives are needed by the student to master performance required on larger tasks by the terminal learning objectives. Instead of addressing a complete task, an enabling step may speak to a task element, which is one component action of a complex task.

The objectives form the basis for developing criterion-referenced tests that measure the performance called for in the learning objectives. Criterion-referenced means that, to pass, a student must meet an objective standard; passing or failing doesn't depend on how other classmates are doing. Criterion-referenced tests usually measure only learning objectives. A terminal learning objective may require a resource unavailable in the testing situation, such as expensive pieces of complex electronic gear. An enabling objective may be a task so simple that it requires no instruction or measurement. Criterion-referenced tests normally measure what is in between those two things.

The design phase includes two other activities. First, a sample of students is tested to see whether their entry behaviors and the learning analysis of required skills and behaviors for job performance match. Entry behaviors are the skills and knowledges a student has before the instruction begins. Since objectives and tests were based on a learning analysis, we want to be sure that they guide and measure the learning of tasks that the student did not know before instruction began.

Second, objectives are sequenced to ensure maximum learning. They can be sequenced by three primary methods. A *job-performance order* arranges objectives in the same sequence in which tasks and task elements are performed on the job. This order is suitable especially for teaching composed of serial, fixed steps.

A *psychological order* seeks to cause learning from the simple to the complex, the known to the unknown, the concrete to the abstract. This order is effective particularly for teaching motor skills. For example, students can be taught to use basic tools on simple tasks before learning to perform complex maintenance tasks with sophisticated equipment.

Sometimes, on particular tasks, neither order works. Some tasks simply do not lend themselves to either sequence. In those cases tasks can be arranged in a logical order such as the whole–part–whole concept. For example, to teach carburetor assembly, it may be best first to demonstrate the entire assembly procedure, then break it into a step-by-step demonstration with step-by-step participation from students, and finally combine all task elements in a complete run-through of the assembly procedure.

Tasks too long to teach as one unit can be divided into several units. But the relationship of each task to the whole task should be stressed, and final practice over the whole task should be given. If a task is broken up, a little effectiveness is lost. If a task is practiced as a whole, the effectiveness is regained.

Phase III: Development

The first step in development is to classify learning objectives into categories of learning. The categories are called *taxonomies.* According to a psychologist's joke, the only things you cannot escape are death and taxonomies. It contains a certain amount of truth. The taxonomies of Bloom (1976) and Gagné (1977) are commonly accepted in instructional design and development.

The second step in this phase is selection of the instructional media and delivery system. This is done by a media selection process that may consider learning categories and guidelines, media characteristics, training setting criteria, and costs. Braby, Henry, Parrish, and Swope (1975) developed a good media selection model for Navy training that may be applied to civilian environments as well. Media and delivery systems are usually known factors. Media almost always include printed and audiovisual material such as programmed tests and slide–tape or tape–filmstrip programs. Delivery systems include group-paced or self-paced instruction. If the instructional system has large numbers of students entering and graduating, computer-based instruction may be needed.

The third step in the development phase is to develop an instructional management plant that allocates and manages all resources required to conduct instruction. Resources are defined very broadly. Instructors, students, and administrative personnel are resources. So are courseware and hardware. So is "other," which may be defined as "everything but."

The final steps in this phase are development and validation of instructional materials. Materials developed in the media specified in the instructional management plan are validated in one or more tryouts. This means that students complete the lessons and/or tests, which, on the basis of subsequent data, are revised for better student performance. Validation data indicate what lessons or tests should be revised, what kinds of revision are needed, where administrative bugs are, and "other" problems.

Validation data are obtained from three sources: criterion-referenced lesson tests, student questionnaires, and student interviews.

Criterion-referenced tests and lessons are based on learning objectives. Thus, they should instruct and measure the same information. Therefore, any lesson-unique problems should show up in the lessons or tests.

Student questionnaires are written measures designed to gather student attitudes toward instruction. The questionnaires indicate whether students feel the lessons are boring, too detailed, unorganized, and so forth.

Written questionnaires do have drawbacks, however. They are a closed loop: What is asked is what is answered. Some students can *speak* attitudes better than they can write them down. For these reasons, student interviews may be conducted to obtain similar information obtained by questionnaires.

Phase IV: Implementation

The analysis, design, and development phases of ISD lead to implementation. It has only two steps: training and conducting instruction. In this first step, key personnel should be subject matter experts who participated in the instructional development effort or instructors who conducted validation tryouts. They require less training than someone totally unfamiliar with the instruction.

Also, the instructional staff must be trained to conduct the actual instruction in the classroom or learning center and to collect evaluation data on all instructional components.

The evaluation data collected here differ from validation data. Data collected during implementation emphasize system operation rather than only instructional material effectiveness. Although some data collected during implementation are used to revise lessons or tests, they are collected as part of the process rather than as its objective. Implementation is also more cold-blooded than validation. In validation, shortcomings are identified so they can be corrected. In implementation, shortcomings are identified so they can be criticized – and then corrected.

The second step in the phase is to conduct instruction. It requires an act of faith. We have to let the instructional product go and see what happens. Since it did not happen without some planning and thought and tryout, we should be somewhat confident about its outcome.

Phase V: Control

The control phase is an orchestration of prior agreements and activities from the previous four phases. It is a most significant phase and is synonymous with evaluation.

Two evaluations are carried out during control. *Internal evaluation* assesses student performance **in the course.** *External evaluation* determines how course graduates perform **on the job.** Internal evaluation intends to identify specific instances of deficient or irrelevant instruction. External evaluation intends to determine the overall effectiveness of instruction. External evaluation sometimes is called *field evaluation.*

Control of a system is so important that evaluation should be administered by personnel who are neither the instructional developers nor the managers. This is called third-party evaluation. It is intended to minimize the influence of interested, biased parties.

Authoring Aids

Every instructional systems development activity has the same ultimate goal: to produce effective instruction. The instruction, whether group-paced or self-paced, is transmitted through materials developed by an authoring process. Therefore, the authoring process is of paramount importance in producing effective instruction.

Although authoring is commonly thought of as an intuition-based activity (Kandaswamy, Stolovitch, & Thiagarajan, 1976) that, by choice, is form-fitted to every instructional effort (Demerath & Daniels, 1973), it is in fact a subsystem of an instructional system and should be approached like any other system. Authoring has an input (job task information), and output (finished instructional materials), a synthesis technique (creative writing, coffee making, pencil chewing), and a means of obtaining feedback on the process (validation tryouts and field tests).

In the context of instructional systems development, authoring may be defined more fully as

> a sequence of activities that obtains supportive information from analyses of jobs, tasks, incoming students, and existing courses and course materials; converts that information into instructional packages of a proper sequence, structure, and format that enables learning to occur; revises those packages during preliminary and large-scale tryouts on the basis of feedback from students, instructors, and publishes those revised packages as finished products by which the largest number of students achieve the greatest number of objectives in the shortest possible time [Logan, 1976, pp. 24–25].

Although parts of the definition may be subject to argument, four processes are inherent in the authoring activity: gathering, conversion, revision, and publication of information. The processes need not be form-fitted to every instructional effort because authoring tools and procedures are available to aid the proper execution of each process.

Authoring tools are defined as evaluated, self-contained products in suitable formats that are applied to the analysis, design, development, implementation, or control of one or more steps of a procedure. Authoring procedures are defined as one or more steps that operationally define one component of instructional systems development; for *component,* you may read *phase.*

Authoring tools and procedures are noted below. They are grouped by numbered steps in accordance with the Interservice Procedures model discussed earlier. For each numbered step, several tools and procedures, which are available from public sources, are discussed. The reader is referred to the original source for more detail, and to other chapters in this book for additional tools and procedures. This review is an updated version of an earlier study (Logan, 1977). The absence of discussion of tools for a particular step indicates that they do not exist in terms of the concept defined above.

I.1 Analyze Job

In the early 1960s, the Air Force initiated an occupational analysis program that led to the development of an effective tool for computer-based job analysis. The Comprehensive Occupational Data Analysis Programs (CODAP) provide individual or group descriptions that specify the percentage of time spent on each job task, describe an actual job at different task performance levels such as apprentice or officer, derive individual and group job differences, and identify specific types of jobs as they exist or **should** exist within a given specialty. Detailed descriptions of procedures, applications, and programming notes are given by Archer (1966); Morsch and Archer (1967); Christal (1972); Weissmuller, Barton, and Rogers (1974a, 1974b); Stacey, Weissmuller, Barton, and Rogers (1974); Mayo, Nance, and Shiegekawa (1975); Stacey and Hazel (1975); and Christal and Weissmuller (1975).

For those doing job analysis manually, Foley (1975) discusses the use of standardized worksheets and illustrates several forms.

Complete occupational and task inventories are collected by the Task Inventory Exchange (TIE, 1975), which has published three task inventories to date.

I.2. Select Task/Functions

McKnight and Adams (1970) report a procedure using a panel of experts to select critical behaviors for driver education training from a pool of 1000 relevant behaviors.

The wording of the standard task statement has been modified by a phrase that aids the selection of tasks for teaching the job of physician's assistant and, presumably, other jobs as well (Powers, 1971). The phrase, *in order to,* was used to indicate an intended outcome of a task and to group students according to required competence levels.

Cline (1973) has developed a multivariate statistical model to predetermine preferable aircraft assignments for Air Force pilots.

I.3. Construct Job Performance Measures

Gael (1974) describes the design and selection of instruments to measure aptitudes and proficiencies for five Bell System jobs. The instruments use both knowledge and performance measures as well as simulation.

I.4. Analyze Existing Course

Lewis, Willow, Brock, Lonigro, Eschenbrenner, and Hanson (1974) analyzed an Air Force Precision Measuring Equipment (PME) course in order to convert it from conventional instruction to self-paced, individualized instruction. The analysis consisted of (a) selecting segments for individualization; (b) analyzing course documentation; (c) choosing the target population; and (d) examining the training environment.

Formal analysis of an existing Air Force course is documented in the Specialty Training Standard (STS), Plan of Instruction (POI), and Course Chart for *Inventory Management Specialist (645X0)* (1975) and *Material Facilities Specialist (647X0)* (1973, 1974). The documents provide codes for various performance levels required at training completion and divide instruction into sequential segments called blocks of instruction. Both cognitive and psychomotor performance levels are identified.

II.1. Develop Objectives

A programmed workbook introduces behavioral objectives and a Navy handbook that teaches the writing of behavioral objectives (Bureau of Naval Personnel, 1968). It is divided into three modules. Module 1 discusses the general concept of behavioral objectives, Module 2 introduces the *Navy's Handbook for Writing Objectives,* and Module 3 provides student exercises for using the handbook and includes testing instruments.

A *Behavior Objectives Training Package* (ESCOE, 1971) serves as a user's guide to writing and implementing behavioral objectives. It also provides an overview of the Evaluation Service Center for Occupational Education, a clearinghouse for behavioral objectives from various institutions.

Dillman (1971) discusses the writing of effective behavioral objectives in a programmed-text format with self-reviews in each section. It is an exceptionally intelligent book.

Programmed texts by Rose, Balasek, Kelleher, Lutz, and Nelken (1972a, 1972b) are designed to help teachers learn how to write performance objectives. An instructor's manual accompanies the programmed text and provides management procedures for inservice training.

Barton (1973) presents a booklet that teaches the recognition and writing of technically correct performance objectives. Validated over a 2-year period, the booklet is in programmed-text format with numerous self-checks.

A compact, multicolor reference wall chart (INSGROUP, 1975) shows the structure of measurable objectives, discusses three applications for them, and presents several learning taxonomies. Also on the chart are addresses where collections of objectives may be obtained.

II.2. Develop Tests

Brown, Brooks, Cocks, and Kersch (1972) report a teacher workshop for defining, developing, and evaluating test items.

The Center for the Study of Evaluation, in conjunction with Research for Better Schools, Inc., has analyzed and evaluated approximately 2600 instruments for measuring higher-order cognitive, affective, and interpersonal skills (Center for the Study of Evaluation, 1972).

A practical guide for preparing and using criterion-referenced tests has been developed by Gronlund (1973). Checklists for evaluating criterion-referenced tests and procedures for item analysis are included in the guide.

Swezey and Pearlstein (1974) have developed an excellent manual that thoroughly covers the design, use, and evaluation of criterion-referenced tests. Four steps are discussed: (a) developing adequate behavioral objectives; (b) developing a test plan and examining practical constraints; (c) building an item pool; and (d) selecting the final test items for instruction.

Stevens and O'Neil (1976b) discuss procedures for generating test items by varying actual instructional sentences according to their syntactic structure. The test items can be used in multiple-choice or constructed-response tests.

Stevens and O'Neil (1976a, 1976c) suggest other procedures for developing and evaluating test items for comprehension-, application-, and analysis-level tests.

II.3. Describe Entry Behavior

Bierbaum and Planisek (1969) have developed an index and procedure for determining the probable academic success of students seeking readmission after academic dismissal.

An interest inventory designed to measure the vocational interests of enlisted men entering the Air Force was developed by Ecternacht, Reilly, and McCaffrey (1973). Called VOICE (Vocational and Occupational Interest Choice Examination), the instrument was intended to be part of an interest inventory for the Guaranteed Enlistment Program.

Mockovak (1974) assessed the literacy requirements of Air Force career ladders in order to determine the reading demands placed upon trainees and job incumbents by instructional materials.

Vitola, Mullins, and Brokaw (1973) found that removal of the draft as a motivator for enlistment affected the Air Force in three ways: (a) decreased accessions completing education beyond the high school level; (b) increased discharge rate for first-term airmen after 4 years; and (c) decreased average difference on mean scores for Airmen Qualifying Examination (AQE) aptitude composites between black and nonblacks. Although the procedure as described is an ex post facto device, it could be used to characterize incoming populations on a continuing basis.

II.4. Determine Sequence and Structure

Dansereau, Evans, Wright, Long, and Actkinson (1974) and Dansereau, Evans, Actkinson, and Long (1974) developed and evaluated a multidimensional scale called INSCAL. It was used to describe the information structure of Air Force instructional materials and to generate effective instructional sequences.

A checklist for determining student positions along a curriculum scale has been developed by the Bucks County Public Schools (1970); it may be useful in computer-based learning systems to assess student performance and determine proper learning sequences.

III.3. Review/Select Existing Materials

The State University College at Buffalo (1972) provides a user's manual describing computer-based resource units in several subject areas and giving directions for obtaining them. A maximum of five units may be requested in terms of individual difference variables listed on the request form.

An annotated listing of curriculum materials that can be obtained from state education agencies is available from the U.S. Government Printing Office (1973). Various curriculum guides cover agriculture, distributive education, health, home economics, technical education, and trade and industrial occupations.

The National Network for Curriculum Coordination in Vocational–Technical Education (1975) develops, publishes, and distributes curriculum guides and support services from six regional curriculum management centers. Curriculum guides are published in brochures, booklets, and microfiche.

The *Special Reserve Components Educational Video Tape Catalog* (1975) lists educational video-tape programs for Army unit training. The materials may be used by Reserve components, Army schools, and other training centers. Tapes may be borrowed from various military Training Aids Support Offices (TASOs) or copied on user-supplied cassette tapes.

The Directorate for Audio-Visual Activities (DAVA, 1975) presents a detailed user's guide of information required to participate in the Defense Audio-Visual Information Network and utilize the Audio-Visual Products Data Base. Appendices give input data guidelines for data coding and other computer-related requirements.

The Department of the Army (1974, 1975) provides two catalogs with annotated films, slides, audiovisual kits, recordings, and tape recordings intended for instructors, information officers, and defense contractors. The second catalog describes films for nonprofit use by government agencies; civic, religious, fraternal and educational organizations; and schools, colleges, and universities. Materials from the first catalog are directed to Army career fields, whereas those in the second catalog cover general subjects such as education, sports, and health.

A detailed *Directory of Collections of Engineering Computer Programs* (1977) provides bibliographic and descriptive information for 54 compendiums of computer programs. An index of the compendiums by major subject and number of programs is also given.

III.4. Develop Instruction

Best (1971) discusses procedures and materials that minimize the cost and time required to prepare and produce computer-controlled films. For local production efforts, the information is sufficient for learning how to process filmstrips into slides for either computer-controlled rear-screen projectors or transparencies.

Thiagarajan (1971) offers a programmed text for learning the write programmed texts. Five stages of the programming process are discussed, and a confirmation section at the conclusion of the book contains correct answers to questions in the text.

How to Design and Produce Individualized Instruction Programs (Minnesota Mining and Manufacturing Co., 1972) is a totally pragmatic workbook for developing audiovisual programs used on the 3M Sound-On-Slide System.

Another user's manual presents guidelines for writing computer-based resource units (State University of New York, 1972). One set of guidelines directs the writing of behavioral objectives, instructional content, activities, materials, and measuring devices. Another set of guidelines addresses the coding of these items for future computer retrieval.

Deterline and Lenn (1972) have developed a self-study course that teaches a process called CISTRAIN (Coordinated Instructional System for Training) for designing, developing, and implementing instruction. The two-volume set of instruction includes a *Lesson Book* and a *Study Resource Materials Book*.

Siegel, Lambert, and Burkett (1974) present a concise, entertaining synthesis of readability research and illustrate findings from that field that are useful to course writers.

Nesbit and O'Neil (1976) provide guidelines for editing programmed texts. The guidelines contain a glossary of terms, explanations of three models for programming texts, and criteria for checking lesson content and author's style.

Tolmie and Gallegos (1976) have developed a practical PDP-11 debugging tool that is applicable to computer-based instructional systems.

Another set of software tools is given by Kernighan and Plauger (1976). The tools, which are presented as complete tested programs, are written in a language call RATFOR (Rational Fortran).

III.5. Validate Instruction

A system for computer-based analysis of lesson tests and course evaluation questionnaires is reported by Aleamoni (1970). The system provides (a) test scores; (b) analysis of scores for groups or individuals; (c) test-item analysis printouts; (d) item analysis data; and (e) analysis of course evaluation questionnaires, attitude scales, and other measures with no known correct response. A manual and other system documentation are available.

Abedor (1972) presents a formative evaluation model intended to function in operational environments. Noting that multiple, iterative revisions of materials can be a monumental and costly effort, Abedor designed the model to generate large amounts of data on instructional problems in a one-time trial of prototype lessons.

Ward (1972) investigated author use of formative evaluation during the preparation of a CAI course and provides several practical development recommendations.

Rayner (1972) has developed a formative evaluation model that provides data for content changes to instructional materials and procedural changes to administrative systems.

Hummel-Rossi (1972) has devised an unusually packaged multiple-choice test for evaluating cognitive knowledge of Bloom's taxonomy. The test includes an instruction sheet, a chemically treated answer sheet, and a testing instrument.

V.1 Conduct Internal Evaluation

The testing of manual procedures for the Bell System personnel subsystem is discussed by Bailey (1972). Data are given for the procedures used to determine the numbers, kinds, and probable causes of errors for various job activities.

Miller and Sellman (1973) developed a student critique form for the Air Force Training Command that employs factor analysis and can be used to manipulate large amounts of questionnaire data and generate reliable subscales for describing student attitudes toward instruction.

V.2 Conduct External Evaluation

Anastasio's (1972) field-test evaluation of the PLATO and TICCIT systems included both cost and educational analyses. Although the evaluation was not fully applied to either system, the discussion of achievement and attitude measures (specifically designed for college students) and the inclusion of the Survey of Instructor Activities and Attitudes (Appendix A of the report) are of interest to instructional evaluators.

INSTRUCTIONAL MATERIALS DEVELOPMENT

It has been said that instructional materials are developed by feel and intuition (Merrill & Boutwell, 1973) and that conscious application of development rules is confused subconsciously with changes in syntax, grammar, and writer's style (Baker, 1970). I have in principle no quarrel with those sentiments, for they hint of a process approaching art, and certainly the most personally effective instructional materials embody some vein or muscle of the artist.

But the most valued art is rare and expensive, and its creative skills are nontransferable and unpredictable. Inevitably, its best qualities run counter to the essential requirements of instructional materials development: first, that materials be reproducible and inexpensive; second, that development skills be generalizable and easily acquired; and third, that products be valid and reliable in a formal sense.

Thus, in the process of developing instructional materials, the artistic notion must be minimized and a more assembly-line mentality adopted. Authoring tools and procedures should be useful for standardizing development methodology. I think there will be disagreement on this point from some readers. Perhaps the disagreement will arise from a philosophical viewpoint, perhaps from our accustomed reliance on the optimal solution that exists for one and only one situation.

As noted earlier, these tools and procedures represent insensitive solutions that consider situational and managemental factors in addition to empirical data. They may not be clearly the best solution to every instructional development problem but they should give reasonably satisfactory performance to instructional developers in widely differing situations.

This is true, I think, because they provide positive answers to three questions that are asked consciously or subconsciously in any evaluation. First, when we consider using something to solve a problem — that is, when we wish to adopt a solution — we ask whether it has been used in similar applications. Since these tools and procedures are essentially how-to, self-help guides developed for specific applications, and since these applications are related quite clearly to an instructional systems development step or phase, it can be concluded that they can be used in the similar situations arising in all efforts using instructional systems development.

Second, we ask whether I as instructional manager or as one who has to persuade other instructional management would support adoption of this solution. This is a purely personal decision. In my case, I can say that in every instructional situation I have ever encountered, developers need guidance — no matter how expert they are — and that management fully supports such guidance if it is in a clearly recognizable how-to format. In my case, these tools and procedures provide the kind of guidance recognized as useful by management.

Third, we ask whether experimental design and data will prove the effectiveness of an adopted solution. Many of these tools and procedures underwent formal evaluation and validation through rigid experimental design. Others were tested under fire, as it were, through many years of development and use. In no case is any tool or procedure merely a theoretical device. I consider them all empirically proven in a first run; additional test and evaluation will have to be undertaken by individual developers.

CONCLUSION

This review defined instructional systems development in terms of a model called interservice procedures. The model breaks down instructional development activities into five phases called analysis, design, development, implementation, and control. Each phase is further composed of steps.

Steps related to developing instructional materials were then associated with tools and procedures that would facilitate their execution and enhance their product. The usefulness of such tools and procedures was considered in terms of insensitive solutions — that is, solutions that may not be the best for any one situation but that should work with satisfactory performance in many different situations. Further research should be conducted to consider the use of insensitive solutions for applying instructional systems development to educational and training programs.

REFERENCES

Abedor, A. J. *Development and validation of a model for formative evaluation of self-instructional multi-media learning systems.* Paper presented at the meeting of the American Educational Research Association, Chicago, April 1972.

Aleamoni, L. M. *MERMAC: A model and system for test and questionnaire analysis* (Research Report 330). Champaign: University of Illinois, Office of Instructional Resources, Measurement and Research Division, March 1970. (ERIC Document Reproduction Service No. ED 055 097).

Anastasio, E. J. *An evaluation of the demonstrations being conducted by the University of Illinois and the MITRE Corporation of their respective computer assisted instructional systems* (ETS PR-72-19). Princeton, N.J.: Educational Testing Service, 1972. (ERIC Document Reproduction Service No. ED 072 070)

Archer, W. B. *Computation of group job descriptions from occupational survey data* (Tech. Rep. PRL-TR-66-12). Lackland Air Force Base, Texas: Air Force Systems Command, Aerospace Medical Division, Personnel Research Laboratory, December 1966.

Bailey, R. W. Testing manual procedures in computer-based business information systems. In W. B. Knowles, M. S. Sanders, & F. A. Muckler (Eds.), *Proceedings of the 16th Annual Meeting of the Human Factors Society,* 1972, 395–401.

Baker, E. L. Generalizability of rules for empirical revision. *AV Communication Review,* 1970, *18,* 300–305.

Barton, G. E. *Performance objectives: A self-instructional booklet.* Provo, Utah: Brigham Young University Press, 1973.

Best, E. *The development of visual materials for CAI* (Technical Memo No. 5). Austin: The University of Texas at Austin, Computer-Assisted Instruction Laboratory, August 1971.

Bierbaum, G. A., & Planisek, R. J. *An index and procedure for readmitting the academically dismissed student.* Kent, Ohio: Kent State University, 1969. (ERIC Document Reproduction Service No. ED 063 555)

Bloom, B. S. *Human characteristics and school learning.* New York: McGraw-Hill, 1976.

Braby, R., Henry, J. M., Parrish, W. F., Jr., & Swope, W. M. *A technique for choosing cost-effective instructional delivery systems* (TAEG Report No. 16). Orlando, Fla.: Department of the Navy, Training Analysis and Evaluation Group, April 1975.

Brown, L., Brooks, G., Cocks, P. J., & Kersch, M. E. *Evaluation for individualized instruction. An operational guide for teacher workshops.* Downers Grove, Ill.: Institute for

Educational Research, 1972. (ERIC Document Reproduction Service No. ED 066 492)

Bucks County Public Schools. *Intensification of the learning process: Diagnostic instruments – Learner state check list evaluation response form.* Doylestown, Pa.: Author, February 1970. (ERIC Document Reproduction Service No. ED 063 345)

Bureau of Naval Personnel. *Preparation of learning objectives.* Washington, D.C.: Department of the Navy, Author, 1968. (ERIC Document Reproduction Service No. ED 058 721)

Butler, F. C. *Instructional systems development for vocational and technical training.* Englewood Cliffs, N.J.: Educational Technology Publications, 1972.

Center for the Study of Evaluation. *CSE–RBS test evaluations: Tests of higher-order cognitive, affective, and interpersonal skills.* Los Angeles: University of California, Graduate School of Education, 1972.

Christal, R. E. *CODAP: Input Standard (INPSTD) and variable generation (VARGEN) programs* (Tech. Rep. AFHRL-TR-72-51). Lackland Air Force Base, Texas: Air Force Human Resources Laboratory, Personnel Research Division, May 1972.

Christal, R. E., & Weismuller, J. J. *New CODAP programs for analyzing task factor information.* Paper presented at the meeting of the Military Testing Association, Indianapolis, September 1975.

Churchman, C. W. *The systems approach.* New York: Dell, 1968.

Cline, J. A. *A multivariate statistical model to predetermine preferable aircraft assignments: A feasibility study* (Doctoral dissertation, Arizona State University, 1973). *Dissertation Abstracts International*, 1973, *34.* (University Microfilms No. 73–20, 494)

Dansereau, D. R., Evans, S. H., Actkinson, T. A., & Long, G. L. *Factors relating to the development of optimal instructional sequences* (Report No. AFHRL-TR-53-51 [II]). Lowry Air Force Base, Colo.: Air Force Human Resources Laboratory, Technical Training Division, June 1974.

Dansereau, D. R., Evans, S. H., Wright, A. D., Long, G., & Actkinson, T., *Factors related to developing instructional information sequences: Phase 1* (Report No. AFHRL-TR-73-51 [I]). Lowry Air Force Base, Colo.: Air Force Human Resources Laboratory, Technical Training Division, March 1974.

Demerath, H. J., & Daniels, L. A. *How to make the fourth revolution: Human factors in the adoption of electronic instructional aids* (Memo No. 75/3). St. Louis: Washington University, Center for Development Technology, December 1973.

Department of the Army. *Index of army motion pictures and related audio-visual aids* (Pamphlet No. 108-1). Washington, D.C.: Headquarters, Author, September 1974.

Department of the Army. *Index of army motion pictures for public non-profit use* (Pamphlet No. 108-4). Washington, D.C.: Headquarters, Author, May 1975.

Deterline, W. A., & Lenn, P. D. *Coordinated instructional system. Study resource materials book. Lesson book.* Palo Alto, Calif.: Sound Education, Inc., 1972.

Dillman, F. E., Jr. *Instructional objectives: Specificity and behavior.* Menlo Park, Calif.: Dillman Associates, 1971. (ERIC Document Reproduction Source No. ED 062 704)

Directorate for Audio-Visual Activities. *Department of Defense audiovisual information system: A user guide for the audiovisual products data base.* Arlington, Va.: Author, Office of Information for the Armed Forces (OASD/M&RA), October 1975.

Directory to Collections of Engineering Computer Programs. Rockville, Md.: EG & G Washington Analytical Services Center, 1977. (NTIS Reproduction Service No. AO A0346 193)

Ecternacht, G. J., Reilly, R. R., & McCaffrey, P. J. *Development and validity of a vocational and occupational interest inventory* (Report No. AFHRL-TR-73-38). Lackland Air Force Base, Texas: Air Force Human Resources Laboratory, Personnel Research Division, December 1973.

ESCOE (Evaluation Service Center for Occupational Education). *Behavioral objectives training package.* Amherst, Mass.: Author, 1971. (ERIC Document Reproduction Service No. ED 060 218)

Foley, J. P., Jr. Task analyses for job performance aids and related training. In T. C. Rowan (Ed.), *Proceedings for the invitational conference on improved information aids for technicians.* Sumner, Md.: Logistics Management Institute, May 1975.

Gael, S. Employment test validation studies. *JSAS Catalog of Selected Documents in Psychology, 1974, 4,* 95 (Ms. No. 711).

Gagné, R. M. *The Conditions of Learning.* New York: Holt, Rinehart and Winston, 1977.

Gronlund, N. *Preparing criterion-referenced tests for classroom instruction.* New York: Macmillan, 1973.

Hummel-Rossi, B. *A formative evaluation of Bloom's mastery learning concept.* New York: Van Valkenburgh, Nooger and Neville, 1972.

INSGROUP. *Objectives for instructional programs, Reference wall chart.* Huntington Beach, Calif.: INSGROUP Inc., 1975.

Inventory management specialist and inventory management supervisor. Specialty training 645XO. Washington, D.C.: Department of the Air Force, Headquarters, August 11, 1975.

Kandaswamy, S., Stolovitch, H. D., & Thiagarajan, S. Learner verification and revision: An experimental comparison of two methods. *AV Communications Review 24,* 1976, *3,* 316–328.

Kernighan, B. W., Plauger, P. J. *Software tools.* Reading, Mass.: Addison-Wesley, 1976.

Lewis, W. E., Willow, J. R., Brock, G. R., Lonigro, J. K., Jr., Eschenbrenner, A. J., & Hanson, A. L. *Precision measuring equipment PME individualized instruction* (Report No. AFHRL-TR-74-46). Lowry Air Force Base, Colorado Air Force Human Resources Laboratory, Technical Training Division, August, 1974.

Logan, R. S., *Instructional Systems Development and Learning Strategies.* Paper presented at the Learning Strategies Conference, Wayzata, Minn., August 1976.

Logan, R. S. *A survey and analysis of military computer-based training systems: A two-part study. Volume I: A survey and annotated bibliography of authoring aids for Instructional Systems Development* (Report No. MDC E 1570). St. Louis: McDonnell Douglas Corp., February 1977. (NTIS Reproduction Service No. AD A036 912)

Material facilities specialist. Course chart 3ABR64730-1. Lowry Air Force Base, Colo.: Lowry Technical Training Center, School of Applied Aerospace Sciences, Department of Logistics Training, September 12, 1973.

Material facilities specialist. Plan of instruction 3ABR64730-1. Lowry Air Force Base, Colo.: Lowry Technical Training Center, School of Applied Aerospace Sciences, Department of Logistics Training, January 2, 1974.

Mayo, C. C., Nance, D. M., & Shiegekawa, L. *Evaluation of the job inventory approach in analyzing USAF officer utilization fields* (Tech. Rep. AFHRL-TR-75-22). Lackland Air Force Base, Texas: Air Force Human Resources Laboratory, Occupational and Manpower Research Division, June, 1975.

McKnight, A. J., & Adams, B. B. *Driver education task analysis. Volume II: Task analysis methods* (Final Report) (HumRRO Tech. 72-13). Arlington, Va.: Human Resources Research Organization, 1970. (ERIC Document Reproduction Service No. ED 075 624)

Merrill, M. D., & Boutwell, R. C. Instructional development: Methodology and research. In F. N. Kerlinger (Ed.), *Review of research in education* (Vol. 1). Itasca, Ill.: F. E. Peacock, 1973.

Miller, G. G., & Sellman, W. S. *Development of psychometric measures of student attitudes toward technical training: Norm group report* (Report No. AFHRL-TR-73-15). Lowry Air Force Base, Colo.: Air Force Human Resources Laboratory, Technical Training Division, October 1973.

Minnesota Mining and Manufacturing Co. *How to design and produce individualized instruction programs.* St. Paul, Minn.: Author, Visual Products Division, 1972.

Mockovak, W. P. *Literary skills and requirements in Air Force career ladders* (Report No. AFHRL-TR-74-90). Lowry Air Force Base. Colo.: Air Force Human Resources Laboratory, Technical Training Division, December 1974.

Morsch, J. E., & Archer, W. B. *Procedural guide for conducting occupational surveys in the United States Air Force* (Tech. Rep. PRL-67-11). Lackland Air Force Base, Texas: Air Force Systems Command, Aerospace Medical Division, Personnel Research Laboratory, September 1967.

National network for curriculum coordination in vocational–technical education. Washington, D.C.: Department of Health, Education and Welfare, Office of Education, 1975.

Nesbit, M., & O'Neil, H. F., Jr. *Guidelines for editing programmed instruction.* Austin: University of Texas Press, 1976.

Powers, L. *The systems approach to functional job analysis: Task analysis of the physician's assistant. Volume 1: Task analysis methodology and techniques.* Winston-Salem, N.C.: Wake Forest University, Bowman Gray School of Medicine, 1971. (ERIC Document Reproduction Service No. ED 059 378)

Quade, E. S., & Boucher, W. I. (Eds.) *Systems analysis and policy planning.* New York: Elsevier–North Holland, 1975.

Rayner, G. T. *An empirical study of a methodology for the revision of systematically designed educational material* (Tech. Rep. No. 24). Tallahassee: Florida State University, Computer-Assisted Instruction Center, March 1972. (ERIC Document Reproduction Service No. ED 067 877)

Rose, B. K., Balasek, J., Kelleher, J., Lutz, J. L., & Nelken, I. *A programmed course for the writing of performance objectives. A constructed response linear program.* Bloomington, Ind.: Phi Delta Kappa, Commission on Educational Planning, 1972. (a) (ERIC Document Reproduction Service No. ED 073 528)

Rose, B. K., Balasek, J., Kelleher, J., Lutz, J. L., & Nelken, I. *Writing performance objectives. Instructor's manual for teachers and administrators. To be used with a programmed course for writing of performance objectives.* Bloomington, Ind.: Phi Delta Kappa, Commission on Educational Planning. 1972. (b) (ERIC Document Reproduction Service No. ED 073 529)

Siegel, A. I., Lambert, J. V., & Burkett, J. R. *Techniques for making written material more readable/comprehensible* (Report No. AFHRL-TR-74-47). Lowry Air Force Base, Colo.: Air Force Human Resources Laboratory, Technical Training Division, August 1974.

Special reserve components educational video tape catalog (Pamphlet No. 350-4). Fort Monroe, Va.: Department of the Army, Headquarters, United States Army Training and Doctrine Command, 25 March 1975.

Stacey, W. J., & Hazel, J. T. *A method of determining desirable task experiences for first-line supervisors* (Tech. Rep. AFHRL-TR-75-23). Lackland Air Force Base, Texas: Air Force Human Resources Laboratory, Occupational and Manpower Research Division, August 1975.

Stacey, W. J., Weismuller, J. J., Barton, B. B., & Rogers, C. R. *CODAP: Control card specifications for the UNIVAC 1108* (Tech. Rep. AFHRL-TR-74-84). Lackland Air Force Base, Texas: Air Force Human Resources Laboratory, Computational Sciences Division, October 1974.

State University College at Buffalo. *Computer assisted planning: A user manual for computer-based resource units.* Buffalo, N.Y.: Author, Faculty of Professional Studies, Research and Development Complex, October 1972. (ERIC Document Reproduction Service No. ED 073 587)

State University of New York. *Guidelines for developing computer based resource units.*

Revised. Buffalo: Author, Educational Research and Development Complex, March 1972. (ERIC Document Reproduction Service No. ED 073 586)

Stevens, J. C., & O'Neil, H. F., Jr. *Some guidelines for development and review of multiple-choice questions.* Austin: University of Texas Press, 1976. (a)

Stevens, J. C., & O'Neil, H. F., Jr. *Suggestions for development of test items.* Austin: University of Texas Press, 1976. (b)

Stevens, J. C., & O'Neil, H. F., Jr. *Suggestions for generating multiple-choice items at the comprehension, application, and analysis levels.* Austin: University of Texas Press, 1976. (c)

Swezey, R. W., & Pearlstein, R. B. *Developing criterion-referenced tests* (Report No. 287-AR18(2)-IR-0974-RWS). Arlington, Va.: U.S. Army Research Institute for the Behavioral and Social Sciences, Unit Training and Educational Technology Systems Area, Performance Measurements and Standards Work Unit, March 1974. (NTIS Document Reproduction Service No. AD A014 987)

Task Inventory Exchange. *Brochure.* Columbus: Ohio State University, Center for Vocational Education, 1975.

Thiagarajan, S. *The programming process: A practical guide.* Worthington, Ohio: Charles A. Jones Publishing Co., 1971.

Tolmie, D. E., & Gallegos, M. E. *PDP-11 Debugging Tool User's Manual.* Oak Ridge, Tenn.: United States Energy Research and Development Administration, Technical Information Center, 1977.

U.S. Army Training and Doctrine Command. *Interservice procedures for instructional systems development* (TRADOC Pamphlet 350-30). Ft. Benning, Ga.: Author, 1975.

Vitola, B. M., Mullins, C. J., & Brokaw, L. D. *Quality of the all-volunteer air force–1973* (Report No. AFHRL-TR-74-35). Lackland Air Force Base, Texas: Air Force Human Resources Laboratory, Personnel Research Division, April 1974.

Ward, M. E. Examination and application of formative evaluation for author utilization during the preparation of a CAI course (Doctoral dissertation, University of Pittsburgh, 1972). (ERIC Document Reproduction Service No. ED 076 056)

Weissmuller, J. J., Barton, B. B., & Rogers, C. R. *CODAP: Programmer notes for the subroutine library on the UNIVAC 1108* (Rep. No. AFHRL-TR-74-85). Lackland Air Force Base, Texas: Air Force Human Resources Laboratory, Computational Sciences Division, October 1974. (a)

Weissmuller, J. J., Barton, B. B., & Rogers, C. R. *CODAP: Source program listings for the UNIVAC 1108* (Rep. No. AFHRL-TR-74-83) Lackland Air Force Base, Texas: Air Force Human Resources Laboratory, Computational Sciences Division, October 1974. (b)

Wong, M. R., & Raulerson, J. R. *A guide to systematic instructional design.* Englewood Cliffs, N.J.: Educational Technology Publications, 1974.

2

CREATE: A Computer-Based Authoring Curriculum

SUSAN S. TAYLOR

INTRODUCTION

The purpose of the CREATE[1] curriculum is to train authors to design and develop instructional materials that are individualized and multimedia. CREATE stands for Computer Resource for Effective Author Training in Education. A major emphasis of the CREATE curriculum is the design, development, and programming of computer-based education (CBE) materials.

The CREATE curriculum itself is an individualized, multimedia, and computer-based curriculum. It is self-paced, competency-based, and designed to adapt to the entry skills and goals of students. The CREATE curriculum utilizes computer-assisted instruction (CAI), printed text and exercises, video cassettes, audio cassettes, and sound filmstrips to present instruction. It relies upon computer-managed instruction (CMI) to monitor students' performance and guide their progress through the curriculum.

The CREATE curriculum was developed by Control Data Corporation in response to several different, but related, needs. The primary need was to train people to use the CONTROL DATA PLATO system for the development of computer-assisted and computer-managed instructional materials. The PLATO system authors would be both internal (from within Control Data) and external, and they would develop materials for use in their own organization.

---

[1] CREATE, PLATO, and CONTROL DATA are all trademarks of Control Data Corporation.

ISSUES IN INSTRUCTIONAL SYSTEMS DEVELOPMENT

At Control Data, the term *computer-based education* is used to describe any teaching or learning activity that makes use of a computer. The Control Data PLATO (Program Logic for Automatic Teaching Operations) system is a multimedia computer-based educational delivery system. The PLATO system provides extremely comprehensive computer-assisted instruction capabilities, including drill-and-practice, tutorial, inquiry, dialogue, simulation, problem-solving, and gaming modes. The PLATO system also provides computer-managed instruction involving complex testing, diagnosis, prescription, and record keeping to facilitate individualized instruction.

A Control Data PLATO system is composed of a large mainframe computer, PLATO terminals, software systems, and special communications equipment. The PLATO terminal is an interactive computer graphics terminal. The student uses it to receive instructional material and interact with the computer; the instructor uses it to create or revise lesson material. Users communicate with the computer by means of the terminal keyboard or a touch panel. Hundreds of users at geographically dispersed terminals can all use the PLATO system simultaneously.

The PLATO author language permits an author to prepare, maintain, and improve courseware. It is a relatively simple language to learn, but it is a powerful language designed to control a very complex instructional system. The author can construct lessons, test for attainment of learning objectives, and change material directly from any PLATO terminal.

In addition to training authors to use the PLATO system, it was desirable to establish a library of high-quality computer-based education materials that were already in existence. These materials could then be made available to users in much the same way that a publishing company distributes textbooks. To achieve this goal there was a need to increase the population of authors qualified to develop computer-based instructional materials. One way to do this was to provide training for potential authors through instruction such as the CREATE curriculum.

Prior to developing the CREATE curriculum, other resources for providing author training were reviewed. There were a number of courses dealing with the various topics, but none that would fulfill the need. Many of these courses were too theoretical and lacked the desired practical orientation. Few author training courses were individualized, and some of these were merely collections of articles on various topics. There were very few courses dealing with the emerging technology of computer-based education, particularly with respect to appropriate utilization of the PLATO system. There were no existing courses that covered all the topics ultimately included in the CREATE curriculum. Consequently, a project was initiated to develop the curriculum.

The initial needs analysis and definition of the CREATE curriculum was accomplished by the Courseware Development Division of Control Data Corporation. The Courseware Development Division then worked with the Center for Educational Design at Florida State University to refine the design and to develop the preliminary edition of the CREATE curriculum. The Center for Educational Design developed 18 of the original 22 modules. The Courseware Development Division developed the other 4 modules.

Because of the short time frame for development and the difficulty of coordinating two development groups that were 1500 miles apart, it was decided that the preliminary edition would be primarily text and it would utilize paper-and-pencil tests. The computer-assisted instruction lessons and audiovisual products that were produced amounted to less than 15 hours of the approximately 250 hours of instructional materials. Each group, however, was asked to identify points where computer-assisted instruction or audiovisual materials would have been more appropriate had more freedom been allowed for media selection.

The first edition was distributed to internal and external subject matter experts to review and to obtain their suggestions for revisions. At the same time, approximately 70 Control Data employees participated as pilot subjects to evaluate various segments of the CREATE curriculum. Students' comments, as well as data on their performance, time, and attitude, were collected and used as the basis for a later revision. During this review-and-evaluation period, a second edition of the CREATE curriculum was produced to correct some surface problems that inhibited instructional delivery. The problems corrected at this time were mainly typographical errors, incorrect answers, and excessive repetition of directions.

A major revision resulting in the third edition of the CREATE curriculum was based on feedback from the review-and-evaluation efforts. During this revision, major changes were made in instructional presentation. This included adding over 40 hours of computer-assisted instruction and major revisions of audiovisual products. A new module was added and all tests were converted from paper-and-pencil delivery to computer-managed instruction delivery on the PLATO system. Although the goals and objectives of the CREATE curriculum have remained fairly stable, the instructional materials have changed significantly since the first version. Less than 20% of the original material remains in the third edition.

To date, over 100 people have contributed to the development, review, and revision of the CREATE curriculum. The remainder of this chapter describes the curriculum as it exists in its current form, with brief allusions to earlier versions.

THE NEED FOR AN AUTHOR-TRAINING CURRICULUM

Several factors had a strong influence on the design and selection of content for the CREATE curriculum. The principal factors were the needs for training,

variations in the target population, and characteristics of the delivery environment. The following sections describe requirements for the curriculum that resulted from each of these factors.

Training Needs

A number of different skills are needed to produce high-quality computer-
based education materials using the PLATO system. The most obvious, of course,
are those skills that are unique to computer-based instruction (such as ability to
program materials and knowledge of the features and capabilities of the PLATO
system). A somewhat more subtle skill involves the ability to use the capabilities
of the computer system (such as branching, feedback, graphics, and recordkeeping)
to enhance the efficiency and effectiveness of instruction.

There are also a number of skills involved in the development of instructional
materials regardless of the delivery medium. These skills include conducting an
instructional-needs analysis, performing an instructional task analysis, writing
objectives, selecting media, designing tests, writing test items, determining appropriate instructional strategies, evaluating instructional effectiveness, and documenting instructional development. Therefore, a curriculum to prepare authors
of computer-based education materials should also contain instruction in these
skills.

The topic of media selection was a particularly critical issue. There was concern that novice authors might inappropriately use the PLATO system. The most
common example is using the computer for "page turning," in which many displays of text material are presented one after the other. This type of presentation does not require the branching and interactive capabilities of a computer
and is best presented via another medium, usually printed text. A related concern was the practice of using new media, such as computer-based education, as
only an adjunct to, and not an integral part of, the total instructional program.
This patchwork approach can lead to inefficient instruction because the materials delivered by the various media are not coordinated with one another. Thus,
it was desirable to include information in the author-training curriculum about
design and development of multimedia courseware. This required provision of
training in media selection and the development of non-computer-based materials
as well.

Miscellaneous topics to be included in the curriculum were also identified.
These included various ways of individualizing instruction, a systematic approach
to the design and development of instructional materials, implementation of
individualized courses, and management of a courseware development project.

In summary, a large number of topics were identified for inclusion in the
CREATE curriculum. The majority of these topics involved general considerations for design and development of individualized, multimedia instructional

materials. Several of these topics, however, were specific to the development of computer-based materials.

The Target Population

A very broad target population was identified for the CREATE curriculum. Primarily, it consists of people who are potential "authors" of instructional materials. The term *author* was very loosely defined to include anyone performing one or more of several major functions involving design and development of individualized instruction. These functions included total courseware design, text development, audiovisual development, computer-assisted instruction development, test development, and PLATO system programming. In the case of a lesson or a small course, a single author might perform all of these functions; in the case of a curriculum or large course, a team of authors might work together to perform different functions. The target population for the CREATE curriculum includes potential authors for either case regardless of a team structure.

In addition to authors, there are other types of people included in the target population. Among them are managers of instructional development projects and subject matter experts who are serving as consultants for an instructional development team. (Sometimes subject matter experts are also authors.) Another audience for the CREATE curriculum consists of executives or administrators of organizations that are either developing or implementing individualized instructional materials.

The members of the target population could come from industry, the military, colleges, universities, vocational – technical school staffs, elementary – secondary school staffs, or any other organization involved in education or training. The majority of the target population could be expected to have a bachelor's degree (or equivalent experience) and a need to learn something about development of individualized materials. The broad range of the target population, however, implies that there are great variations in entry skills. Some may be experienced designers and developers of individualized materials who just need to learn about computer-based instruction. Others may be subject matter experts with no formal training in the development of instruction. Some students may be familiar with computer programming techniques; others may not.

In addition to variations in entry skills, there are also variations in needs and goals among members of the target population. Executives may need only an awareness of the total process; some students may need to perform only some of the functions as members of instructional development teams; other students may need to perform all of the functions themselves. These differences among members of the target population required that the CREATE curriculum be adaptable to both varying entry skills and varying needs and goals of its students.

The Delivery Environment

The environment in which the CREATE curriculum would be delivered also imposed design requirements. The primary environment consists of a network of learning centers, which are operated by the Control Data Education Company, scattered across the country. Each learning center is equipped with video cassette players, audio cassette players, sound–filmstrip projectors, and PLATO terminals. Thus, the equipment available in the learning centers defined the media that could be used in the CREATE curriculum.

The learning centers' staff included an education consultant and learning center technicians. The technicians helped students locate materials and operate the equipment, but generally did not have subject matter expertise. The education consultants, however, were qualified in the field of instructional technology, but their available time was limited. Thus, it was necessary for the CREATE curriculum to be as instructor-independent as possible, with consulting support provided by the learning center staff only when necessary.

The CREATE curriculum may also be delivered in an environment other than a learning center as long as comparable equipment and support are made available to the student.

Other Requirements

Several other requirements were established for the CREATE curriculum. First, the curriculum was to be practical and not theoretical in nature. The purpose was to train people to be functional and efficient developers of individualized instructional materials and not to debate various instructional issues. A second requirement was for students to have the experience of developing actual instructional materials as a part of their training. This meant that they were to apply what they learned to the development of a lesson in their own subject matter area. Finally, the CREATE curriculum itself was to be an example of the kind of individualized, multimedia instruction that it was training people to develop.

DESIGN FEATURES

In order to accommodate the various requirements previously described, considerable thought went into the design of the CREATE curriculum. This section describes each of the principal design features that resulted.

Flexible Structure

The CREATE curriculum is large; it is unlikely that the typical student will need to study every module and every lesson within this curriculum. To meet the goals and needs of most students, only parts of the CREATE curriculum will usually be required. Consequently, the curriculum uses a modular structure. The parts that are needed can be selected and combined into an individual, specific course of study that meets each student's needs.

The CREATE curriculum is divided into courses, modules, units, and learning activities. Each course is an instructional package consisting of one or more modules designed to train a student to meet a specific job function. A student's study program is composed of one or more courses. Each module deals with a specific subject in detail. The 25 modules in the CREATE curriculum range in length from 1 to 50 hours in average completion time. Each module consists of one or more units. Units can be thought of as the chapters of a book. Units contain a group of learning activities and generally correspond to test sections. Learning activities are the smallest segments of instruction in the CREATE curriculum. Learning activities may employ one or more of the following media: text, filmstrip, audiotape, videotape, and computer-assisted instruction.

Nine Basic Courses

The nine courses that comprise the CREATE curriculum and the modules within each course are shown in Figure 2.1. Courses can be combined to form study programs that include training in the job functions students need or desire for future roles in curriculum development. The CREATE curriculum is designed with certain subjects prerequisite to others. All courses of study should begin with the CREATE Fundamentals course.

The CREATE Fundamentals course is an introduction to the CREATE curriculum and an introduction to and an overview of a systems approach to designing, developing, and evaluating computer-based educational programs. It provides a rationale for the use of computers in instruction, explains the purpose and uses of documentation, and describes a specific systems-approach model for designing, developing, and evaluating curricula.

The Design, Design/Development Interface, and Development courses provide training in the design, development, and evaluation of individualized courseware. These courses are intended primarily for designers and developers who will be working with any media.

The next four courses (Computer-Assisted Instruction Design and Development, PLATO Author Language: Part I, PLATO Author Language: Part II, and Computer-Managed Instruction) deal specifically with the design, development, and programming of computer-based materials.

The Management course introduces the concerns that are specific to the management of instructional development projects. It also discusses the needs of the learning centers that are likely to use the instructional product. The Management course is designed to be taken by persons who will be working as project

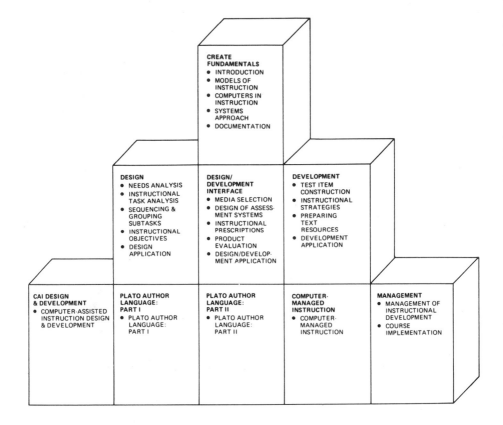

Figure 2.1 Nine basic courses.

managers. It may also be of interest to those who work as learning center managers.

A description of the modules within each of the nine courses in the CREATE curriculum is provided later in this chapter.

Levels of Instruction

Some members of the target population need to learn only the basics about each topic; others need more in-depth instruction. To accomodate these differences, three levels of instruction were defined for each module in the first and second editions of the CREATE curriculum. Level A was intended to provide an awareness of the topic; it defined basic terms and provided examples of the topic. Level B was intended to provide a working knowledge of the topic and gave rules for performing a particular step in the instructional design and development process. Level C was an application level in which the student actually worked on a project. Although the modules are no longer broken into levels in the third edition, the concept of providing different levels of instruction has been retained. Those who need only an awareness of each topic would take only the CREATE Fundamentals course. The instructional modules provide a working knowledge of each topic. The application modules at the end of each course correspond to level C.

Competency-Based Curriculum

In order to make the instruction more efficient and adaptable to the needs of each student, the CREATE curriculum is competency-based. All test items and learning activities are keyed to objectives. Diagnostic pretests are used as a basis for prescribing instruction. Only those learning activities corresponding to un-mastered objectives are assigned and only unmastered objectives are tested again in the progress checks. Students who fail the objectives a second time are directed to review appropriate learning activities or are prescribed alternative activities when available. A student must master each objective before proceeding to the next unit.

Multimedia

The learning activities in the CREATE curriculum are presented through a variety of media. In the entire curriculum, there are 243 text activities (including both text readings and exercises), 17 filmstrips, 7 videotapes, 19 audiotapes, and 80 computer-assisted instruction lessons. In the two PLATO Author Language courses there are also 41 programming practice activities. In addition, there are several reference tools both on-line and off-line.

Computer-Managed Instruction

In addition to using computer-assisted instruction as a medium of instruction, the CREATE curriculum utilizes computer-managed instruction as the primary means of managing instruction. All tests are delivered on-line, automatically scored, and recorded. Students receive immediate feedback on their test results as well as directions on what they can do next. Study prescriptions based on the test results are also assigned by the computer-managed instruction system. The education consultants can check the progress of their students even when the students may be working in another location. Through the PLATO computer-managed instruction system, students may access the computer-assisted instruction lessons as well as lists of objectives, learning activity descriptions, and reports on their progress. Most of the guidance a student must have to proceed through the CREATE curriculum is provided by the PLATO system.

Instructional Projects

As students proceed through the CREATE curriculum, they are directed to work on the development of a small instructional product. These projects typically represent less than 1 hour of instruction and are in a subject area of the student's choice. The purpose of these projects is to give students an opportunity to apply what they are learning as they learn it and in their own content areas. The application modules and units that are found at the end of most of the CREATE courses provide step-by-step directions for students to perform the instructional design and development process that was taught within the course. The application modules also provide students with guidance on documenting their projects and criteria for evaluating their performance. Essentially, the application portions of the CREATE curriculum serve as authoring aids as defined by Logan in Chapter 1 of this volume.

In order to place as little burden as possible on the learning center staff to deliver the CREATE curriculum, almost all of the directions that students need are contained within the materials themselves; however, a learning center technician is needed to help students get started, distribute materials, show them how to operate equipment, and register them on the PLATO system. When students start working on their projects, the education consultant helps evaluate the projects and provides guidance for revisions. Thus, although the CREATE curriculum is not entirely instructor-independent, the need for an instructor is minimized through the use of the PLATO computer-managed instruction system to handle routine delivery. The role of an instructor then becomes more like that of a consultant.

CREATE MODULES

There are 25 modules in the CREATE curriculum. Twently-two of the modules are strictly instructional in nature. The other 3 are called application modules and provide guidance to the students as they work on their projects. This section provides a description of each of the modules in the CREATE curriculum from the standpoint of the approach taken and the topics addressed.

The instructional modules within the CREATE curriculum require approximately 250 hours to complete, although the overall time varies from student to student. Students may also spend up to 100 additional hours working on their projects. Project times vary considerably, depending on the scope and complexity of the projects.

Introduction

The Introduction module is very short and is designed to aid students in proceeding through the CREATE curriculum. It discusses the organization of the CREATE curriculum and introduces the PLATO system. After completing this module, students should understand how to use the CREATE curriculum, including registering for a course, completing a course, and using the PLATO system to receive tests and instruction.

Models of Instruction

Models of Instruction discusses the advantages and disadvantages of two models for presenting instruction. One is designed to accomodate individuals; the other is designed to accommodate groups. The module presents five basic categories of student differences that affect learning and describes how those differences can be accommodated by individualized instruction. The five variables discussed are learning rates, entry knowledge levels, instructional methods preferred, goals, and proficiency levels. The underlying philosophy of this module is similar to Bloom's (1968) concept of mastery learning. The purpose of this module is to indicate that there are many different ways of individualizing instruction and to stress the importance of well-developed materials to accommodate the five variables. This module also introduces current terms relating to individualized instruction and warns the student that there are sometimes several different interpretations for the same term.

Computers in Instruction

Computers in Instruction examines the ways in which computers can be used for instruction, including record keeping, testing, instruction, and information resource. The module examines strengths and weaknesses of computers for instruction. It also defines four terms basic to the discussion of computers in instruction: computer-based education, computer-managed instruction, computer-assisted instruction, and computer-supported learning aids. The module provides an overview of the applications and usefulness of computers in individualized instruction. More in-depth presentations of computer-assisted instruction and computer-managed instruction occur in later modules.

Systems Approach

The Systems Approach module presents a workable system for designing, developing, and evaluating instructional materials. When an instructional process is considered a system, it is possible to establish and sequence specific steps that facilitate the courseware production process. The systems approach advocated by this module is a three-phase approach (design, development, and evaluation) consisting of 20 steps. The purpose of each step, as well as the input and output of the steps, is described. The importance of the effective use of feedback within the system is stressed. The systems approach in this model is very similar to that explicated in Chapter 1 of this volume.

A second unit in this module addresses how the systems approach can be used by both an individual author and development teams. This unit reflects Control Data's experience with the evolution of systems approach models in order to accomodate variations in development-team configurations, media alternatives, and project size (Taylor & O'Neal, 1978). Appropriate ways of modifying steps in the model to fit the situation are described. The module contains an activity that students use to identify other modules in the CREATE curriculum pertinent to their interests and needs. This activity helps students choose their final course flow through the CREATE curriculum.

Documentation

The Documentation module discusses the documentation of the design, development, and evaluation of instructional materials. It explains the need for producing a complete and permanent record, for future reference, of all the steps in creating instructional materials. The topics covered include the need for documentation, the standards for documentation, the contents of general documentation, and the specifics of documenting the instructional process. A documentation checklist (Control Data Corporation, 1976) is provided along with criteria for what is documented and how it is documented. More detailed information on documenting each step is included in later modules.

Needs Analysis

The process of identifying problems and clarifying needs is called needs analysis. The Needs Analysis module introduces a two-phase process for the needs analysis of instructional problems. It discusses the products of needs analysis, which are an instructional goal statement, a target population description, a list of constraints, and a solution statement. After completing this module, students should understand the needs analysis process and be ready to conduct their own needs analysis.

Instructional Task Analysis

Once the general goals of a course have been determined, the tasks the student must learn to reach those goals must be defined. This can be accomplished through an instructional task analysis. The task analysis process, presented in the Instructional Task Analysis module, can help students determine the tasks to be taught and the relationships among those tasks. This module defines both the purpose and the process of task analysis. Three different approaches to task analysis are presented. These are job task analysis (Mager & Beach, 1967), information-processing task analysis (P. F. Merrill, 1971), and hierarchical task analysis (Gagné, 1965). The second unit teaches the student to interpret and judge the accuracy of learning maps. The last unit presents seven steps in conducting an instructional task analysis.

Instructional Objectives

This module contains three units. The first unit introduces the concept of instructional objectives and describes their uses and purpose. Some common misconceptions regarding objectives are also discussed. The second unit describes the critical components of well-written objectives based on Mager's (1962) approach. It also discusses alternative approaches and variations in format (Gagné & Briggs, 1974; Gronlund, 1970). The third unit addresses classifying objectives into domains of learning and levels of behavior (Bloom, 1956; Gagné, 1970; M. D. Merrill, 1972).

Sequencing and Grouping Subtasks

The sequencing and grouping process organizes the content of a course in a way that facilitates learning. Sequencing and Grouping Subtasks defines this process and offers guidelines to enable the designer to present instruction in a well-organized manner.

Design Application

Design Application focuses on applying the principles of design discussed in the Design course. It is a step-by-step guide to designing a project of the student's choice. The student is guided in conducting a needs analysis, conducting an instructional task analysis, writing instructional objectives, and sequencing and grouping subtasks. This module also includes criteria for evaluating and documenting the design steps in their project.

Media Selection

Instruction can be presented through many different media. The media selected should be chosen with a number of considerations in mind. These include characteristics of media, instructional considerations, impact on the learner, learning center equipment, product costs and time, and available resources. The Media Selection module examines these considerations. Students are given an opportunity to select various media based on specific instructional situations, and to evaluate existing instructional products in various media. The production of various media is also briefly discussed. After completing this module, students should understand the media-selection process and the many factors that contribute to good media selection. Students should also be able to distinguish between good and poor samples of media use.

Design of Assessment Systems

An assessment system is an established set of activities through which information concerning individual or group performance is obtained. The purpose of such information is to make decisions or conclusions about the students. Design of Assessment Systems examines the role of assessment systems in individualized instruction. It discusses when to test, how to test, how to score tests and translate the scores into meaningful decisions, and how to design a good assessment system.

The first unit introduces the concept and purpose of assessment systems, distinguishes between criterion-referenced and norm-referenced testing, and discusses some common problems with testing. The second unit discusses the role of testing before, during, and after instruction; the role of feedback; and choosing a delivery system. The third unit presents characteristics of good tests, such as clarity, number of items, cultural bias, relevance, reliability, validity, and how these may differ between norm-referenced and criterion-referenced tests. The last unit provides a step-by-step procedure for designing assessment systems and includes a number of worksheets. This unit includes a computer-assisted instruction lesson on how to improve test validity and reliability. Tables of probabilities of passing by guessing are also provided.

Instructional Prescriptions

Instructional prescriptions are a direct communication to the learner, based on the individual's performance level; they specify what is to be learned and how the student should go about learning it. The Instructional Prescriptions module examines the use of such prescriptions and their contribution to good individualized instruction. Various prescription strategies and formats are discussed. Factors that influence the generation of prescription strategies are discussed. These are learner population, information-monitoring system, level of instructional activities, diagnostic mechanism, prescription-components match, testing system, and delivery mechanism. The module also includes a detailed checklist for evaluating instructional prescriptions.

Product Evaluation

Product evaluation is a process used to determine whether a product helps students attain instructional goals and whether an instructional product solves the problems for which it was designed. This module, Product Evaluation, is intended to make students aware of the need for product evaluation and of the steps involved in the process. It is an overview of evaluation procedures (Glass, 1973) that will enable students, once they have designed or developed their own course, to work with a professional evaluator to evaluate their course. The various procedures used for collecting information in expert reviews, one-to-ones, pilots, and field tests are described. Specific emphasis is placed on one-to-one evaluations, which are often conducted by the developers. One activity specifically addresses the formative evaluation of computer-assisted instruction lessons.

Design/Development Application

Design/Development Application gives students the opportunity to complete such tasks by following step-by-step guides for media selection, designing an assessment system, and planning a one-to-one evalution. This module contains step-by-step procedures, worksheets, quality-control checklists, and guidelines for documentation.

Instructional Strategies

Effective instruction requires the use of a variety of procedures that combine to form an instructional strategy. The appropriate strategy depends on the activity's objective and the pupose of instruction. The Instructional Strategies module introduces the subject of instructional strategies and presents procedures and techniques for implementing them. More detailed discussion of implementing instructional strategies occur in the Preparing Test Resources and Computer-Assisted Instruction modules. The Instructional Strategies module is based on Gagné's (1970; Gagné & Briggs, 1974) theory of events of instruction.

Test Item Construction

Test Item Constuction provides guidance in the construction and use of test items. It contains a discussion of the various test-item formats, the mechanics of their construction, and their advantages and disadvantages. Guidelines similar to those defined by Wesman (1971) are given for writing and using seven different types of test items: alternate response, multiple-choice, matching, short-answer, completion, essay, and performance tests. In addition, there is a discussion of the various scoring procedures and factors influencing the selection of appropriate test-item formats.

Preparing Text Resources

The Preparing Text Resources module discusses the writing process from the general to the specific — from analyzing overall course structure to eliminating sexist language. It provides an introduction to structuring strategies and the purposes of the basic types of text materials; it explains the purpose of defining, gathering, organizing, and obtaining permission to reprint the content of text materials; it describes the components of each type of text activity; it contains techniques for implementing instructional procedures and improving paragraph and sentence structure; and it introduces the concepts of reading levels, basic techniques for drawing up formats, the role of the editor, and sexist language in text materials. After completing this module, students should understand the importance of the structure of text materials and be able to research and organize content effectively and to write text materials that meet the basic requirements of instructional activities.

Development Application

This module, Development Application, is a guide to applying the principles of development as taught in the Instructional Strategies, Test Item Construction, and Preparing Text Resources modules. The module describes the documentation received and produced by the developer and provides a step-by-step procedure for applying the techniques of development. The module also contains documentation guidelines and quality-control checklists.

Computer-Assisted Instruction Design and Development

This module prepares students for designing and developing their own computer-assisted instruction lessons, introduces a six-phase process for developing computer-assisted instruction. The course explains and provides practice in the process of designing, developing, and evluating computer-assisted instruction lessons. It describes when and how computer-assisted instruction should be used, details a 12-step procedure for designing computer-assisted instruction lessons, introduces a six-phase process for developing computer assisted instruction lessons, gives guidelines for evaluation, and offers students an opportunity to design and develop a computer-assisted instruction activity. After completing this course, students should be able to design and develop a computer-assisted instruction lesson up to, but not including, programming. Students should also be able to evaluate a lesson after it has been programmed.

The first unit addresses the characteristics and modes of computer-assisted instruction, causes of frustration in computer-assisted instruction, and the selection of computer-assisted instruction as the appropriate medium of instruction. The next three units address the design, development, and evaluation processes for computer-based lessons. Unit 5 is analogous to the application modules for other courses. It contains worksheets and quality-control checklists.

PLATO Author Language: Part I

PLATO Author Language: Part I introduces the topic of programming instructional activities on the PLATO system. In this course, students learn the capabilities of the PLATO system, the relationship of programming to design and development terminology and documents, basic instructions used in programming on the PLATO system, and methods of obtaining information about the PLATO author language. After completing this module, students should know how to use approximately 50 instructions and be able to program many types of computer-assisted instruction lessons using these instructions. This course is intended for those students who wish to learn how to do the actual programming of computer-assisted instruction activities. This module contains a number of programming practice exercises.

PLATO Author Language: Part II

PLATO Author Language: Part II expands upon programming concepts presented in PLATO Author Language: Part I. It also presents new topics including single and multiple character creation, animation, relocatable graphics and graphs, touch-panel processing, judging and arrow processing, pause processing, argument passing in subroutines, curriculum creation through the use of routers, and additional instructions. After completing this course, students should be able to program more complex computer-assisted instruction.

Computer-Managed Instruction

The Computer-Managed Instruction module discusses a computerized method of testing, record keeping, and decision making that assists administrative, classroom, and individual learner management. The course examines how computers can solve the management problems of individualized instruction and describes the role of computers in testing and record keeping; it also describes prescription-generation components of computer-managed instruction systems in general and the Control Data computer-managed instruction system in specific. To show the full range of capabilities of the Control Data computer-managed instruction system, several alternative pathways through this module were developed using different media.

Management of Instructional Development

This module, Management of Instructional Development, introduces a four-phase process for managing an instructional development project. The first two phases constitute the planning function during which project objectives, constraints, and requirements are determined. The final two phases, which make up the coordination function, deal with implementing and controlling the project. The use of communication networks (Cleland & King, 1968) is briefly discussed. The module also provides a reference section for the manager to use on the job.

Course Implementation

Course Implementation examines how the development team aids the learning center in implementing a course. The nature, responsibilities, and operating needs of typical learning centers are explained to help the development team understand the setting in which its product will be implemented. The concept of an administration guide is also explored; such guides tell the learning center staff what they must know to implement courses.

AVAILABILITY OF THE CREATE CURRICULUM

The CREATE curriculum is a proprietary product of Control Data Corporation. It is available through any of the nearly 50 learning centers operated by the Control Data Education Company. It may also be delivered at any customer facilities that have Control Data PLATO terminals and the required audiovisual equipment. The pricing structure for the CREATE curriculum takes into consideration the delivery location (learning center versus customer site) and its individualized characteristics by enabling the customer to purchase only those components of the CREATE curriculum that are needed. More detailed descriptions of the CREATE curriculum and its delivery may be found in the CREATE Curriculum Description (Control Data Education Company, 1978b) and the CREATE Administration Guide (Control Data Education Company, 1978a).[2]

FUTURE OF THE CREATE CURRICULUM

It is very unlikely that the CREATE curriculum will remain static. It will undergo continuous evaluation, maintenance, and updating. Discussions have already begun about future enhancements to be developed based on needs and demand. These enhancements could include additional modules, the inclusion of more interactive tools to aid the author (even after completing the CREATE curriculum), or the addition of new features such as placement tests. Whatever

[2] Information on pricing and availability may be obtained by writing to Control Data Education Company, Attention: CREATE Product Line Manager, HQA03Y, Box 0, Minneapolis, Minnesota 55440.

happens, the CREATE curriculum is a product of what it preaches and will continue to be revised based on feedback and changing requirements.

REFERENCES

Bloom, B. S. Learning for mastery. *Evaluation Comment,* 1968, *1* (2), entire issue.

Bloom, B. S. (Ed.). *Taxonomy of educational objectives. Handbook: Cognitive domain.* New York: David McKay Co., Inc., 1956.

Cleland, D. I., & King, W. R. *Systems analysis and project management.* New York: McGraw-Hill, 1968.

Control Data Corporation. *Documents for education: Quality assurance.* Minneapolis: Control Data Corporation, February 1976.

Control Data Education Company. *CREATE administration guide.* Minneapolis: Control Data Corporation, 1978.(a)

Control Data Education Company. CREATE *curriculum description.* Minneapolis: Control Data Corporation, 1978.(b)

Gagné, R. M. The analysis of instructional objectives for the design of instruction. In R. Glaser (Ed.), *Teaching machines and programmed learning II: Data and directions.* Washington, D.C.: Department of Audiovisual Instruction, National Education Association, 1965.

Gagné, R. M. *The conditions of learning* (2nd ed.). New York: Holt, Rinehart, and Winston, 1970.

Gagné, R. M., & Briggs, L. J. *Principles of instructional design.* New York: Holt, Rinehart, and Winston, 1974.

Glass, G. V. Design of evaluation studies. In *Educational evaluation: Theory and practice.* Worthington, Ohio: Charles A. Jones Publishing Co, 1973.

Gronlund, N. E. *Stating behavioral objectives for classroom instruction.* New York: MacMillan, 1970.

Mager, R. F. *Preparing instructional objectives.* Belmont, Calif.: Fearon Publishers, 1962.

Mager, R. F., & Beach, K. M. *Developing vocational instruction.* Belmont, Calif.: Fearon Publishers, 1967.

Merrill, M. D. *Content and instructional analysis for cognitive transfer tasks* (Working Paper 40). Provo, Utah: Brigham Young University, 1972.

Merrill, P. F. *Task analysis – An information processing approach* (Technical Memo No. 27). Arlington, Va.: Personnel and Training Research Program, Office of Naval Research, April 1971.

Taylor, S. S. & O'Neal, A. F. *Authoring systems and large-scale instruction development for CAI.* Paper presented at the annual meeting of the American Education Research Association, Toronto, March 1978.

Wesman, A. G. Writing the test item. In R. L. Thorndike (Ed.), *Educational measurement* (2nd ed.). Washington, D. C.: American Council on Education, 1971.

3

An Authoring System for On-the-Job Environments[1]

WILLIAM P. HARRIS

The authoring component of a technology-based system for performance training in on-the-job environments is described here. The conditions for authoring differ in three major respects from those associated with preparation of instructional materials in a school environment. First, the area of application is training to perform the work procedures involved in the operation and maintenance of technically sophisticated equipment and systems. Second, the author is a subject matter expert, a person highly skilled in the performance of work but neither trained as an instructor nor skilled in the design and implementation of training materials. Third, the authoring is carried out under the direction of work managers and the lessons are produced to satisfy immediate work needs. Thus, this authoring system for on-the-job environments differs markedly with respect to subject matter, author qualification, and management from those usually found in school environments. These circumstances define a new area for the application of technology to authoring and demand a fresh application of the principles of instructional system design.

[1]This work was performed by the Lincoln Laboratory of the Massachusetts Institute of Technology and was sponsored by the Defense Advanced Research Projects Agency, the Department of the Air Force, and the U.S. Bureau of Mines. However, the views and conclusions contained in this document are those of the author and should not be interpreted as necessarily representing the official policies, either expressed or implied, of the U.S. government.

ISSUES IN INSTRUCTIONAL SYSTEMS DEVELOPMENT

THE AUTHORING SYSTEM REQUIREMENTS

The Setting for Training

In terms established in Chapter 1, the following three conditions prevail:

1. A subject matter expert, as contrasted with an educational specialist, is the primary author of the materials.
2. Aid is given to authors on computer facilities.
3. Materials are designed for delivery by a computer-based delivery system.

The area of application is Formal On-the-Job Training (FOJT) as defined in the Interservice Procedures for Instructional System Development (TRADOC, 1975). The conditions assumed are those listed as favorable to the on-the-job environment as the setting: Few trainees are in training at a given time, training resources are available on site, and there is time to train new personnel.

The focus is on the training of novice technicians to operate and maintain equipment and systems. It is the kind of training that bridges the gap between technical schooling and readiness to perform actual work. The usual method of training follows the ancient tradition of the master indoctrinating the apprentice. The setting is the factory, shop, or field, where learning must occur in a disruptive atmosphere and the materials used to support training tend to be inadequate. It is often said that the results are rather poor and the system is inefficient. Yet it is one of the most common forms of instruction, and since it needs improvement it deserves attention from instructional systems engineers.

Identifying the Training Problem

Work managers tend to feel that better preparation in technical schools would solve the problem of on-the-job training. However, training on sophisticated systems and equipments that are not available in school environments must be done on site. The Interservice Procedures (TRADOC, 1975) suggest that on-the-job instruction be improved by establishing training standards, upgrading instructional materials, and training the trainers, but these suggestions seem off the mark. It is the unavailability of qualified personnel to serve as trainers that seems to be the prevalent problem. It is a difficult one. Operational responsibilities must take precedence over training. Yet there is no substitute for the expert: In almost every work situation there is practical knowledge essential to effective work performance that only the expert has to convey. Under these circumstances the primary need is to make better use of the existing qualified personnel.

The Authoring Component for the Proposed System

The authoring procedures reported here are part of a system to remove availability of the trainer as the limiting factor in technical performance training on-the-job. Since the demand for this kind of training is widely distributed in time and space, a system is proposed to capture it in lesson materials and to deliver it as some form of computer-based instruction when it is needed The standard of performance for the system is to teach task proficiency in the absence of a qualified expert. To achieve this goal, there are two difficult requirements to be met, an efficient way to capture expert knowledge and an effective way to deliver it.

The expert must serve as author but it is not practical to take the time to train the expert to become a lesson designer. Qualified personnel in short supply for training are also in short supply for authoring and must be used sparingly. Fortunately experts need not be trained as authors in order to produce sound lesson material. The educational technique used by experts as trainers is at times primitive but their efforts are nonetheless effective. It seems likely then that the training experience of the experts would enable them to prepare materials by following a procedure if the design of the lessons is patterned after the authors' usual tutorial mode of instruction. This is the approach developed here, and the kind of material produced is called a *task lesson*.

Of course the development of a source of materials would be fruitless if there were no means of delivery. The features essential to an effective delivery unit are described in the next section. Implications of the means of delivery for authoring are examined before proceeding to a description of the lesson preparation procedure.

The Delivery Component for the Proposed System

The delivery unit requirements are based on a task analysis of what the expert does while training the novice:

1. Presents information useful in performance of the work
2. Tests and remediates learning of relevant information
3. Presents task instructions and safety warnings
4. Evaluates and corrects task performance

To the extent required, each of the four functions is performed at each step of the task. The authoring procedure must enable the subject matter expert to program a machine that has a capacity to provide these training services.

A unit suited to the delivery of task lessons must have the capability to

1. Display detailed visual information such as that contained in technical manuals and other documents
2. Monitor task performance and related knowledge at each step and branch to remedial material when required
3. Keep a log of training to evaluate lesson quality and to certify trainee proficiency

What is needed is a kind of "instructional robot," one providing intellectual rather than physical services in this case. A computer has the capability to monitor, as in Computer-Assisted Instruction (CAI), but lacks graphics display and mass information storage capacity. Text and conventional audiovisual devices lack a performance-testing capability vital to task learning: The effect of each step in the task on the system that is the object of training must be checked to assure that the system is in a normal state before proceeding to the next step. A delivery unit is needed that meets both requirements 1 and 2 above. Moreover, it must be designed to minimize the demands on subject matter experts as authors.

The robot need not simulate all the capabilities of a human trainer to be effective. It is enough to evaluate performance at a level that makes learning, not guessing, the more attractive way for the trainee to work through a lesson. However, it is mandatory to test understanding of critical facts and concepts and to check the performance of difficult steps in the task. Occasionally, this may necessitate human intervention. A degree of human assistance is tolerable as long as the services of the expert are only occasionally needed or a less qualified person can act as a substitute. Sophisticated monitoring capabilities on the part of the delivery unit are not absolutely essential, and therefore elaborate programming skills on the part of the author are not required.

Accuracy, completeness, and clarity with respect to technical content are crucial, and achieving them is by far the most difficult aspect of lesson preparation. Some talent on the part of the author is assumed, but special skills in the design and implementation of information displays cannot be expected. Authoring procedures themselves must promote an orderly presentation of goals, facts, concepts, and task instructions, and conventional display techniques must be employed. If these things are done, a subject matter expert, without formal training in educational technology and with little help from professionals, should be able to prepare effective materials.

At least one form of instructional robot is available that seems to meet all the requirements listed above. It is the delivery unit of the Lincoln Terminal System, the LTS-5 (Butman, 1978). A microfiche film card projector provides random access to a large store of frames of audio, visual, and control-data information. It is controlled by a microprocessor that interprets user inputs, logs training data, and selects frames of instruction. Visual displays that include text, drawings, and gray-scale photographs are projected, accompanied by brief audio messages. Test modes, such as analysis of the responses to a multiple-choice quiz or evaluation of the magnitude of a numerical entry, are programmed into the unit. An optional feature to allow the user to branch on his own is also provided. A record of training performance is kept in digital form on a magnetic tape cassette. The preparation of materials involves conventional artwork, audio recording, and data entry techniques, easily mastered by authors. Only a small fraction of the authoring procedures is specific to this unit, and materials produced can readily be adapted to any other system with a similar delivery capability.

THE AUTHORING SYSTEM

The system is presented in terms of the lesson-development procedures. The five stages of task lesson development are shown in Table 3.1, listing the locale, product, duration, and participants at each stage. They are consistent with the principles underlying the Interservice Procedures for Instructional System Development (TRADOC, 1975) but are not the same. Phase 1 of the Interservice Procedures, Analysis, combines similar tasks from different job assignments into training clusters. It does not apply here because the task itself in its natural sequence of steps is the topic of each lesson. The Design, Development, and Implementation phases of the Interservice Procedures are narrowed in scope and rearranged to meet practical limitations of the on-the-job environment. Control of both authoring and training is incorporated into the regular work management system.

Stage 1: Training Program

In general planning the content of task training is not altered by the advent of the new technology. Task lessons are organized around standard work procedures or other typical work processes. A program of training is a list of task lessons arranged in priority according to formal precedence relations, difficulty for the learner, and relevance to pending operations. Of course, the work manager always looks for a less difficult way to deal with work deficiencies than training, such as improved job aids and prior schooling. Training mediated by an instructional unit is planned when there is likely to be a significant shortage of trainers, when experts are available as authors, and when the size of the student population justifies the authoring effort.

Stage 2: Lesson Specification

A task lesson specification is a description of the requirements for a lesson in a given topic area. The kind of lesson is one that instructs the trainee how to perform actual work. It differs from the kinds of lessons that precede and follow it. It is not a lesson intended primarily to prepare the trainee for work by teaching component skills or relevant concepts. Nor is it a lesson to practice or rehearse an established skill. The task lesson specification defines the mission of the author, who must be an expert in the execution of the task that is the subject matter of the lesson. It is also included later as part of the lesson itself to guide

TABLE 3.1
Summary of the Five Stages of Task Lesson Development[a]

Stage 1. Training program planning

Location:	Work site	
Product:	List of lesson topics	
Duration:	1–2 days	
Personnel:	Work manager	1[b]
	Training manager	1

Stage 2. Lesson specification

Location:	Work site	
Product:	Lesson specification	
	Lesson validation plan	
Duration:	2 days	
Personnel:	Author	4
	Technical advisors (2)	8
	Educational advisor	4
	Training manager	4

Stage 3. Lesson preparation

Location:	Authoring center	
Product:	Lesson in draft form	
Duration:	30 days	
Personnel:	Author	200
	Educational advisor	8
	Technical advisor	4
	Trainees (4)	4

Stage 4. Conversion to medium (Lincoln Terminal System)

Location:	Authoring center	
	Fiche production facility	
Product:	Lesson on microfiche	
Duration:	30 days	
Personnel:	Author	4
	Artist/typist	32
	LTS technician	8
	Photo technician	20

Stage 5. Lesson evaluation

Location:	Work site	
Product:	Lesson revisions	
Duration:	10 days	
Personnel:	Author	8
	Educational advisor	8
	Technical advisors (2)	8

---

[a]Duration and man-hours for preparation of a lesson.
[b]Numbers refer to man-hours.

course planners, training supervisors, and trainees in the program of instruction.

The specification describes the conditions of training, the general training goals, work problems to be remedied by the training, and source documents for both work procedures and relevant explanatory material. A team that includes the course development manager, work manager, and subject matter experts is formed to prepare a task lesson specification. The team follows the procedure presented in Appendix 1. A typical product for an elementary lesson on "Changing Tires" is shown in Table 3.2. Items 1–4 describe the conditions and resources and 5–9 constitute an assignment for the author. The principal training objective is always to perform the task specified. A general standard of performance is given in terms of requirements for safety, dependence on manuals, detection and correction of faults, and so forth. The work standards at each step of the task, however, are established by the author in the course of preparation of the lesson. Also the explanations given at each step are determined by the author; the list of work problems in the specification provides important clues as to what needs to be explained. The lesson specification is very much an external one, except that the work procedure itself must be agreed upon in detail before proceeding to preparation of the lesson.

Stage 3: Lesson Preparation

The main procedure for drafting a task lesson is given in Appendix 2. The purpose of the procedure is to enable a subject matter expert to develop an effective task lesson with little outside help and no prior training in educational technique. The lesson is prepared on the basis of the lesson specification and work manuals. Authors work largely on their own, aided at times by an educational advisor, experienced author, or course development manager.

Part I: Outlining the Task

This consists of breaking the task into parts, that is, major steps in the work performance. A part of the outline for the lesson "Changing Tires" is shown in Figure 3.1.

Part 2: Preparing Block Diagrams

This provides a means for the author to lay out the general design of the lesson before drafting the frames. It is based on making notes on a generalized block diagram for each part of the lesson. Eight training fuctions are represented by the blocks and the author fills in notes in those considered essential to achieving the training goals. An example is shown in Figure 3.2, for Part 3 of "Changing Tires."

```
   f.  _ _ _ _ _ _

Part 3. Jack up the car.
   a.  Place plate and jack at corner nearest flat tire.
   b.  Place jack lever in the UP position.
   c.  Manipulate jack up and down until bumper hook is just touching bumper.
   d.  Insert jack handle and jack car until tire clears ground.

Part 4. Remove tire.
   a.  _ _ _ _ _ _
```

Figure 3.1 Part 3 of the outline of the lesson "Changing Tires."

The first section is made up of the four blocks at the top:
Block 1. Explanation: statements of purpose, relevant facts, concepts, etc.
Block 2. Explanation help: more details about content of Block 1
Block 3. Explanation test: test of knowledge of contents of Block 1
Block 4. Explanation test correction: remediation of erroneous responses

The second four blocks are related to the task itself:
Block 5. Task instructions: step-by-step actions
Block 6. Task instructions help: more details about Block 5
Block 7. Task evaluation: check on task performance
Block 8. Task correction: directions to remedy the faulty performance

The blocks may be grouped in pairs according to the general training function they serve:
Blocks 1 and 5   present information.
Blocks 2 and 6   present additional information.
Blocks 3 and 7   evaluate behavior.
Blocks 4 and 8   present corrective information.

If all four functions are served well for both the explanatory and task phases of each part, then the trainee will have the opportunity to learn. Continuous monitoring will assure that learning does in fact occur.

The design, of course, reflects a procedure that a live trainer might follow in training. All the possible training functions are provided for, although rarely will all be required in one part of the lesson. Nor is the arrangement always the best; by way of a counterexample, if operational definition of new terms seems important, then the task might precede the explanation.

Part 3: Making a Rough Draft

Three kinds of information make up a frame: visual, comment, and interac-

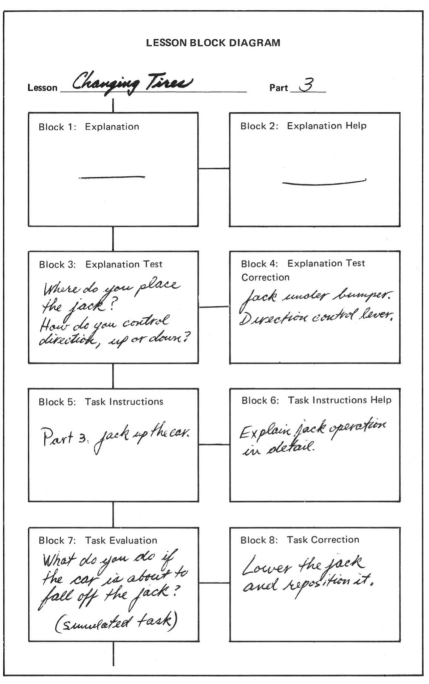

Figure 3.2 An example of a Lesson Block Diagram for Part 3 of the Lesson "Changing Tires."

49

FRAME CODE: 3.3.1

VISUAL:

Quiz

The next stage of the procedure is to jack up the wheel that has the flat tire.

Before doing this work, however, answer these two questions:

Where is the jack placed to raise the car?
1. Under the hub of the wheel with the flat tire.
2. Under the bumper near the flat tire.
3. Under the body frame next to the flat tire.

What is wrong if the jack goes down when the handle is pumped?
1. The lever is not in the UP position.
2. The jack is upside down.
3. The jack is broken.

COMMENT:

"Before proceeding, answer these questions."

INTERACTION:

Test Mode: QUIZ

On correct answer (2,1), go to the instructions, frame 3.5.1.
On wrong answer, go to the test correction, frame 3.4.1.

Figure 3.3 Example of a draft of an Explanation Test frame in the lesson "Changing Tires."

tion. The visual contains all the basic technical information in the lesson. Comment, in audio or printed form, directs the attention of the trainee to certain information to enhance training. Interaction is determination of the next frame based on either (*a*) an option expressed by the trainee or (*b*) an outcome of a test specified by the author.

The purpose of this procedure is to convert the lesson design in the block diagrams to a set of frames in rough-draft form. Some important matters are introduced here, such as the optimum size of frames, the need for clear instructions, the format of the visuals, ways to use audio or other comment, modes of interaction, and instructions to the training assistant.

A draft of a frame of the lesson "Changing Tires" is shown in Figure 3.3. The frame code at the top, 3.3.1, indicates the content of the frame: It serves Part 3 of the work procedure; it is a Block 3, explanation test, type of frame; and it is the Number 1 frame of that part and type. Thus, the frame code relates each frame to the outline and the block diagram. A test of knowledge is presented

---

FRAME CODE: 3.7.1

VISUAL:

[Insert a photograph of a car taken from the rear, raised on a jack and leaning to the left.]

PROBLEM: As the wheel is being lifted off the ground, the car leans to the left as shown above.

Which of the following is the first step of the proper procedure to correct this condition?

1. Drive the car forward to escape the jack.
2. Kick the jack from under the car.
3. Place the direction lever on the jack in the DOWN position.
4. Push on the car from the left side to straighten it up.

COMMENT:

"How would you cope with this trouble?"

INTERACTION:
Test Mode: QUIZ
On a correct answer (3), go to the next part, frame 4.1.1.
On a wrong answer, go to the task correction, frame 3.8.1.

Figure 3.4 Example of a Task Evaluation draft frame in the lesson "Changing Tires."

first because, it is felt that most trainees will already be familiar with the facts. A trainee who fails this quiz is sent to remedial frames and returns to try the quiz again. The next frame is the task instructions and it is followed by the performance test shown in Figure 3.4. For reasons of safety, the equipment malfunction is simulated in this case.

Part 4: Finishing Materials for the Delivery Unit

This part is not included in the appendices. It contains many detailed instructions on laying out the visuals, writing out comment for transcription to audio, and specifying frame data to support computer-assist functions. Some of these are quite specific to the Lincoln Terminal System mode of delivery but most are not. Roughly 50% of the author's effort in lesson preparation is in this part of the process, the "getting it right" after "getting it down."

The Lincoln system includes an author-support facility, a minicomputer with a special audio-data tape unit attached. The audio message and the data associated with each frame are recorded on magnetic tape. A simulated mode of running lessons is supported with computer control of audio playback, computer interpretation of user inputs, and manual access to visuals in the lesson notebook. Checkout by the author and tryouts on trainees are feasible before commitment to final form. These aids improve the efficiency of the lesson-production process, but they have an impact on only a small fraction of the total work involved in lesson preparation.

Stage 4: Conversion to Medium

The finished materials — audio or printed comment, visuals, and frame logic — are converted to the medium of the instructional delivery unit. In the case of the Lincoln Terminal System, the materials are returned on microfiche film cards, 12 frames of audio, visual, and computer data per card.

Stage 5: Lesson Evaluation

The lesson is installed in the delivery unit and tried out on a number of trainees. Given that the materials were subject to the recommended peer review and training tests during development, a good result may be expected. The conventional pre-and posttest formative evaluation of training probably can be dispensed with in this context since a record is kept automatically by the delivery unit of the time per frame and errors. Long dwell times on explanatory frames and consistent errors on the tests reveal the faults in the lesson.

Also, summative evaluation — that is, validation of training — is routinely provided for. Work records and other sources of information, indicated in Item 10 of the lesson specification, establish the validity of the lesson in terms of its effect on work performance. The mere fact that trainees complete a lesson is also an indicator of validity because the lessons represent an actual work sample, and learning is assured by the performance monitoring built in.

APPLICATION STUDIES

In order to give perspective to this type of authoring as a component in an instructional system, an applications study is reviewed. The new technology is being tried out in the Tactical Communications Area command of the Air Force Communications Services. A recent management study revealed a number of serious problems in task performance training. There is a chronic excess of trainees relative to the available trainers. The loss of qualified personnel through rapid turnover and reassignment has a marked adverse effect on training capability. And the manpower and training facilities to deal with these conditions are lacking. As a result a program has been initiated by the command to modernize performance training. An attempt to capture expert technical knowledge in training materials and use the Lincoln Terminal System unit to deliver it has been included as part of the program.

The training is task-oriented and hands-on to equipment. It has not been feasible to provide this training in technical school. Currently, qualified experts are assigned to train novice technicians who arrive on site at an average rate of about one per week. Duties other than training occupy almost all of the time of the qualified personnel except during a few slack periods in each year. Under these circumstances there is often a long delay between the time when a novice appears on site and when he completes training and becomes a qualified journeyman worker. The goal of management is to provide trainees with better access to training, and since trainers seem to be the limiting resource, the Lincoln technology is being adopted on a trial basis to overcome this problem.

Clearly a valid study must include both trials of the authoring procedures and tests of the materials produced in the on-the-job environment. Thirty lessons are being developed to train recent electronics school graduates to be proficient in the execution of basic maintenance procedures for a mobile radio communications set. These lessons are being prepared by technical sergeants using the authoring procedures described here. Records of the use of manpower and other costs of lesson development are being kept. A formal test will be conducted of the effectiveness of the lessons delivered by LTS-5 units at the work site.

This is research in progress and about twenty lessons have been completed. The estimates in Table 3.1 for Stages 2 and 3 are based on these efforts. These numbers are very approximate but nonetheless suggest a magnitude of effort typical of the production of individualized instruction. Other observations to date include the following:

1. Authoring a lesson is a time-consuming and difficult duty requiring uninterrupted and dedicated effort.
2. Novice authors need day-to-day help from experienced personnel in an "authoring center" established for this purpose.
3. Almost all lessons conform to most of the design requirements inherent in the procedures.

Senior personnel among the authors are of the opinion that few lessons will require substantial revision and that trainees will learn with little assistance from expert technicians. The fraction of the total training requirement met by the lessons and the labor costs will be determined in the study. These numbers will be used to decide whether this form of instruction is a practical means to relieve the chronic shortage of qualified trainers.

Another study, application of the technology to training electricians in coal mining, is planned by the U.S. Bureau of Mines. Training in this industry is done

TABLE 3.2
Example of a Lesson Specification

1. Course: Basic auto maintenance
2. Topic: Changing tires
3. Training conditions:
   Trainee: Auto mechanic, driver
   Prerequisites: Driver training
   Location: Shop, parking area
   Mode: Hands-on to equipment
   Aids:
       Training supervisor: Auto mechanic
       Subject matter expert: Auto mechanic
       Equipment: Tools, auto (U.S. manufacture)
       Documents: Manufacturer's manual
4. Medium: LTS-5 instructional unit
5. Objectives
   a. Change tire
   b. Learn safe methods and precautions
6. Work problems
   a. Auto falls off jack
   b. Lug nuts too tight or too loose
   c. Tools left at roadside
7. Typical work sequences
   (See auto manuals for makers A, B, and C.)
8. Related documents
   a. Manufacturers' manuals
   b. Zeblick, V. N. *Safe Driving.* Platt, Ohio: Bard Press, 1972
9. Planned lessons
   a. Changing tires on level ground
   b. Changing tires under adverse conditions
10. Validation plan
   The first 20 trainees to complete the course will be required to change a tire on a
   slope, and they will be rated on this performance by their supervisor. A rating check
   list based on the two lessons will be used.

at a large number of scattered locations adjacent to mining operations. The trainers are senior personnel who are constantly in short supply. The authoring procedures provide a means to capture expert knowledge of the maintenance of mining equipment for use throughout the industry.

APPENDIX 1: LESSON SPECIFICATION PROCEDURE

This is the procedure for preparation of a task lesson specification. It is Stage
2 in the development of task lessons. Stage 2 involves a team of qualified experts

who plan one or more lessons in a topic area and specify how the lessons will serve the overall training requirements.

The product is keyed to the items on the task-lesson-specification form. Because the entries in the form vary a great deal in length, make up the form and fill it out as you go. (An example is shown in Table 3.2.)

Prepare Validation Plan

Begin with Item 10, validation plan. Write out a brief plan to test the impact of the proposed training on actual work performance. Compare performance measures before and after training, such as

1. Work records, logs, production sheets, mission reports
2. Reports on equipment failures, down time, parts orders
3. Ratings and performance evaluations by supervisors

Prepare a rough validation plan; it will be revised later. If one cannot be devised, the course development manager should reconsider the need for the lesson.

Specify Course and Topic Area

Fill in Item 1, the course or courses that will use the lesson, and Item 2, a brief description of the topic area as given.

Indicate Training Conditions

Indicate in Item 3 the conditions under which training will be conducted. Under "trainee," describe very briefly the prior training and experience of the trainees; indicate the range, from least to best prepared.

Show the prerequisites, the prior lessons within the training program and other skill qualification necessary to profit from the lesson and to perform the tasks involved.

The location is the training site: classroom, shop, yard, field, etc.

Mode refers to hands-on or simulated relative to the tasks performed in the lesson. *Simulated* means that each task is described but the trainee does not actually do it. Use this mode only if performance is not feasible or if the task is already totally familiar and well rehearsed by all trainees.

List each of the four kinds of aids to the trainee. The training supervisor assigns lessons, schedules equipment, provides manuals, and monitors trainee progress. The subject matter expert is a qualified person who can be consulted by the trainee for help if necessary. The equipment includes the operational unit for hands-on instruction, training aids, tools, test instruments, etc. The documents are manuals, technical orders, work cards, training cards, printed lesson material, diagrams, charts, forms, etc.

One outcome of this step in the authoring procedure may be that the requirements cannot be met in the training environment. The course development manager may have to revise the course plan to accommodate the training requirements and impose limitations on the scope of the task lesson.

Decide on the Medium

The medium, Item 4, is the manner of presentation of the lesson:

1. Oral presentation by a qualified trainer
2. Text, with instructor support
3. LTS-5 or other computer controlled audiovisual unit

Set Objectives

Task lesson objectives, Item 5, fall into two major categories:

1. Performing the task:
    a. Working with speed, accuracy, and safety
    b. Working from memory or with the aid of manuals, work cards, etc., as allowed
2. Dealing with troubles:
    a. Recognizing troubles as deviations from normal system performance when they occur
    b. Diagnosing the source of trouble as faulty equipment, incorrect procedure execution, or false information such as messages or meter readings
    c. Knowing when to proceed to correct a fault and how to do it
    d. Knowing when *not* to proceed and how to get help

List the applicable objectives and the level of performance expected — how fast, which troubles, etc. Give objectives and performance standards for the lesson as a whole and for the parts for which safety or other critical matters occur.

Check the feasibility of achieving the objectives against the training conditions in Item 3 and the availability of qualified authors. One outcome may be that the requirements cannot be met in the training environment. The course development manager in this case will decide whether to revise the course plan, impose limitations on the lesson objectives, or postpone lesson implementation — whatever is best.

The basic work procedures and the standards of performance of each part must be agreed upon by the team before proceeding to prepare the lesson. At this point agreement must be reached on the basic steps in the procedure that define the task. In Steps 6 and 7 the levels of performance required will become more clearly established.

List Work Problems

List the major work problems in Item 6 that the lesson is intended to prepare the trainee to handle. Review the work process step-by-step to recall actual problems that have occurred and to uncover ones that have significant potential for trouble. List only the major problems, ones that are critical to the overall goal or are likely to occur; include problems that arise from faulty work performance and from false information as well as those due to equipment failure. Include hazards to equipment and personnel.

Specify the Task

A task lesson is always organized around the work process that is the subject of the lesson. Usually the work process is a standard procedure obtained from a work manual. If none exists, prepare one (or more), write it out, and attach it to the lesson specification. Provide at each step of the work process an indication of the level of the performance, if not obvious. Provide enough different sequences to cover all aspects of the topic area listed in Item 2. List the sequences and specify the source of Item 7.

Cross-check the work process in Item 7 against the training conditions in Item 3, the objectives in Item 5, and the work problems in item 6; modify the items to make them consistent with one another.

In complex systems and especially in maintenance operations it is often true that there are several decision points in the work process and thus a large number of different processes. It is not sensible to have the trainee memorize a procedure for every possible case; he or she must learn how to make the correct decision at each point. The skill knowledge required to do so, unless it is rather elementary, is usually acquired in training prerequisite to the task lesson. In such a case make certain that the prerequisite is given in Item 3; pick sequences for the task lesson that challenge the trainee to demonstrate proper decision making.

At another extreme some tasks can be reduced to pure procedure — little understanding is required. Training is in most cases the most costly way to improve work performance. Provide improved procedure as an alternative to training whenever possible. Provide it in the form of job performance aids, manuals, work cards, etc., whenever permissible in order to avoid reliance on memory, the most fallible of all human capacities.

Refer to Documents

List related documents in Item 8 that will help the author in preparation of the lesson.

List Lessons

Make a list of lessons in Item 9 that cover the topic area. Usually there is one lesson for each procedure or each variant of the procedure listed in Item 7.

Assign Author

A member of the team is assigned to author each lesson. The author prepares a task lesson specification for the assigned lesson; it is based on the original version and prepared by going back over the steps in this procedure. The specification is reviewed and revised by the team.

The team reconsiders the validation plan for the topic area. It may be revised to check on the validity of several lessons; it may eventually become part of a larger plan to determine the value of lessons from a set of related topics within a program of training.

APPENDIX 2: LESSON PREPARATION PROCEDURE

This is the procedure for Stage 3 in the development of task lessons. Stage 3 is the preparation of a lesson by an author who is highly qualified in the performance of the task and has at least a modest capacity to make an orderly presentation of information.

A task lesson guides a novice through an actual work process in the same manner that a master indoctrinates an apprentice. This authoring procedure is used to prepare task lessons that capture in instructional materials the capability of a qualified expert to conduct work proficiency training. The resulting lessons when administered to novice personnel induce work proficiency and free qualified personnel of training duties. The kind of lesson produced is particularly suited to the training of personnel on the maintenance of technically sophisticated systems.

The underlying lesson structure is one especially designed to simulate the live trainer, in terms of both informing the trainee and monitoring the learning behavior. The author is guided by experience in one-to-one training and by technical judgment to provide what is best for the trainee at each step. The lesson produced can be most efficiently delivered by a machine that stores within itself all the information required for learning and has its own computer-based capability to test and remediate the learning of related facts and concepts and to check on the performance of tasks. The product of this procedure is a finished and tested version of the lesson in notebook form ready for conversion to an automated delivery system.

A Warning to Authors. In the procedures that follow there are several places where the instructions to the author tell how to evaluate lesson materials through tryouts. No lesson is too simple to justify skipping these empirical checks. Trial on one or two persons is the only means to discover many errors in lesson design, even for experienced authors. It is far more efficient to spend a few hours testing and editing a legible draft than to correct the errors in the lesson in final form.

Part 1: Outlining the Task

The first part of lesson preparation is to make an outline of the task procedure upon which the lesson is based. All task lessons are linear in organization — the trainee progresses through the lesson following the steps of the procedure in order. The sequence is broken into parts so that explanations about the task can be placed at convenient points along the way. (An example is shown in Figure 3.1.)

Write the Procedure

Refer to the work sequence in Item 7 of the lesson specification. The procedure in step-by-step form is required next to test its effectiveness.

If the procedure is written in detailed form, suitable for an experienced technician or operator, proceed to Step 2. If the procedure is abbreviated, expand it to a level of detail suited to the need.

Test the Procedure

If the procedure as written has not been in regular use, get an experienced technician or operator not familiar with the procedure to execute it. Have the person work on the basis of the written instructions and under training conditions given in the lesson specification. Note difficulties encountered, make changes, and retest the procedure on another person. It is essential to prove at this point that the procedure is workable and that it leads to the desired result.

If the revised version is significantly different from the one in the lesson specification, consult with the course development manager and members of the team for approval of the changes.

Partition the Procedure

Break up the list of steps into meaningful parts. Each part usually contains on the order of two to five steps and requires an expert no more than 5–10 minutes to execute. Make a note for each part that gives

1. The effect of performing the part on the equipment or system
2. How doing the part contributes to the overall goal of the task

If these notes seem difficult to prepare, try regrouping the steps. The best definition of parts may not be apparent and one plausible partitioning may be as good as another at this point.

Name the Parts

Make up a name or phrase for each part describing the action or the outcome and write it on the outline.

Make a Job Aid, as Required

The task instructions in abbreviated form will be required if

1. The technician or operator relies on it regularly under normal work conditions (work card)
2. It is used as a temporary aid to memory during an intermediate stage of training but not allowed under normal work conditions (training card)

Check in the lesson specification under Item 5, objectives, to see whether using a job aid is approved and look under Item 3 to see whether one already exists. If a new job aid is needed or an old one needs revision, prepare one by condensing the steps in each part of the task into a one- or two-sentence instruction. Test the job aid on recently trained personnel to determine that it is adequate.

Part 2: Preparing Block Diagrams

The task lesson is organized around the parts of the procedure as defined in the outline just prepared. Each part of the task is expanded and becomes a part of the lesson.

An orderly procedure to design a part of a lesson is given here. It is based on making notes on a block diagram. (An example of a block diagram is shown in Figure 3.2.)

At this stage the goal is to make a set of notes as a preliminary to the drafting of frames of lesson material. The primary objective is to provide a detailed specification of the content of the lesson. A secondary objective is to introduce a scheme that makes keeping track of revisions of material easier. It involves a code for each frame in the form of P.B.F., where P is the part of the task, B is the block within the part (see Figure 5.2), and F is a frame number within the part and block. Because referring to blocks by number is a convenient shorthand, it is necessary eventually to learn the meaning of the block numbers.

The procedure follows.

Heading, Block 5

Obtain copies of the block diagram form. Fill in the heading for the part of the lesson.

Copy the name of the part of the procedure and the steps in abbreviated form from the outline to Block 5 of the block diagram.

Block 1

The purpose of Block 1 is to provide a place to make notes about information that will help the trainee to understand the procedure.

List the facts and principles in Block 1 required to perform this part of the task to the standard established in the objectives in the lesson specification. Do the following:

1. Define the product of this part of the task.
2. Relate how the part contributes to the overall goal.
3. Give facts, rules, principles, etc. that help the trainee to
   a. Avoid hazards to man and machine
   b. Commit details of the procedure to memory
   c. Check his own performance of the task
   d. Detect failures of the equipment and other abnormal conditions

Consider the work problems listed in the specification that relate to the present part of the task. Add to the list if necessary by reviewing the steps, and ask what are the likely and serious things that can go wrong at each step. Derive a list of relevant facts, concepts, etc. that would help the trainee to solve those work problems that he is required to solve. Discard matters that are inessential because they are

1. Irrelevant or unimportant
2. Already well known by all trainees
3. Needed only to perform tasks that are not permitted

Indicate the reamining items in Block 1.

One possible outcome is that there are no significant matters because the procedures are straightforward, failures are unlikely, or the training standards are not high. If so, simply note the product and overall goal for the part, delete Blocks 2, 3, and 4, and skip to preparing Block 6.

Block 2

Block 2 is a place to note optional help material for the trainee.

Expand in Block 2 on some of the matters dealt with in Block 1. Choose facts and concepts that inexperienced trainees might need to have explained in more detail. Optional explanatory material that the trainee is not required to master is placed here. If there is none, omit Block 2.

Block 3

The purpose of Block 3 is to provide a test of learning of facts and concepts.

Plan a test for Block 3 on material contained in Block 1. The function of Block 3 is not to provide a complete test of all the content of Block 1: The training objective is to keep the trainee on his toes and to raise the level of assurance that learning will take place. Try to make the questions or problems difficult ones in order to make learning, not guessing, the easier way to get through the lesson.

If it seems likely that trainees will almost always answer even the most difficult questions correctly, omit Blocks 3 and 4 and skip to Block 6.

Block 4

The purpose of Block 4 is to provide correction when the trainee makes errors in the test in Block 3.

Provide material in Block 4 that explains the correct answers to the test in Block 3.

Block 6

In Block 6 make notes of matters in the task instructions in Block 5 that are likely to require more detailed presentation for the inexperienced trainee.

Block 7

The purpose of Block 7 is to provide for an objective evaluation of the performance of the task instructions in Block 5.

Make notes to check the performance by a method such as the following:

1. The trainee obtains data such as meter readings, and these data are tested against standard values.
2. Photographs or drawings of good and bad results are presented, and the trainee selects the one most like his or her result.
3. The trainee is instructed to obtain the services of a subject matter expert, and the latter is instructed to evaluate the result.

It is often necessary to add a step or two to the procedure in order to obtain data or other information to use to evaluate task performance.

Block 8

Block 8 represents information to help the trainee cope with a failure detected in the task evaluation, Block 7.

Make notes on likely sources of difficulty and how the trainee should proceed. Have the trainee get expert help if needed and provide instructions to the expert on what to do.

Block 9

When the first block diagram is complete, have it reviewed by the educational advisor.

Return to the first step and repeat the process until all parts are done. Have the completed set of block diagrams reviewed by the educational advisor.

Part 3: Making a Rough Draft

The product of this part of the authoring procedure is a rough draft of the frames of the lesson. A frame is a unit of information display that the trainee acts upon in the course of taking a lesson.

The standard visual consists of a maximum of 250 words of text, usually 25 lines, 10 words per line. Illustrations subtract from the total text in proportion to the areas they occupy. Comment is on the order of one to three sentences of about 50 words or less, in printed or spoken form. Interaction is supported by options for the trainee to go on to the next frame, call for help frame, or respond to one of the following test modes:

1. QUIZ. Take a multiple-choice test.
2. CHOOSE. Select an item from a list.
3. FIXORD, ANYORD. Make several selections from a list and enter them in a fixed or in any order.
4. NUMBER, MULNUM. Enter single- or multiple-decimal numbers within defined limits.

Rough out the content of each frame in the lesson as follows:

1. Visuals. Write out the text and sketch in or describe the illustrations required.
2. Comments. Make notes on the content, for now.
3. Interaction. Indicate how actions by the trainee determine the selection of the next frame.

Make this draft on $8\frac{1}{2} \times 11$-in. or $8\frac{1}{2} \times 14$-in. paper, one page per frame. Leave the upper three-fourths or so of each sheet for the visual and the remainder for notes on the comment and interaction.

Get it down here. Do not take time to correct errors and polish. You will do that at a later stage when the content of the lesson has stabilized.

(Examples are shown in Figures 3.3 and 3.4.)

Block 5 Frames

Start with Block 5 of Part 1, the task instructions. Use the outline of the task prepared in Part 1 of this authoring procedure. If the trainee normally works with a job aid such as a manual, work card, or other printed matter, have it on hand to refer to or copy each step on the visual display exactly as printed in the job aid. In most cases the procedure in the job aid is written at the level of a qualified person, not a trainee. Each task instruction must, of course, be rewritten in sufficient detail to support the novice; often one job-aid instruction becomes several steps in the procedure for novices. Present as much detail in Block 5 frames as most trainees will require. Refer to prerequisites listed in the lesson specification to see what the trainee should be able to handle.

Specify photographs and drawings to define terms, to show the location of parts, and otherwise to illustrate the operations wherever practical.

Review the material to see whether there are any lengthy instructions that most trainees do not require. Replace these steps with brief instructions and move the details to Block 6, task instructions help. Put a notice that a help option exists immediately following the instruction it explains.

Put safety precautions and other warnings just ahead of the step to which they apply. Set them off in a box.

Put several steps on a frame if there is ample space. Allow 25 lines of 10 words each per page, reduced in proportion to the space occupied by illustrations.

Make notes at the bottom of each sheet of one or two points that might be called to the trainer's attention to enhance learning as a comment at the start of the frames.

Number the first frame 1.5.1 for Part 1, Block 5, Frame 1, and subsequent frames 1.5.2, 1.5.3, etc., if needed for further steps in the task instructions.

Block 6 Frames

Write out one or more frames for Block 6 as specified, task instructions help for inexperienced trainees. Only one help frame is allowed for each Block 5 task instruction frame.

One outcome is that there may be many frames derived from Blocks 5 and 6; if so, it may be desirable to break this part of the task procedure into two or more parts to permit a check of performance before all steps are done. If so, revise the outline, add two new block diagrams to replace the previous one, and return to the first step to design the frames for the first of the two new parts.

Conversely, if the frames for Block 5 and 6 are short, combine them into one frame, with the Block 5 material at the top and the Block 6 below.

Make notes at the bottom of each sheet of one or two points that might be called to the attention of the trainee in comments at the start of the frame.

Number the task instructions help frames with the part number, 6, and the frame number — as 1.6.1, 1.6.2, etc. Make a note at the bottom of each Block 5 task instruction frame of the number of the Block 6 help frame it calls, if any. Note on the help frame the next frame to go to — almost always a return to the frame that called it.

Block 1 and 2 Frames

Prepare the Block 1 explanation frames. The content of Block 1 includes statements, drawings, diagrams, charts, photographs, etc. that summarize

1. The nature of the result or product of this part of the task
2. How the part relates to the whole task
3. What may happen if safety precautions are ignored
4. Facts, rules, concepts, and the like relevant to the next part of the task

Assume that the trainee is familiar with most of the facts and concepts. Review each matter briefly and point out how it may be used to achieve the kind of task performance expected of qualified personnel.

Prepare Block 2 explanation help frames to elaborate on one or two points some trainees might have difficulty with.

One outcome is that the material in these blocks is excessive, more than a few frames. Consult with the course development manager to determine whether some of it should be moved to prerequisite training.

If there are only a few lines of Block 1 material, consider combining frames from different blocks into one frame. If there is a Block 2 frame, combine it with Block 1, with the Block 1 material at the top and the Block 2 below. If there are no Blocks 2, 3, and 4 and Block 1 is brief, put it at the top of the first task instructions frame, Block 5.

Make notes at the bottom of each sheet of one or two points that might be called to the attention of the trainee as comments at the start of the frame.

Number each new frame with the proper part, block, and frame number. Make a note of the Block 2 explanation help frame at the foot of Block 1 explanation frame sheet. Note on every Block 2 explanation help frame the next one to go to — almost always a return to the frame that called it.

Block 3 Frame

Prepare a Block 3 explanation test frame. Review the definitions of the test modes — CHOOSE, FIXORD, ANYORD, QUIZ, NUMBER, and MULNUM — given previously. Prepare a short test frame in one of these test modes covering the material in Block 1. Test the more important and difficult points, including all matters of safety. Make certain that there are enough possible answers that the trainee cannot pass easily by guessing. Do not test matters that are presented only in the help frames of Block 2, in fairness to trainees who do not use the help option.

Comment is usually a simple statement that a test is being given.

Note at the bottom of the sheet the name of the test mode, the correct answer to the test, the next frame given a right answer, and the next frame given a wrong answer.

(An example is shown in Figure 3.3.)

Block 4 Frame

Explain the correct answers in a Block 4 frame. However, if the original explanation in the Block 1 seems adequate, omit the Block 4 frame and return the trainee to Block 1 on a wrong answer. If a Block 4 frame is needed, repeat information in Block 2, explanation help, if it is relevant.

Comment is usually a brief statement that an error has been made and that remedial information is being presented.

Note whether the trainee is to go next to the explanation, to the test, or to the task instructions.

Block 7 Frame

Provide the task evaluation frame specified in Block 7 for the part.

If the trainee enters data that indicates the outcome of the task performance, use one of the standard test modes — CHOOSE, FIXORD, etc. If an assistant such as a subject matter expert is called for, provide a detailed procedure for the assistant to follow to perform the evaluation. Let the assistant determine the next frame to go to by a CHOOSE action.

Comment is usually a simple statement that performance is being evaluated.

(An example is shown in Figure 3.4.)

Block 8 Frame

If the task evaluation was performed in a test mode, give information in a Block 8 task correction frame that suggests what may have gone wrong and tells what to do next. If the task evaluation is done by an assistant, tell the assistant to explain the error and give corrective instructions. The assistant may demonstrate the proper procedure.

Make a note at the bottom which frame will be next.

Comment is in the form "You seem to be having trouble," "Get help," etc.

Review Draft with Advisor

This completes the draft of frames for one part of the lesson.

At the completion of the first part, review the material with the educational advisor. When all parts of the lesson have been drafted, review it with the educational advisor.

Choose Next Procedure

Refer to Item 4 in the lesson specification to determine the next authoring procedure to follow. If the medium is LTS-5 or an equivalent computer-based delivery unit, go on to Part 4 of the manual. (Part 4 is not included here.) To finish materials for other media, obtain instructions on how to proceed from the educational advisor.

ACKNOWLEDGMENTS

Major contributions to the development of the authoring procedures were made by Robert C. Butman, Frederick C. Frick, Terrill A. Mast, Timothy A. Smith, and Raymond A. Wiesen. This account of the work, however, is solely the view of the author.

REFERENCES

Butman, Robert C. *The Lincoln Terminal System (LTS-5), a brief description* (Technical Note 1977-13). Lexington, Mass.: Lincoln Laboratory, Massachusetts Institute of Technology, 1977.

U.S. Army Training and Doctrine Command. *Interservice procedures for instructional system development* (TRADOC Pamphlet 350-30). Ft. Benning, Ga.: Author, 1975.

Author Management Systems

A. F. O'NEAL and H. L. O'NEAL

MANAGEMENT SYSTEMS FOR SYSTEMATIC DEVELOPMENT OF TRAINING AND INSTRUCTION

This chapter will briefly explore the need for more sophisticated management support capabilities for the design and development activities in instructional systems development (ISD) efforts. It will outline the desirable characteristics of a system providing those capabilities and will describe a prototype system being developed in both manual and automated modes.

The scope and complexity of major ISD programs and the sophistication and detailed level of definition of particular ISD models utilized have greatly increased in the last few years. The advanced planning and day-to-day management necessary for such programs have become commensurately more difficult and complex. The interactions between the many resource, personnel, and schedule requirements involved increase the difficulty of identifying specific sources of problems and responding to them without causing problems elsewhere (Faust & O'Neal, 1977a, 1977b; O'Neal, 1977a, 1977b; O'Neal, Monsees, Cary & Smith, 1977).

In response to this management challenge, interest is greatly increasing in comprehensive, real-time, integrated information management systems that incorporate a variety of flexible management projection and simulation capabilities. It is becoming essential to give managers the tools to test the impact of their decisions *before* they commit project resources to courses of action whose consequences are not completely understood (Taylor & O'Neal, 1978).

ISSUES IN INSTRUCTIONAL SYSTEMS DEVELOPMENT

ISD is maturing as a discipline and a method. The models being used tend to have an increasing number of engineering rather than artistic attributes. That is, they are characterized by increasingly well-defined procedures and techniques, and modification primarily involves refinements, not basics. With this increasing process definition comes the potential for even more efficient use of personnel and resources (U.S. Air Force, 1970; Smith, 1971; TRADOC, 1975).

Today's ISD activities tend to reflect more the differentiation of staff and efficient application of specialized skills — characteristic of what might be termed an instructional analogue to the industrial revolution — and less and less the heavy dependence upon the idiosyncratic experiences and artistic intuitions of "renaissance man" types of generalists (Bunderson, 1972; O'Neal, 1977b). This evolution of the discipline holds the promise of great potential for better planning and management, and as the process and the roles involved become well defined, progress monitoring and evaluation decision making will become more effective. However, this process tends to be somewhat obscured by the details of its own definition. That is, as ISD efforts become more complex and larger in scope, and as the ISD models applied become more sophisticated and detailed, effective management and implementation become extremely difficult (Hartley, 1968; Montemerlo, 1975; Rankin, 1975).

Two ongoing ISD activities with which the authors are familiar are offered as examples of this problem. The first is the ISD effort to support the air crew training for the SH2F LAMPS antisubmarine warfare helicopter (Gibbons & Hymes, 1977). In this activity (now in the final phases of evaluation in both the East and West Coast training squadrons), almost 900 instructional and/or performance check packages were developed and validated in eight different media-delivery modes including workbook, computer-assisted instruction, simulator activities, and several still and motion audiovisual formats.

This effort progressed very quickly. It took a little over 2 years to complete the entire ISD cycle from analysis (initiated by Naval Training Equipment Center under their Systems Approach to Training study) through implementation and final evaluation. A large and constantly shifting ISD team that sometimes numbered as many as 50 people (both contractor and Navy personnel) and involved more than 100 different individuals over the course of the project was required to support this ambitious and effective ISD activity. About 30 major professional role classifications can be identified on this team (e.g., instructional psychologist, subject matter expert, scriptwriter, artist, photographer, and secretary). Many of the problems encountered in the management of this activity have served to underscore the benefits to be incurred through the types of automated management programs to be discussed in this paper.

The other major ISD activity that illustrates the need for more sophisticated management tools for ISD is the P-3 Orion air crew-training ISD activity now being carried out at Moffett Field (DOD Contract Number N00123-77-C-0792). In this activity the scope is greatly amplified. For example, instead of 900 instructional and/or performance check packages, nearly 6000 are involved.

The mix of media for the P-3 project is at least as complex as that used on the SH-2F project, and the audiovisual effort is one of the most ambitious ever undertaken on this type of training. It will take almost 4 years to complete this activity, and the combined contractor–Navy ISD team will run consistently more than 100 on-board personnel with several hundred different people having participated at one phase or another by the end of the project. When one realizes that each step in the ISD process requires the dedication of a different mix of these personnel and other resources and that production of one audiovisual package may involve management of nearly 100 identifiable individual activities (such as holding design conferences, holding artist–author conferences, writing specifications, and writing a first draft) the true scope of the management problem involved can be appreciated.

ISD clearly needs sophisticated management support. While this management system must obviously contain such functions and capabilities as resource, component, and personnel monitoring, as well as report generation, there is a serious need for at least two other essential functions: the establishment and maintenance of a historical data base and a set of modeling or simulation capabilities.

Historical Data Base

We were recently involved in the performance of a needs analysis pertaining to ISD management in which more than a dozen ISD activities within the Department of Defense (mostly Navy) were analyzed under a current ongoing Defense Advanced Research Projects Agency (DARPA) contract (DOD Contract Number MDA-903-76-C-0216). It was found almost without exception that these efforts possessed no useful historical data base on their development experiences. That is, when ISD representatives were asked how much it cost them to carry out various instructional development activities, they could quote numbers of objectives treated and total fiscal year budgets, but they were generally unable to document any detailed breakdown of the personnel or the lengths of time or costs involved in carrying out any specific ISD subfunction within their projects. They simply had not kept such records, probably because of the difficulty in doing so without some model and sufficient support (Bunderson, 1977).

For the same reason, detailed documentation of the training needs of individual personnel or comparisons between the efficiency and effectiveness of different personnel on the same team doing the same jobs were lacking. Without this data base, planning for each subsequent ISD activity will essentially proceed repeatedly from the same perspective. Each ISD group will, by and large, be destined to repeat past mistakes except insofar as their personal experiences and impressions can be taken into account. With increasingly well-defined and more detailed ISD models this data will be available (sometimes for the first time). But without a system for collecting and storing it, planning will be no better served than before.

Modeling and Simulation Capability

And now to the second — and perhaps most interesting — tool that should be included in any ISD management system: the set of modeling or simulation capabilities. These are dependent in part upon both the current and historical data bases for their effectiveness.

For example, through the development of a current data base one can obtain an accurate picture of available resources, the status of the development of the project components, specification of ISD event sequences and their resource-personnel requirements, identification of the roles and skills of the team, and an up-to-date picture of the schedule. From the historical data base come the cumulative record of personnel efficiency and effectiveness, the actual amount of time any individual ISD task has required for the lifetime of the project, and some ideas as to the actual availability (versus planned availability) of the personnel required.

As one example, in the Navy S-3 and SH-2F aircraft ISD activities extensive planning was predicated upon the availability of full-time Navy subject matter experts. There was some consternation when these were supplied in the numbers requested, and yet production of instructional materials fell behind schedule. In both cases accumulation of a small historical data base over several months revealed that by the time so-called "full-time" subject matter experts from the antisubmarine warfare community took physicals, stood watches, met minimum flight requirements, and stood inspections, they were available only about 65% of the time (Gibbons & Hymes, 1977). When these subject matter expert projections were corrected on the basis of this small historical data base, the problem was solved, and better plans could be made for the future.

What is needed then is a complete set of models with which to manipulate copies of both current and historical data bases for management purposes. With these tools management can determine the projected start-to-finish dates for any or all tasks–events in the ISD program. They can ask such questions as, With current personnel and resource conditions, when will the course be finished? How much of each skill available will be used? How many of personnel X, Y, and Z can be protected while the projected completion date is maintained?

As copies of the current and historical data base are manipulated by management to simulate revised conditions, the system can answer a variety of management questions, many dealing with the consequences of proposed decisions. For instance, if a planned media alternative is unavailable for some reason, what is the effect of its alternative(s) on the program? What if specified personnel need to be reserved for some other effort? What effect does that have on the completion date? What if a new completion date is desired? Management can then estimate the conditions necessary to meet the deadline (hiring more artists, for instance), and the system will calculate the effect of that change in personnel on the completion date. The completion date calculated by the system can be compared with the desired completion date and further changes made if necessary. In addition, the system assists management in deciding that hiring more artists rather then hiring more writers is the best way to meet an earlier deadline by indicating the limiting factors in any project organization. The system does this by indicating such things as how much of each skill available is being used and how much of each person's time is being used.

The effect of unforeseen contingencies (always a factor in the world of fiscal-year-to-fiscal-year funding and constantly changing weapons systems) could be explored as they come up using these models. The authors know from experience that it is not always easy in a complex ISD activity to determine the real cause of problems or delays. With manipulative models it would be possible to ask a variety of "what if" questions based on changing personnel mixes and therefore to examine more thoroughly the real limitations or problems faced by a project. For instance, it may be found that the hiring of two more instructional psychologists will have no effect on production rate or completion deadline. With the help of some exploration, using the management simulation, it might be revealed that the real bottleneck is in review and editing personnel.

Characteristics of Simulation–Management Systems

There are a variety of general-purpose and even training-program-specific simulation–management systems becoming available. These are currently finding their most effective use in planning and training support requirements analysis of major programs. Among these are such program/systems as Method of Designing Instructional Alternatives (MODIA), Logistics Composite Model (L-COM), and Decision Oriented Scheduling System (DOSS) (Carpenter-Huffman, 1977; Fisher, Drake, Delfausse, Clar & Buchaman, 1968; Hillestad, 1977). These programs, though they reflect varying degrees of sophistication and power, do not offer the solutions and support required for the real-time, on-line management of major ISD activities.

Systems whose responsiveness, user orientation, general architectural characteristics, and training-related missions are more appropriate as starting places for development of management support for ISD include the Navy's Versatile Training System (VTS) (Versatile Training System Functional Description for Naval Aviation Activities, 1977) and the Air Force Operations Resource Management System (AFORMS) (AIR Force Operations Resource Management System, Functional Description, 1976). However, though these systems would be good candidates for development into ISD management functions, neither of them currently incorporates anywhere near the full range of the necessary specific application programs (Hughes, O'Neal, & Hymes, 1977; O'Neal, 1977a).

Characteristics of the management systems that are required now and that will be required in the near future are fairly straightforward. Because of the compressed time frames of most ISD activities and the great number of short-term deadlines and simultaneous activities, the systems implied must be automated. They must be real-time and should support the capability for routine data collection, project monitoring, and report-generation activities while at the same time supporting the types of management simulation activities discussed here. Another important characteristic of these systems is their human engineering for users such as project managers, secretaries, and ISD team personnel — *not* computer programmers.

An illustration of the problem here might be MODIA, one of the most powerful and flexible of the simulation–projection systems currently available. The use of MODIA requires at least two expert teams of personnel. One team should be experts in the system being simulated or analyzed; the other should be specifically trained and experienced in the use of the MODIA program itself. In other words, this system, though powerful and sophisticated, is not human-engineered to the class of users involved in most ISD activities.

Finally, though there is increasing agreement on many ISD functions, interpretation of specific techniques and procedures and the types and number of personnel available to each ISD activity vary widely. Therefore, the management system to be provided (and specifically the basic data base and simulation components) must allow considerable local definition of critical parameters. These systems must be generalizable to a variety of settings and installations by the users at the setting — *not* by a team of systems or management experts. Let us now discuss some of the factors involved in establishing the data bases for such systems.

DEFINITION AND MAINTENANCE OF DATA BASES FOR MANAGEMENT OF SYSTEMATIC DESIGN AND DEVELOPMENT OF TRAINING

The effective management of any complex activity involving sequencing of tasks taking place within time and resource constraints, and requiring multiple personnel with different skills, implies the necessity for establishment and maintenance of a data base with certain generalizable characteristics. Detailed procedures and specific personnel assignments will vary widely between ISD activities, depending upon available assets and/or constraints and upon the particular ISD model being followed.

Therefore, if the data base and management system to be outlined shortly

Calendar	Personnel	Course Definition	Task Definitions
	• Personnel	• Identifiers	
	• Biographical/Person	• Objectives	• Event Definitions
	• Skill(s)/Person	• Key Words	
	• Availability/Person	• Media	
		• Instructional Classifications	• Skill(s)/Event
		• Event Hierarchy Identifier	• Person Loading/Event/ Skill
		• Status Vector	
• Project Working Days Definition	• Current Assignments	• Deadlines	• Definitions of Event Hierarchies

Figure 4.1 Author management system (AMS) data base.

appear as well suited to managing the manufacture of widgets as to managing design and development activities within ISD, this is a strength — not a weakness — of the system. It illustrates the adaptability of the system to a broad range of local procedures and constraints. Regardless of the specific procedures used or personnel available, however, certain managment decisions must be made and certain data must be identified and collected to manage any complex activity properly. This basic data structure can be represented in many ways, but for purposes of this discussion the conceptual organization shown in Figure 4.1 will be followed. Let us define these four basic data areas (calendar, personnel, course definition and task definitions) in more detail.

Calendar

Given that most development activities take place within some sort of time constraints and that in any event some historical record of the start and finish of activities would be desirable, an early activity of project management would be the establishment of a calendar. This involves the identification of some start date and the identification of the deadline for all design and development activities. Within these two dates, all holidays, weekends, and other nonworking days should be identified, and a one-to-one correspondence established between the remaining days and the number of each working day within the project. It is then easy to establish clearly that Working Day 15 of the project falls on Tuesday, December 13, etc. This greatly simplifies calculations, assignment of intermediate deadlines, and a variety of internal projections. In the absence of such a calendar data base, all too frequently miscalculations involving the amount of time actually available to perform major portions of the work will ensue. In addition, mere performance of the calendar exercise is valuable in that it lends a sense of perspective and scope to the participating management staff in terms of the real (versus apparent) time resources available.

Personnel

As reflected in Figure 4.1, the personnel data involve a slightly more complex set of management decisions and determinations. However, if the project is to be systematically carried out and managed, these decisions should be made and these determinations accomplished at the very beginning of the project working period, if not before.

Obviously, one set of data required is a determination of just what personnel will be applied to the project's activities. An array of biographical and personal information on each of the personnel identified for the work may be included at management's discretion. Certainly, such data as phone number or address for contact purposes would seem to be warranted as a minimum. The particular skills of all personnel and their usefulness to the project should also be clearly identified.

This means that within the personnel data base there will exist a master list of the skills the project will require (instructional designer, artist, photographer, editor, etc.) If this master list of skills is ordered and numbered, then, of course, the skills represented by each person will be a short string of numerical codes attached to the individual personnel records.

The personnel identified then become project resources and their skills are assets that can be applied to the solution of each management–design–production problem. In the event some personnel represent multiple skill areas, some priority ranking should be identified − probably in the order in which their skills are listed − that represents the priority of their skills application. That is, if a person is first an editor and then (as a lower-priority skill) a proofreader, and if a proofreader is needed at a particular point in the project's activities, the editor would not be assigned to that task unless all personnel whose first priority was proofreader were assigned. This ranking of skills according to priority helps ensure that each person's expertise is applied as optimally as possible.

In addition, there should be some indication in the personnel record as to the availability of that person. Some people will be available for full-time work on the project; others should never be assigned more than half-time, as they are also working on other projects.

With that information, it becomes possible to keep accurate track of the current assignments of all personnel, and it becomes easier for management to determine accurately where each new project task should be assigned. Notice that with the information given, this determination can be made on the basis of assigning the task to the most skilled person or assigning the task to that qualified person with the shortest job queue.

Course Definition

It is, of course, necessary to establish as soon as possible some representation of the work to be done. One of the first steps is to identify the structure of the course or that part of the course being worked on. The management system should be given a set of identifiers that represent the various components of the course (objectives, tests, special activities, etc.) and their relationship to one another.

This represents the structure, and to a certain degree the scope and complexity, of the work to be done on the project. To each of these identifiers can be assigned a variety of descriptive data. For example, titles, the actual wording of objectives, and lists of key words may be appended. These descriptors can be used in a variety of reports, lists, and searches; they will help to describe the course and its components to all concerned. For each identifier (course component) the instructional media to be used should be identified.

The resulting detailed definition of the media for all course components is necessary for training-support requirements analysis and figuring costs, and helps to define the resources, personnel, and skills required for the design and development effort. It should be apparent that the detailed subtasks and design and development events for writing and producing a videotape may be quite different from those required for the design and development of a workbook.

Every course component should also be identified in terms of the instructional classification of the component if applicable. Note that it does not matter which instructional classification scheme is applied in any given project. Bloom's taxonomy, Gagné's levels of learning, or Merrill's classification scheme are some examples that might be used (Bloom, 1956; Gagné & Briggs, 1974; Merrill & Boutwell, 1973). The important thing is that, as is the case with media, the design and development subtask (hence skill and personnel requirements) for a component with one instructional classification may be quite different from those required for a component with a different instructional classification, even within the same classification scheme. Otherwise, one would expect that, regardless of the type of learning objective encountered, one would always design and develop the same instructional sequence and components and that all instructional segments would require the same mix of skills and level of effort.

Given that each medium and instructional classification implies a different set of personnel, skills, and design and development subtasks, some sort of event-hierarchy identifier should be included within each component of the course. This would be an indicator of the mix and level of personnel and skills and, therefore, the amount of assets and resources required for the design and development of that course component (see task definitions for definition of event hierarchy).

As can be seen by the examples cited in the introduction to this chapter, ISD

efforts can be extremely complex and can involve thousands of course components. It is sometimes very difficult in a large and complex project to tell exactly
where you are, what has been finished, what is currently in process, and what
has yet to be started. And in the detailed and sophisticated ISD models now being pursued, the full design and development of each course component may require that a large and complex mixture of personnel, skills, and resources be applied to a large number of complex and interactive (and, it is to be hoped, well-
designed) subtasks.

Therefore, some sort of status vector should be appended to each course component within the course definition data base. This status vector would provide
information as to whether a course component had been completed or was in
process. For those in process, it would delineate which of the many different
subtasks (defined specifically in the master definition of the hierarchy being followed for the instructional component) had not yet been started, had been assigned but not finished, or had been finished. And finally, attached to each
course component in the process of being developed (started but not finished),
the deadlines for event subtasks currently under way would be listed to provide
management information as to when activities are expected to be concluded and
when, therefore, critical personnel-resources might become available for other
assignments.

Task Definitions

As part of systematic design and development of training and instruction,
the assumption is made that design and development will proceed on the basis of
well-defined procedures and techniques. These procedures and techniques should
be operationalized by management personnel as a set of clear and unambiguous
event definitions. These constitute the set of procedures and techniques to be
applied to each identifiable subtask in the design and development process for
every media-instructional classification problem to be encountered within the
course being worked on. (Remember, the assumption is that the activity being
managed is a *systematic* instructional development activity, not an amorphous,
undefined artistic-intuitive approach.)

This planning activity is valuable for several reasons. First, it clearly opera-
tionalizes the procedure and techniques to be used, resulting in easier personnel
training and more consistency across personnel and components. And second, it
clearly reveals what you do and do not "know how to do." The procedures or
event definitions generated are a working list to be utilized and applied for the
many advantages their definition implies. However, they may be modified and
updated at any time to reflect experience or better understanding of the processes and techniques involved.

Each event definition should include a clear statement of the personnel skills required to accomplish the event and the amount (person-loading) of each skill required for each event. This definition allows from the very beginning much better planning in terms of personnel and resources required by the project when you need it most.

Finally, an underlying assumption of a systematic approach to developing instruction and training is that common classes of instructional problems are frequently encountered and that considerable savings and efficiencies can be accomplished through the application of similar solutions to those problems. One implication might be that for any media–instructional classification encountered, there will be some well-defined combination of subtasks (events) with attendant personnel and person-loading implications that will represent that set of detailed procedures, techniques, and personnel required to complete the design and development of that instructional component.

These sets of subtasks (events) are defined as a set of event hierarchies (each component in the course definition includes a statement of which event hierarchy is to be followed for that instructional component). Each event hierarchy includes a listing of all the events, and therefore, requires indirectly a listing of all those personnel and skills for the design and development of that instructional component. Equally important, it includes a definition of the hierarchical relationship between those events (i.e., which events must be completed before other events can be begun, etc.).

It should be noted that the establishment of the data bases outlined in this section constitutes no more than the minimum set of those management decision-determinations that should be made at the outset and maintained for the lifetime of any complex activity operating within time and resource constraints and utilizing a differentiated staff of personnel. In other words, whether management of the activity proceeds from a manual (paper) or from automated representation of this data, the decisions and definitions implied by the data bases defined are very representative of those that must be done anyway.

AUTHOR MANAGEMENT SYSTEM–MANUAL
AND AUTOMATED

Two versions of an author management system have been developed, a manual (paper) version and an automated version.

Both versions depend upon the same set of management decisions and definitions (data base) completed at the beginning of the project. Both deliver from that data base essentially the same set of reports (briefly outlined in the next section). However, the complexity and scope of the project to be managed and the frequency and facility with which the reports can be provided depend greatly on whether the manual or automated version is available. In addition, the

Manual/Paper Version	Automated Version
• Form driven-manual system. (Programmable calculator helpful, not necessary.)	• Form driven-minicomputer based.
• Allows each user to define course, task, and personnel structures.	• Allows each user to define course, task, and personnel structures.
• Can be maintained and operated by managerial/secretarial personnel.	• Can be maintained and operated by managerial/secretarial personnel.
• Major reports available within two hours. (1000 objective course) 25 personnel.	• Any report available within 15 minutes. (1000 objective course, 100 personnel) Most available within 3-5 minutes.
• System 'human engineered' using simple, well-defined and documented procedures (flowcharts, checklists, etc.).	• System 'human engineered' using simple, well-defined and documented procedures (flowcharts, checklists, etc.) and supported by on-line interactive protocols with many automatic error detection/ reduction routines.
• Basic set of management/projection reports. Has a limited modeling capability.	• Rich set of management/projection reports with very good modeling capability.
• Provides historical data base for planning/ auditing support.	• Provides historical data base for planning/ auditing support.
• Model is 'tuneable' to reflect current data.	• Model is 'tuneable' to reflect current data, and may be allowed to be automatically 'self-tuning'.

Figure 4.2 Author management system.

levels of specification and detail of events, skill areas, and course structure that can be easily managed differ greatly between the manual and automated versions.

It should be easily seen that there is a point at which the number of interactions required by a large staff on a finely detailed set of events would generate so many transactions per unit time, that it would become an almost impossible clerical task to keep the system up to date. Likewise, if hundreds of personnel were interacting at any given time, manual generation of the reports and summation of the data would become very time-consuming.

One of the strengths of the author management system is its ability to manipulate the data base in a variety of modes to test the effect of different management decisions. This manipulation consists primarily of modifying the data base, then generating reports on the basis of the modification.

It should be clear that the practical scope and frequency of modifications are much greater with the automated version than with the manual. That is, where two or three such modifications might be reasonable in a several-hour period on the manual version, dozens per hour might be practical on the automated version. This could allow much greater exploration of alternatives and much finer tuning of management decision making under the automated system.

Figure 4.2 is a simplified representation of some of the major comparisons between the manual and automated versions of the author management system. Both versions are primarily form-driven systems. That is, in the manual version a set of self-explanatory forms is used in collecting and recording data and in the generation of reports. For some of the standard reports a set of calculator programs has been developed as a demonstration, but the system may be used effectively without them. In the automated version, the analogue to the manual system forms a series of user menus displayed on a screen, outlining the services and choices available to the user.

An advantage of the automated system is that, in most cases, ambiguities concerning the choices and services available can be clarified by requesting help, whereupon on-line supplementary explanatory material will be displayed.

Both the manual and automated versions allow (rather than require) each user to define his course, task, and personnel structures as outlined previously. Both systems, within their constraints and limitations, are designed to be maintained and operated by managerial and secretarial personnel. The automated version does not require computer programming–operating personnel, and the manual version can be easily learned by secretarial personnel from the user manual and its examples.

In the manual version of the author management system, major reports are available within 2 hours. This is based upon the assumption of a 1000-objective course and a development team of around 25 personnel. Some infrequently required reports may take longer than this and most reports will take 15-20 minutes to generate, with the exception of those reports that require no manipulation but rather merely a listing of a section of the data base.

In the automated version (depending upon the hardware implementation) it is anticipated that any report available for a 1000-objective course and up to 100 personnel will be available within a maximum of 15 minutes. Almost all will be available within 3 to 5 minutes and many will be available instantly. Of course, on the automated version, all reports may be viewed on the screen and/or printed on the line printer as hard copy backup.

The manual version has been human-engineered through the forms and checklists to be used. These are as self-explanatory as possible, and examples are provided in the user manual for their use.

The automated version has several advantages in terms of human engineering. The on-line procedures include interactive protocols with many automatic error detection and reduction routines. These include immediate, specific instructional feedback when many errors (e.g., domain errors) are detected.

Both the manual and the automated versions include some modeling capability as outlined previously, the major difference being that the automated version will have distinct advantages in terms of turnaround time and, therefore, practical frequency of iteration.

Both versions provide a good historical data base for planning and auditing support. Both models may be modified to reflect current data. That is, when the data base is established, management will provide its best guesses based on experience and/or intuition concerning how long different events will take and how many personnel will be required. As the historical data base accumulates, these planning parameters can be frequently compared with actual data and the model can then be tuned to reflect the real numbers or some compromise figure. The automated version, of course, has the advantage that this comparison can be made at every new data point and, subject to management approval, the parameters can be automatically modified by the system to reflect real data.

The manual version of the author management system was developed at Brigham Young University by Dean Black and C. Victor Bunderson, who worked from specifications. It consists primarily of a set of well-defined procedures and forms supported by a few calculator programs and a reference manual (Rodi, Black, & Bunderson, 1978).

An adaptation of this manual system is being tested on the P-3 ISD activity at Moffett Field. As previously mentioned, this ISD effort is aimed at development of about 6000 instructional components and requires a staff of over 100 people, including different subject matter experts for the 13 or 14 different crew positions and five different models of the aircraft involved. About 10 different course tracks must be monitored. This activity should provide a thorough test of this version of the author management system.

The automated version of the author management system was developed in the San Diego offices of Courseware, Inc. This version has been implemented at the initial Navy Instructional Program Development Center, Naval Education and Training Support Center — Pacific. This group is responsible for the large scale, systematic design and development of Navy "A" school courses.

Since the goal was to design and develop a system that could be maintained and operated by managerial and secretarial personnel, the hardware selected requires no high level of expertise to run or maintain.

The current automated author management system is designed for a Wang 2200T (32K) minicomputer with a terminal and keyboard supported by two floppy discs (265K bytes each). The complete configuration includes a printer and a single-card reader and costs approximately $19,000. The minicomputer functions essentially as another piece of office equipment to be turned off and on. The automated version is programmed in BASIC and would be easily transferable to many different hardware configurations with very little work.

ISD MANAGEMENT SYSTEM REPORTS

Basically, the reports that have been defined in the author management system are the reports that, in common experience with the ISD project, yield the most valuable kinds of management information. The goals are a well-defined set of basic management projection reports with some limited modeling capability even in the manual version of the system.

In other words, the author management system will generate reports based on current, realistic information or it will allow you to play "what if" games and project the possible consequences of various courses of action.

In undertaking the design and development of a system such as the author management system, several approaches were possible. The approach taken consists primarily of spending the time and effort to form a clear definition of the data base and its attendant utilities with the result that the data base structures are easily manipulable and simple to set up and maintain. It then becomes much more straightforward in either the manual or the automated version to clearly define procedures and/or develop utilities for the summary and extraction of information from the data base for any desired report.

The description in this section will outline a representative set of those reports that are provided. It should be emphasized, however, that if the data base is properly set up, any number of special-purpose reports can be simply generated with a minimum of effort. Since these reports are primarily simple manipulations of the data base, Figure 4.1 is again referenced as a helpful, conceptual aid.

Utilizing the calendar part of the data base is a very straightforward way to determine what project working day falls on any calendar date and vice versa. In addition, it is possible to equate a level of effort (e.g., 5 person-days) starting at any given time with a calendar date through use of the calendar, and to establish deadlines. From the data base it is possible to generate a variety of personnel reports, including but not limited to reports answering requests for such things as lists of all personnel with a particular skill, lists of all full-time personnel, the current assignments of any person or list of people, or phone numbers and addresses.

Reports generated from the course-definition data base are many. One is a report of the course structure, that is, a list of all identifiers and their prerequisite relationships with one another. During course design and development this is an extremely important capability, since the development team may frequently identify needed instruction that must be inserted or instructional components that should be combined, thereby interrupting or revising the numbering scheme for the total data structure.

This is an extremely tedious problem in a manual mode, and documenting course structure through representations such as course maps may be very time-consuming. (For example, the initial course maps on P-3 required over 2 person-months to generate one copy showing all course components and their prerequisite relationships.)

The automated version of the author management system has some definite advantages here in terms of automatically documenting with the high-speed printer all changes to the course structure. It is also possible to obtain lists such as these giving all segments of instruction using slide-tape media or listing all memory-level instructional segments. Of course, it is also important to obtain such reports as a list of all segments that are finished, a list of all segments that are not yet started, or a list of all segments that are now in process (mentioning at which stage of development each segment is). All these reports are available.

In using the automated version of the author management system, it is possible to run key-word searches on all objectives and key-word lists. You can ask for a report such as a list of all segments of instruction that might be affected by a recently received change in the radar system through searching for the word *radar*. Of course, this is possible in the manual version, but it would be much more tedious and time-consuming and would probably result in a greater error rate.

Lists by media and instructional classification, by specific event hierarchy to be used, and so on are straightforward reports generated from the course-definition data base. From the task-definition data base, one can get reports such as a list of the title and/or definitions of all events, or a list of all events utilizing any skill and how many hours of that skill are required for any event.

Another important report is a list of the event structure and definitions of the events used in a specific design or development procedure or event hierarchy. You may find through experience that you need to add or subtract events to any hierarchy, in which case the master event definition list must be updated, and the revised procedure will then structure and manage all instruction modules based on that procedure.

From checking the historical data base associated with the course definition data, you may find that some event is taking much longer than you had anticipated, in which case you may want to go into the task definition data base and modify the person-loading per that event for each skill involved. Some complex reports use a combination of all the data bases. A good example is the course-completion projection report, which looks at all course components either in process or not yet started. It calculates, on the basis of the event hierarchies and the event definitions, how many person-hours of every skill required will be necessary to complete the course. It will then calculate, based on the personnel data, how many person-hours of each skill area are available and project on what calendar working day the project will be finished.

A similar, related report would list what percentage of the total pool of person-hours available for each skill area would have been utilized in meeting that completion date. Obviously, one or more skill areas would have been utilized at a 100% rate. Other skill areas would have been used at some lesser rate.

Figure 4.3 shows the staffing report for an imaginary course before any work has been done. The course calls for a diverse staff with many skills; notice that in the case of Resource 22 a piece of equipment is being managed, instead of a staff

MONDAY, MARCH 6, 1978

RESOURCE	HOURS TO COMPLETE THE PROJECT		
	ESTIMATED	PROJECTED	AVAILABLE
01 Instructional Psychologist	85.00 −	85.00 −	3464.80
02 Subject Matter Expert	653.00 −	653.00 −	2828.64
03 Author	511.50 −	511.50 −	2183.96
04 Typist	213.00 −	213.00 −	2527.60
05 Instructional Technologist	82.00 −	82.00 −	2646.88
06 Editor	317.00 −	317.00 −	2022.08
07 Artist	944.50 +	944.50 +	744.08
08 Production Manager	46.50 −	46.50 −	886.08
09 Word Processor	201.50 −	201.50 −	806.56
10 Paster-Upper	77.50 −	77.50 −	715.68
11 Media Expert (S/T)	120.00	120.00	-----NA---
12 Scriptwriter	310.00 +	310.00 +	56.80
13 Photographer	100.00	100.00	----NA---
14 Media Expert (S/D)	89.00 −	89.00 −	482.80
15 Lyricist	70.00 −	70.00 −	681.60
16 Composer	70.00 −	70.00 −	227.20
17 Choreographer	301.00 −	301.00	----NA----
18 Director	91.00 −	91.00 −	238.56
19 Kazoo Player	91.00 +	91.00 +	56.80
20 Singer	91.00 −	91.00 −	181.76
21 Dancer	91.00 −	91.00 −	170.40
22 DEC	186.00 −	186.00 −	204.48

ASSIGNMENTS REMAINING TO COMPLETE: 2067
TASKS REMAINING: 1298

ASSUMING AVAILABLE SKILLS AND
EXCLUDING ANY SKILLS PRESENTLY NOT AVAILABLE
OR NOT APPLICABLE (---NA---), THE PROJECTED
DATE OF COMPLETION IS MONDAY, FEBRUARY 23, 1981

THE THREE SKILLS TAKING THE LONGEST TIME
WITH THE PRESENT PERSONNEL ARE, IN ORDER: 12 19 7

Figure 4.3 Manpower for course completion using present rate of completion.

skill pool. In this case, since no work has yet been done on the 1298 tasks involving a total of 2067 team-member assignments that are to be managed, the estimated resource hours (based on management estimates) and the projected resource hours (based on the teams' "task record" on all events finished to date) are equal.

This report reveals that if you wish to finish the project you must hire at least the estimated levels of skills 11, 13, and 17, since at present you have none of these people.

In addition, to finish any sooner than February 23, 1981, you must hire more people with Skills 12, 19 and 7, since they are the limiting factors. The number of hours of these skills available is less than that estimated to be needed. Hiring more instructional psychologists (Skill 1) will get you finished no sooner and will leave a greater percentage of personnel with that skill sitting around with nothing to do (unless they also have other skills that can be more profitably applied).

The author management system should assist management by, for example, providing reports and information such as that based on the prerequisite relationships in any event hierarchy (e.g., these three subtasks have had all prerequisite subtasks finished and any or all of the three may now be assigned in the design and development cycle for course component A.1.7). Furthermore, the system could provide information such as what the personnel skills required are and who the personnel with these skills who have the shortest job queues are.

Another report that could be of great value would be a nightly report listing all subtasks not finished by the deadline (projected finish time) on any given day.

It is clear that many more reports are possible and could easily be added to either system upon demand. In either system, the main historical and current data bases can easily be copied. They can easily be copied by machine in the form of the manual version or by duplicating a floppy diskette in the case of the automated version.) Then the copies may be safely manipulated in a variety of ways and reports generated for simulation and management modeling purposes.

No special reports are required using this procedure. For example, by manipulating the personnel data base, you may hire imaginary people with arbitrarily defined skills and investigate which personnel mix will most shorten the time required to complete the project.

SUMMARY

As ISD efforts become more complex and sophisticated, it becomes increasingly important and more difficult to manage them efficiently. Based on a needs analysis of typical Department of Defense instructional development sites and upon the aggregate experience of the development team in a range of Department of Defense ISD projects, an author management system has been developed and is described here that will help to facilitate process-and-product tracking and personnel assignment and will establish a historical data base for planning and projection purposes.

The system described is generalizable to the management support of any systematic authoring–production project and can be implemented in either a manual–paper mode or an inexpensive automated version that greatly increases responsiveness and system-modeling capabilities. The automated version is written in BASIC on a Wang 2200T minicomputer system.

This chapter outlines major data bases and reports common to both the manual and automated versions of the system as it now exists. The automated version is now installed and in use at the Instructional Program Development Center at the Naval Education and Training Support Command Pacific in San Diego, California. It is projected for use in a slightly modified form on the ISD effort for the Air Force's F-16 pilot training program, now underway. It is currently being enhanced and modified for internal corporate use on large-scale development activities by Courseware Inc., and it has been recommended as a major subsystem for inclusion in the sophisticated Computer-Aided Training System Development and Management System now being designed under Naval Training Equipment Center Contract Number N61339-77-C-0018.

REFERENCES

Air Force Operations Resource Management System. *Functional description.* Gunter Air Force Base, Alabama: Air Force Data Systems Design Center, December 1, 1976.

Bloom, B. S. (Ed.). *Taxonomy of educational objectives, handbook: Cognitive domain.* N.Y.: : David McKay, 1956.

Bunderson, C. V. *Team production of learner-controller courseware: A progress Report,* Provo, Utah: Brigham Young University, 1972.

Bunderson, C. V. *Analysis of needs and goals for author training and production Management systems* (Tech. Rep. 1). (DOD Contract Number MDA-903-76-C-0216 Courseware, Inc.) San Diego, Calif.: Courseware, Inc.: March 1977.

Carpenter-Huffman, P. *MODIA: Vol. 1, Overview of a Tool for Planning the Use of Air Force Training Resources.* (R-1700-AF). Santa Monica, Calif.: The RAND Corporation, March 1977.

Faust, G. W., & O'Neal, A. F. *Instructional Science and the evolution of computer assisted instruction systems.* Paper presented at the meeting of the Institute of Electrical and Electronic Engineers, (Electro 77), New York, April 1977.(a)

Faust, G. W., & O'Neal, A. F. *Computer-based management of instructional development, or how to keep track of the players and pieces while you play a good game.* Paper presented at the meeting of the Association for Educational Communication and Technology, Miami, April 1977.(b)

Fisher, Capt. R. R., Drake, W. F., Delfausse, J. J., Clark, A. J., Buchaman, A. L. *The logistics composite model: An overall view* (RM-5544-PR). Santa Monica, Calif.: The RAND Corporation, May 1968.

Gagné, R. M., & Briggs, L. J. *Principles of instructional design.* New York: Holt, Rinehart and Winston, 1974.

Gibbons, A. S., & Hymes, J. P. *SH-2F LAMPS Instructional systems development: Phase II final report,* (NAVTRAEQUIPCEN Technical Report 76-C-00SS-1). Orlando, Fla.: NAVTRAEQUIPCEN, September 1977.

Hartley, H. S. Twelve hurdles to clear before you take on systems analysis, *American School Board Journal,* 1968, *156,* 16–18.

Hillestad, R. J. *Review of the DOSS research: A briefing* (WN-9771-AF), Santa Monica, Calif.: The RAND Corporation, April, 1977.

Hughes, J. A., O'Neal, A. F., & Hymes, J. P. *ISD Task Priorities for CATSDM* (Courseware Tech. Rep., Data-Item 004). San Diego, Calif.: Courseware, Inc., 1977.

Merrill, M. D., & Boutwell, R. C. Instructional development: Methodology and research. In F. Kerlinger (Ed.), *Review of research in education.* Itasca, Ill.: F. E. Peacock, 1973.

Montemerlo, Melvin D. *Instructional systems development state-of-the-art and directions for the future.* Paper presented at the eighth Naval Training and Equipment Center Industry Conference, Orlando, Fla., Naval Training Equipment Center, Nov. 1975.

O'Neal, A. F. *Specification of computer aids to ISD.* Paper presented at the meeting of the American Educational Research Association, New York, 1977.(b)

O'Neal, A. F., Monsees, Capt. J. H., Cary, Capt. J. L., Jr., & Smith, L. H. *F-16 training management system needs analysis and design concept* (F-16 Development Report 12). San Diego: Courseware, Inc., December 1977. (DOD contract number F02604-77-C0075).

O'Neal, A. F. *Analysis of existing programs for CATSDM* (Courseware Tech. Rep., Data-Item 005, 61339-77-C-0018). San Diego, Calif.: Courseware, Inc., 1977.(a)

Rankin, William C. *Task description and analysis for training system design* (Training Analysis Evaluation Group Technical Memorandum 74-2). January 1975.

Rodi, L., Black, D., & Bunderson, C. V. *Author management system reference manual* (Courseware Technical Memo). San Diego, Calif.: Courseware, Inc., May 1978.

Smith, Robert G., Jr. *The engineering of educational and training systems.* Lexington, Mass.: D.C. Heath, 1971.

Taylor, S., & O'Neal, A. F. *Authoring systems and large scale instructional development for CAI.* Paper presented at the meeting of the American Educational Research Association, 1978.

U.S. Army Training and Doctrine Command. *Interservice procedures for instructional systems development.* (TRADOC Pamphlet 350-30). Ft. Benning, Ga.: Author, 1975.

U.S. Air Force. *Instructional System Development* (AFM 50-2). Washington, D.C.: Department of the Air Force, December 1970.

Versatile training system functional description for naval aviation activities (REG 31408-88-76). China Lake, Calif.: Naval Weapons Center, April 15, 1977.

5

Automated Data on Instructional Technology (ADIT)

T. E. COTTERMAN

INTRODUCTION

For a good many years the instructional process has been a primary target of alert thinkers, researchers, and developers. They have worked at the problem of producing effective learning, so necessary to the success of society and individuals, from a variety of vantage points and with slightly differing purposes. Those directly concerned professionally with the management and conduct of institutional education have given myriads of person-hours' attention to it. They have focused especially on such practical considerations of classroom technique, testing methods, curriculum planning, and the like. Psychologists with a research orientation have emphasized the learning process within the individual. Over nearly a century of data collection they have elaborated the characteristics and parameters of that process and helped to foster innovative methods. A still more heterogeneous group of individuals scattered about in business, industry, and government has tended very practically to concern themselves with what works best and most economically and is available. Their focus is on accomplishing the needed personnel training at minimum expense within the context of a larger system.

All of these people have been verbal (if not sometimes verbose) and have freely shared their findings and their thoughts in a variegated professional literature. Thus, it is fair to state that today there is, in one sense, no lack of information on training: On the contrary, there is an enormous amount of information. The problem is, instead, how to use it and how to access it efficiently for the purposes at hand. What one needs to know at the moment may not be known, but that can only be determined from a knowledge of available information.

WHAT IS A D I T ?

- COMPUTERIZED INFORMATION SYSTEM
- COMPREHENSIVE ABSTRACTS
  (DISCUSSION & RESEARCH)
- INSTRUCTIONAL TECHNOLOGY DOCUMENTS
- NUMBERING 10,712 (AND GROWING)
- INCLUDING 36 KINDS OF INFORMATION
- FOR DOD TRAINING ORGANIZATIONS

AUTOMATED DATA ON INSTRUCTIONAL TECHNOLOGY   **Figure 5.1** ADIT: General description.

What this chapter describes is not an innovation in instructional system development, but rather an innovative computer tool to assist in the process of such development and in research on the supporting technology. Since their inception some years ago computer systems have been used in a variety of now familiar ways. They have been used to handle information on costs, on management, and on logistics; to control industrial processes; and to provide or control instruction. Computers also are being used to facilitate various aspects of scientific research in all disciplines. More recently, they have been introduced into our libraries for managing and controlling the resources of the library.

What is briefly described here is a computerized system intended to improve upon the handling of scientific information. The domain is, of course, instructional technology. To my knowledge there is no other such system at this time, although there certainly are other relevant scientific information systems (e.g., The Educational Resource Information Centers, The National Technical Information Service, and Lockheed Data Systems). What is different from these is the kind of information made available. However, conceptually similar systems are being created by general news media organizations for their purposes or as a commercial service — for example, *The New York Times* information bank (Full-page advertisement, 1973: "The New York Times, information bank," 1973). The innovative information-science aspects of the system being described here were elaborated earlier by Scheffler and Cotterman (1976).

BRIEF OVERVIEW OF ADIT

I have organized this chapter around six questions that you might ask if I have aroused your curiosity. The first and obvious question is, "What is this information system called ADIT?" (see Figure 5.1). It is a computerized, on-line system. It is a real-time system, fully interactive, with the capability of retrieving any or all of any record. It is a full-text retrieval system. It is part of a massive storage and retrieval system operated by the Air Force Aeronautical Systems Division at the Wright–Patterson Air Force Base, Ohio. The hardware presently used is an ITEL AS/5; the software is leased from Mead Technology Laboratories, Inc. In Air Force contexts and elsewhere throughout the Department of Defense, where the basic storage and retrieval system is used widely, it is called Information Central (INFOCEN). The ADIT system is a part of and operates on INFOCEN.

What is involved? Comprehensive abstracts of two kinds: those that deal with sources relating original research and those that deal with discussion articles, books, theoretical writings, and the like. A fundamental feature of ADIT is that the abstracts (or records) are intended to be comprehensive — at least so far as original research is concerned — so that for many purposes you do not have to look for the original source to know what was done or found or concluded, or even to know how good the work was. The abstracts are surrogates for or stand in lieu of instructional technology documents of a great variety — journal articles, technical reports, books, house publications, and the like — with emphasis on Instructional Systems Development (ISD). It is our intention, as we build this system, to reach out comprehensively to include almost everything of a substantive nature available in English language publications relating to human learning. We even include items concerning early childhood that seem relevant to understanding the learning process. We also include information on task analysis, some descriptions of tasks, and documents on measurement that seem closely related to the training concern; but, we do exclude animal learning studies.

On June 1, 1978, we were operating with 10,712 records on-line. Additional records are to be added in ensuing months so that by January 1980 we expect to have approximately 14,000 abstracts (or records). I have supposed that the domain we are interested in might approximate that number, and so we are operating on the assumption that the system will be virtually complete at that time. For that reason, I prefer to talk of records within the system rather than just abstracts.

Who is the system for? It is for anyone in the Department of Defense concerned with training, whether the concern is research, development of the technology, or the application of the technology in any way. It may be used in curriculum planning, in defining the requirements for or characteristics of training equipment, or in the development of particular courses. We think that this kind of information — particularly for one who needs to apply it quickly and has little time to go to libraries and scrabble through shelves — offers an immediacy, a specificity, a currency, a completeness, and overall an efficiency that cannot be found elsewhere. It is automated data on instructional technology.

WHAT INFORMATION IS IN A D I T RECORDS ?

BIBLIOGRAPHIC :

- CITATION, AUTHOR, TITLE, DATE, ORGANIZATION
  SPONSOR, REPORT NUMBER, OTHER NUMBER, SOURCE ID.

- CONTRACT / PROJECT, DISTRIBUTION, CLASSIFICATION,
  DECLASSIFICATION, NOTES, SUPL. NOTES

- TYPE PUB., PAGES, NUMBER REFERENCES

- UPDATE, LOCATION

TECHNICAL :

- ABSTRACT, CONCLUSIONS, RESEARCH NEEDED

- EVALUATION, QUALITY INDEX, COMMENTS

- TYPE, KEYWORDS, UNIQUE WORDS, CROSS REF.

- METHOD, APPARATUS / MEDIA, SUBJECTS, INDEP. VAR.,   **Figure 5.2** Information in ADIT
  DEPEND VAR., MEASURES / STAT.   records

CONTENT OF ADIT RECORDS

What information is in ADIT records? As may be seen in Figure 5.2, the content of a record can be conveniently sorted into two categories — bibliographic and technical. However, not all the kinds of information or segments included are independent of one another. Those that do provide the unique information are underlined. Obviously, the author, title, date, and organization are included in a normal citation. Consequently, when these items appear separately, they are redundant. They and the other redundant information are included for convenience in searching and retrieval.

It should also be noted that different documents involve differing amounts of information. For example, *contract-project* and so forth typically are not applicable to a book. The file does not include classified information. *Update* and *location* are simply convenience segments or fields used by us in managing the system. Similarly, *method, apparatus-media,* and the like are applicable only to the research documents.

EQUIPMENT AND MATERIALS FOR USE

What is needed for access to the system? As is shown in Figure 5.3, one needs only a common computer terminal and an ordinary telephone. If you are within the Department of Defense, AUTOVON will do it, or the WATS system will do it, or you can access the system through regular commercial lines. AUTOVON is the automatic voice switching network of the Defense communications system; WATS is the commercially available Wide Area Telephone Service.

WHAT IS NEEDED FOR ACCESS TO A D I T ?

● COMMON COMPUTER TERMINAL
  ($2,000 AND UP)

● CLASS A TELEPHONE
  (AV., WATS, COMMERCIAL)

● USER IDENTIFICATION
  (IO - DIGIT NUMBER)

● GUIDE TO USE
  (FOR TRAINING AND AIDING

Figure 5.3 Equipment and material needed for using ADIT.

You do need a unique identification number and you probably will need, unless you are very familiar with such systems, a guide to the use of it that gives you the necessary information about the segments and the procedures. We have prepared such a guide (Cotterman, 1977). With diligent effort a person can come a long way toward proficiency in using ADIT simply by reading the guide, using the adjunct questions in appendices, and following through with the practice exercises that are included. The guide also provides information that you need occasionally at the terminal even if you are proficient with the system. From time to time the guide will be changed to reflect system changes and user experience. Additional system information of a complex nature or subject to frequent change will be provided by letter.

METHOD OF USE

Your next question might be, How is ADIT used? Those of you familiar with computers may find this very simplistic. It is really very easy, as Figure 5.4 illustrates. You dial up, establish a linkage with the computer center, identify yourself with the 10-digit number, and state which of the numerous files accommodated by the INFOCEN system you want. At that point, you are ready to make a search. (Incidentally, the Navy's file catalog of Navy training courses [CANTRAC] can be selected in the same way: it is on the same computer system and the same general procedures apply.)

There are some particular procedures that you have to learn, but they are not very complicated. After entering your request, the answer you get is always in the form, "X many answers satisfy your request." For example, with respect to your question, "What records were authored by so-and-so?" the system response might be that there are 17 answers. You then have a choice. You can go on and display those answers, or you can modify your search. Suppose you had asked for information on computer-aided instruction (CAI). You might then decide, rather than looking at all of CAI (which is a large field), that you will look only at items dealing with both CAI and programmed learning. You could then modi-

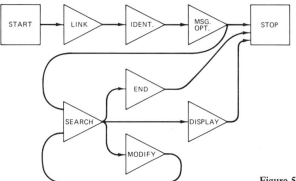

Figure 5.4 Method of using ADIT.

fy the search without displaying what you had first called out. In that fashion, modifying either by *and,* with which you add additional requirements and restrict the search, or by *or,* with which you expand the search, you can obtain precisely what you want. If there are no answers and you feel it is not likely you would get any by a modification, you can instead make a new request. Or, of course, you can just stop there. Thus, several choices are possible when the system reports the number of answers to your query.

You can elect to look at any part of or all of the records that you have retrieved. You can look at only the author information, or the citation, or the abstract. Or you can look at the search term in the textual context and expand that context very flexibly. You can display the whole record. You can display the record at your terminal — on the cathode ray tube, or with your printer — or, alternatively, you can ask that it be printed off-line at the computer center and forwarded to you by mail. You can modify your search even after displaying some of the records, perhaps deciding that was not all you wanted or that you did not need all you were getting. In short, it is a very flexible system.

DVELOPMENT AND MANAGEMENT

Now you may be curious as to how ADIT was developed and how it is managed (see Figure 5.5). To summarize briefly, the program is an Air Force Human Resources Laboratory (AFHRL) effort that we began formally in 1974, although there were some years of related activity before it. It follows an interest that we have had for many years in systematically organizing information on learning and training. For example, some may recall that we defined and worked on the problem of task classification a number of years ago for that purpose (Cotterman, 1959; Stolurow, 1964). Shortly prior to formally beginning this program, we arranged for the production of a *Handbook for Designers of Instructional Systems,* which is designated Air Force Pamphlet 50-58 (1974).

HOW IS A D I T DEVELOPED AND MANAGED?

● AFHRL PROGRAM, FORMALLY BEGUN 1974

● CONTRACTOR - PREPARED ABSTRACTS

● IN - HOUSE INTEGRATION AND OPERATION

● PARTICIPATIVE JOINT SUPPORT BY   **Figure 5.5** ADIT development and man-
ARMY (ARI), NAVY (NPRDC), AND ARPA   agement.

Our development policy has been to secure the abstract records on a contractual basis. The same group that supplied the Air Force pamphlet, Applied Science Associates, delivered the first nearly 2700 records under a separate contract. The history and certain products of this effort were documented in a series of technical reports (Schumacher, 1973; Schumacher, Pearlstein, & Martin, 1974; Schumacher, Swezey, Pearlstein, & Valverde, 1974; Schumacher & Wiltman, 1974). At about the same time the feasibility and utility of a computerized system were being examined by the University of Dayton (Sheffler, DaPolito, McAdams, & Gee, 1974). Having decided to proceed with the system, we have secured subsequent records continuously over a period of years from the University of Dayton. We do not have the resources and people to prepare them ourselves even though we might like to do so.

The records are costly and so it has been necessary to sacrifice a bit of quality. To keep costs down our contractor has employed recent graduates or students in psychology to do the abstracting. Not being fully qualified professionals, these abstractors do occasionally introduce errors in the abstracts, and they lack an adequate perspective for making the evaluation of the work. Nevertheless, because each draft record is fully reviewed by a senior, experienced staff member, the majority of the records produced and introduced in the system are of a uniformly high quality.

At our laboratory, we integrate the information, see that it gets on the system, and manage the various details of development. Financial support for ADIT has come from the Army Research Institute for the Behavioral and Social Sciences, form the Navy Personnel and Training Research Center, and from the Cybernetics Technology Office of Defense Advanced Research Projects Agency, as well as from the Air Force Office of Scientific Research. From the formal beginning in 1974 ADIT has been a jointly supported effort.

PROSPECTS FOR THE FUTURE

Perhaps your next question is, What is the future of ADIT? Several current and future activities are summarized in Figure 5.6. We are in the process of improving and refining our existing records. There are some annoying typograhical

WHAT IS THE FUTURE OF A D I T ?

●   REFINEMENT OF EXISTING RECORDS

●   COMPLETION OF COVERAGE
    (85 % JULY 78)

●   COMMERCIAL NET ACCESS ?

●   CONTINUING OPERATION AND SUPPORT BY
    DOD AND JOINT SERVICES COMMITMENT

●   DEVELOPMENT OF PRINCIPLES / PRESCRIPTIONS
    CAPABILITY   **Figure 5.6** The future of ADIT.

errors and some technical inaccuracies that are being corrected. There also are occasional difficulties with the retrieval process, which we expect to remove. We are trying to make the records a highly accurate, useful, and dependable source of information.

We are continuing also to move twoard the completion of coverage and, as already stated, we expect to do so by January 1980, with a total of about 14,000 records. During the process of completion and as the system becomes more ready for use, still more people and agencies within the Department of Defense probably will become interested in using ADIT. (There already are some two dozen users.) With increasing usage it may be that, as an economy measure on behalf of users, we will make the system available through a commercial net. This would have the pleasant result of substantially reducing access costs to perhaps half of commercial long-distance toll charges. That would be advantageous to those who find AUTOVON and WATS unacceptable because of time limts or other reasons.

Even before the coverage is complete — that is, by April 1979 — we hope to have made firm arrangements within the Department of Defense for the continued operation and support of the system. Although clearly intended as a technical library-at-your-fingertips rather than as a retrieval service, still a minimal staffing of perhaps two persons will be required. There also will be continued costs of computer support and the need for updating with the addition of 500–600 records per year. We do not know quite how that will be accomplished, but we certainly hope that it will be arranged because we believe that ADIT is a unique and valuable system.

Incidentally, apart from hearsay and the informal enthusiasm of users, some evaluative information has been obtained tending to substantiate that belief. In March of 1977 data were gathered at Lowry Air Force Base, Colorado, from 12 individuals who might, in the normal course of their work activities, use such a system. Some were members of the Technical Training Division, Air Force Human Resources Laboratory, and some were members of the Air Force Air Training Command, which operates the Technical Training Center there. What we did, simply, was to ask the people to learn how to use the system. They used the guide and had the benefit of low-key tutorial assistance by an experienced person if they needed help. Otherwise we left them on their own.

When they were finished with the guide, we gave them a job-performance test to see how well they could operate in a representative fashion. It was a fairly extensive and demanding test. We also gave them two short questionnaires to obtain their reactions to the guide as a training and aiding handbook as well as to the overall system. We found that the people did learn the system: Some of them learned it extremely well. They represented a very heterogeneous group — all the way from GS-3 to GS-11 and from airman to captain. One of the best performances was turned in by a GS-4, secretary-clerical aide. That was a 61 out of a possible score of 67, where 67 represents a level of expertise that one would not expect of a novice. Judging from the questionnaire responses, the participants apparently were reasonably satisfied with the guide and quite pleased with the system. These results will be documented in an AFHRL technical report (Cotterman & Thomas, in preparation). Parallel evaluations are being conducted by the participating Army and Navy agencies.

The ADIT system is, of course, being developed within the Department of Defense for internal use in facilitating the extensive planning, development, and decisions relating to training that must be accomplished, as well as for training research. There probably would be no difficulty in arranging access by other agencies of the federal government. However, at present there are no plans to extend access to civilian organizations or persons. To do so according to current regulations would necessitate some arrangement for recouping at least 50% of the cost and would probably require an elaborate accounting system with considerable administration expense. Nevertheless, one may surmise that if the system is found as useful as can be expected, some way will be found to share it more widely. Note that civilian contractors or grantees of Department of Defense agencies can now secure the benefits of ADIT indirectly through requests to their program monitors.

EXTENSIONS OF ADIT

Finally, in regard to the future of ADIT, one other expectation should be mentioned. It is our plan to extend the system's capabilities in a way that will make its use for typical purposes even more efficient. Think of training information needs in a system-analysis way for a moment. As a training planner–developer, you want information about selecting training devices and choosing course content, course organization, and so forth relevant to a particular problem. Depending on available time, you will look in handbooks, review articles, and maybe original reference documents for findings and generalities that apply. What you are really looking for is not the documents but the information that the documents contain. You are looking for the applicable and creditable facts. The existing ADIT system allows you to gain access to that information a good deal more quickly. It is a highly efficient fact-retrieval system.

But for matters of application even the facts of specific studies are not what you use directly. Rather, what you use and need are the consensual assertions (i.e., general rules) derived (often by yourself) from the facts. With these you can then accomplish the final step — a choice or a decision about the particular problem at hand. In other words, you can use the generality to arrive at a prescription for this instance.

We believe that we can extend the ADIT concept and build upon the data base of the system to go beyond fact retrieval and provide such principles and prescriptions. The principles capability would allow a user to make a query like "When are slides useful?" What would be obtained are the kinds of general statements summarizing the existing knowledge that you might like to have available in a handbook on your desk for frequent reference. They would be computed on the basis of existing evidence, and if the evidence warranted no general assertions, that too would be known.

Then, if principles can be provided, we can probably go one step further to provide a capability for prescriptions and guidance about particular training problems. For example, one might ask, "What sound-slide or movie presentation would be best for this segment of instruction?" Obviously, the system would not be able to answer a question such as that without some elaboration: What kind of people? What kind of training? For what purpose? Through a sequence of such interaction the query would be specified and narrowed so that available principles could be applied.

These refinements, you may well imagine, involve an extensive conceptual development, some recoding of the data base, and considerable system analysis and programming. We think we see the way to do this. We hope that it will be possible to do it within the next few years. Not only would the resulting capabilities be helpful to practitioners; they would be equally helpful to researchers in clearly defining what is known and what is yet to be learned.

SUMMARY

In summary, ADIT is a large information storage and retrieval system being developed within the Department of Defense that provides for efficient, direct access to the enormous amount of information on human learning and training. Rather than providing document-location and ordering services, as is typical of other scientific information retrieval systems, this system is a library at your fingertips giving direct user access to the information. This is accomplished by (*a*) comprehensive textual abstracts of original research that generally can be used in lieu of the reference documents; (*b*) extended records with detailed, partially redundant retrieval information; and (*c*) use of an interactive, real-time, on-line computer system providing highly flexible full-text retrieval either directly or off-line. Access is by ordinary telephone and requires only a common computer terminal and appropriate user identification. Procedural operation is rather simple and easily learned in a single day with the use of an available guide.

Routine operation of ADIT for access by Department of Defense personnel and agencies concerned with training is expected to begin about April, 1979. However, record refinement and full coverage of the instructional technology domain, estimated to involve about 14,000 records, will not be completed until January 1980. Arrangements for continuing operation and file updating are anticipated. Informal reaction and comment from potential users and some formal data suggest that the system will be very useful to and well received by those having a serious interest in the technical data it affords.

In addition to the existing fact-retrieval capability of ADIT, two extensions or refinements in capability are planned for development over the next several years. The first of these is the capability to request and obtain consensual assertions on specified instructional issues based upon the available data. These will be validated principles or generalities applicable to various training design or development situations. The second, related capability will be that of obtaining data-based prescriptions or guidance about particular situations. Together these capabilities will allow training practitioners to use instructional technology still more efficiently and will allow researchers to define precisely and explicitly what is yet to be determined.

REFERENCES

Cotterman, T. E. *Task classification: An approach to partially ordering information on human learning* (WADC Technical Note 58-374). Wright–Patterson Air Force Base, Ohio: Wright Air Development Center, Air Research and Development Command, January 1959. (NTIS No. AD 210716).

Cotterman, T. E. *Automated data on instructional technology (ADIT): Guide to use* (rev. ed.). Wright–Patterson Air Force Base, Ohio: Advanced Systems Division, Air Force Human Resources Laboratory, February 1977.

Cotterman, T. E., & Thomas, D. L. *An evaluation of typical users capability to learn operation of ADIT and their reactions to the system.* Wright–Patterson Air Force Base, Ohio: Advanced Systems Division, Air Force Human Resources Laboratory, in preparation.

Full-page advertisement. *The New York Times,* September 30, 1973, p. 4.

The New York Times information bank. Seventy years of news online. *Modern Data,* September 1973, pp. 70–71.

Scheffler, F. L., & Cotterman, T. E. Technical information retrieval – What do we really want? In *Information interaction. Compendium of presentations of the 5th ASIS midyear meeting,* Washington, D.C.: American Society for Information Science, 1976.

Scheffler, F. L., DaPolito, F. J., McAdams, R. L., & Gee, M. J. *Feasibility of computer processing of technical information on the design of instructional systems* (AFHRL-TR-73-40). Wright–Patterson Air Force Base, Ohio: Advanced Systems Division, Air Force Human Resources Laboratory, January 1974. (NTIS No. AD 778073)

Schumacher, S. P. *Development of a technical data file on the design and use of instructional systems* (AFHRL-TR-73-41). Wright–Patterson Air Force Base, Ohio: Advanced Systems Division, Air Force Human Resources Laboratory, December 1973. (NTIS No. AD 775 149)

Schumacher, S. P., Pearlstein, R. B., & Martin, P. W. *A comprehensive key word index and bibliography on instructional system development* (AFHRL-TR-74-14). Wright–Patterson Air Force Base, Ohio: Advanced Systems Division, Air Force Human Resources Laboratory, February 1974. (NTIS No. AD 777192)

Schumacher, S. P., Swezey, R. W., Pearlstein, R. B., & Valverde, H. H. *Guidelines for abstracting technical literature on instructional system development* (AFHRL-TR-74-13). Wright–Patterson Air Force Base, Ohio: Advanced Systems Division, Air Force Human Resources Laboratory, February 1974. (NTIS No. AD 777757)

Schumacher, S. P., & Wiltman S. *A compendium of research and development needs on instructional system development* (AFHRL-TR-74-15). Wright–Patterson Air Force Base, Ohio: Advanced Systems Division, Air Force Human Resources Laboratory, February 1974. (NTIS No. AD 777196)

Stolurow, L. M. *A taxonomy of learning task characteristics* (AMRL-TDR-64-2). Wright–Patterson Air Force Base, Ohio: Behavioral Sciences Laboratory, Aerospace Medical Research Laboratories, January 1964. (NTIS No. AD 433199)

United States Air Force. *Handbook for designers of instructional systems* (Air Force Pamphlet 50-58). Washington, D.C.: Author, January 1974.

6

TRAIDEX: A Proposed System to Minimize Training Duplication[1]

JOHN W. BRACKETT

The Training Resources, Applications and Information/Data Exchange (TRAIDEX) is a proposed information storage and retrieval system that has not yet been implemented. It was designed by SofTech to reduce the cost of developing technical training courses within the Armed Services by allowing the developer to have timely access to a comprehensive, up-to-date catalog of well-described and validated courseware. This chapter describes both the information collection and analysis that form the basis for the TRAIDEX design and the functional design of an information exchange system that could fulfill the requirements uncovered by the information needs analysis. Although the TRAIDEX system has not as yet been implemented, important aspects of the system design are in use in a system developed by SofTech for the U.S. Army.

The study indicated that the interservice sharing of validated technical course units can significantly decrease the time and cost required to produce courses for which identical or similar units must be developed. This view is supported both by qualified development personnel and by the experience of course developers who have actually reused course material from other services.

During late 1975 a series of interviews was conducted at over 12 separate

[1]This project was jointly funded by the Army, Navy, Air Force, and the Defense Advanced Research Projects Agency (DARPA), and was conducted under the auspices of DARPA and the Interservice Training Review Organization (ITRO) by SofTech and Educational Testing Service under Contract MDA903-75-C-0224. Additional information on the project can be obtained from the final report, which is available from the National Technical Information Service as document AD-A024861.

headquarters and training development locations, with personnel ranging from senior headquarters and technical school staff through education-and-training specialists to course developers. The interviews indicated that major obstacles that currently prevent this type of information sharing from taking place are

- The lack of a catalog of up-to-date, descriptive information that identifies well-validated course material
- The lack of a uniform and responsive system for obtaining course material after it has been identified

The TRAIDEX system design addresses the information needs identified. Furthermore, the functional requirements of the system can be met by utilizing an existing hardware–software information-processing system currently operated by the government. Based upon accepted estimates of technical course development costs, the system need reduce the development costs of the courses impacted by TRAIDEX by an average of only 2% in order to pay for itself in 5 years (SofTech, 1976b).

INFORMATION NEEDS ANALYSIS

The information needs analysis focused on technical training because it has the following characteristics:

- It is characterized by high cost per student and high student volume.
- Course content is likely to possess a high degree of commonality across services.
- Changing weapons system technology base is causing the production of new courses and the modification of existing ones at a rapid rate.

Other areas such as human goals (e.g., race relations) and general military training (e.g., unit leadership) were believed to possess a high degree of commonality, but the dollar costs per student for these programs are not as high as for technical training and were deemphasized during the information needs analysis. At the start of the information needs analysis the benefits projected for the potential TRAIDEX system were

- Reduced course development effort and cost
- Increased productivity and effectiveness of the course developer
- Support of instructional system development (ISD) methods

Cost–Benefit Analysis Approach

The planned cost–benefit analysis involved the collection of design and development costs for each of the various stages of the instructional systems development process. However, as the information needs analysis proceeded, it became apparent that it would be impossible to obtain representative analysis, design, and development costs. The reasons for this lack of cost data are essentially these:

- Personnel costs for learning material development are often not separated from costs incurred for instruction.
- Estimates of the ratio of development to presentation time vary widely and are heavily impacted by the introduction of new instructional technologies such as self-paced instruction in its various forms.
- Development time is also strongly correlated with developer experience. Given the emerging state of the newest (and presumably most effective) technologies and the relatively high rate of developer turnover, most developers have had relatively little experience in applying these technologies.

We were therefore hesitant to accept the few development costs that were obtained as representative.

In spite of the problems cited above, the following general cost trends appear clear:

- The same instructional technologies that are proving so effective in reducing the training time required to produce a qualified graduate are demanding an increasing investment in the learning-material-development phase.
- As the trend toward more specialized course modules proceeds, the total number of course hours that must be developed is increasing.

As a result of this information deficiency, the study team chose the following approach:

- Design and specify an information exchange system that is functionally capable of providing the required course development assistance and of handling the projected volume of stored information and data transactions.
- Estimate the costs of developing, integrating, and operating this system, making maximum use of existing hardware and software systems, and translate these costs into the development resources that would have to be saved in order to have the system pay for itself.

The decision of whether to implement the system would partially depend on whether such savings appeared realizable.

Interview Results

The requirement that TRAIDEX be oriented primarily toward improving the technical training course development process implied that the information needs analysis task must gather at least the following basic data:

- Descriptions (both qualitative and quantitative) of current course development practices
- Descriptions of current information sources used by developers, and identification of those phases of the development process that would benefit most from the introduction of new sources
- Estimates of the direction of future developments in instructional technology and their requirements for new information

In addition, it was felt that verification of many of the fundamental assumptions about the utility of a TRAIDEX facility should be obtained from its potential end users. The analysis of training information needs was accomplished in the period May–August 1975 by interviewing a cross-section of training personnel in the four services in the following areas:

- Course development process
  - Describe the training process, management, and support provided by your organization.
  - What is the role of a formal ISD methodology in this process?
  - What is a typical ratio of course development time to course presentation time?
  - What are the most difficult or time-consuming phases in the ISD process?
  - What are typical course development costs?
  - Describe the inputs and outputs of the development process as practiced by your organization.
- TRAIDEX information content and concept
  - What information would substantively aid the developer? How would the information be used, and how much would it help?
  - Describe user-to-system interface requirements and possibilities, timeliness, indexing, form, and format. Describe possible relevancy measures of TRAIDEX outputs.
- Other information sources
  - What sources are currently used?
  - What sources would be used if access were available?

In addition, representatives of the training community were questioned regarding the assumptions behind TRAIDEX, such as the possibility of reducing development time and increasing developer efficiency and the existence of a high degree of interservice commonality. Hypotheses on the content, interface, and function of a possible TRAIDEX were continually tested. Feedback on problems for an operational TRAIDEX were generally contributed with little need for formal questions or prompting from the study team.

In order to present the results of a large number of interviews in a coherent manner, we have restated the original projected benefits and goals of TRAIDEX, along with some underlying assumptions about the nature of the technical training development process, as a set of hypothetical statements. The hypotheses are followed by a summary of interview responses both pro and con and the study team's conclusion.

Hypothesis: *Exchange of information will save course development time.*

A limited number of course developers have successfully borrowed courseware from another service and saved their own course development time as a result. For example, developers in the Department of Army-Wide Training Support at the Signal School (Ft. Gordon) cited a case in which 1 month of development time was saved on a 3-4 month effort by using material borrowed from the Air Force; furthermore, this time was saved in spite of ostensible interservice differences in maintenance and training philosophy. An interesting aspect of this particular development experience is that the developers tended to be technically oriented generalists who relied upon the assistance of subject matter experts, rather than subject matter experts with experience in a particular kind of course development.

However, the reuse of shared learning material is an infrequent occurrence, and how frequently sharing can be done and how much time can be saved are in doubt. A portion of those people interviewed felt that a significant amount of content duplication in course development exists and that most developers would find it helpful to see what other developers with similar objectives have produced. Another portion felt that because of a variety of interservice differences, the interservice exchange of curriculum materials would seldom be worthwhile. And a third portion felt that because of the time needed to understand and absorb another developer's material, the time savings would be minimal though the exchange would be helpful.

The possibility that the exchange and review of relevant learning materials might result in indirect reduction of effort became apparent as the study progressed. A number of developers interviewed felt that looking at the results of another's development effort would be a source of inspiration on presentation technique, format, and so on even though the material itself was not directly borrowed. Support for this point varies between the experienced and the inexperienced developer, with the strongest support coming from those who are relatively inexperienced in applying a particular technology. The experience factor may be particularly critical in services where there is a rapid introduction of new learning technology or a high rate of developer turnover.

Although estimates of potential development time savings varied widely, the study concluded that the exchange of course material will indeed save course development time; however, the quantification of this time savings is a difficult issue. The savings appear to depend heavily upon the relative experience of the developer, the ability to submerge one's own ego sufficiently to borrow relevant material, and the ability to locate relevant and properly validated instructional material quickly.

Hypothesis: *Exchange of information will increase course effectiveness.*

This point depends upon the ability of the course developer to obtain (through TRAIDEX) material that may be more effective than can be produced within time and budgetary constraints. Many of those interviewed were concerned about the quality of material that TRAIDEX would cause to be shared. A large percentage of the sample mentioned the use of professionally recognized validation methods as a criterion by which to judge the worth of learning material. Internal validation results, showing that the course material is consistently successful in meeting the original learning objectives, have been specified as a requirement for inclusion in the TRAIDEX data base.

With respect to a developer's obtaining more effective material than might be produced on one's own, there will be a variance between those who are experienced and those who are inexperienced in the application of a particular technology. In areas of the services with rapid turnover of course developers, one would expect the strongest positive effect.

Hypothesis: *Perceived benefits can be cost-analyzed.*

Any model used to analyze the impact of a TRAIDEX on the course development process by cost–benefit analysis assumes the existence of cost data for the various phases of the process. However, hard and comprehensive course development cost data could not be obtained from any site. In most cases, development costs for a school were not separated from instruction costs. In one case, development costs were merged for several courses. Factors such as the impact of the introduction of new instructional technology (such as self-pacing), differences between initial and subsequent development of a course, developer time taken from other duties, and experience of developer also made cost comparisons impossible.

Thus, conventional approaches to the costing of development activities could not be applied, because the necessary data are simply not being tracked. The closest we were able to come to real cost data was in the Air Force, where we were able to obtain some **sampled** data. Chanute Air Force Base records fairly extensive data on the ISD process; Table 6.1 summarizes this data for three sample self-paced courses. The problem with projecting from this data is that it is not comprehensive and therefore cannot provide a true picture of *all* course development activity, even at Chanute. Moreover, because of the difficulties inherent in tracking the time of instructors and part-time personnel, it is not clear that all of the personnel involved in the development process were tracked, or that their time was precisely allocated.

Rule-of-thumb estimates of the development ratio range from 30 hours (per hour of instruction) to 300 hours. A reasonable estimate for a comprehensive ISD effort within the Air Force is 100–150 hours. The Naval Air Maintenance Training Group representative to the Interservice Training Review Board (ITRB)

Table 6.1
Sample Course Development Costs, Chanute

	Course		
	A	B	C
Contact hours	232	231	384
Phase I	594	80	534
Phase II	721	16	13
Phase III	531	1,642	560
Phase IV	9,673	9,477	3,880
Total hours	11,519	11,215	4,995
Ratio	49.7	48.5	13

estimated development time at about 200 hours. At the instructor level we heard estimates of between 30 and 70 hours.

In Table 6.1 the phases correspond to four or five phases of the Air Force ISD process (Phase I — Analyze System Requirements; Phase II — Define Education and Training Requirements; Phase III — Develop Objectives and Tests; and Phase IV — Plan, Develop, and Validate Instruction). The ratio is the number of development hours to the number of contact hours. It is interesting that in these particular examples Phase IV (where TRAIDEX should be most useful) consumes approximately 80% of the development process. A few of those interviewed in relation to these cost figures estimated that TRAIDEX could save 25-50% of the production time (Phase IV). The important issues, however, are the rate of development and the number of courses for which TRAIDEX would be useful.

Hypothesis: *Benefits of TRAIDEX are important because of a high rate of new course development and course modification.*

Most of those interviewed who supported the TRAIDEX concept agreed that benefits would be apparent in new course development. However, the benefits perceived for course modification were not as great. For example, course revisions to cover minor equipment changes are usually not major enough to warrant reuse of other than the original material. However, there are cases, such as the addition of a new subject or the conversion to a new type of training technology (self-paced instruction, for example), when the ability to look at previously developed material is a real asset.

We received conflicting reports on the amount of new course development and the rate of revision involving a new training technology. The Navy has about 2000 full-time people involved in course development or redevelopment, the Air Force revises approximately 75,000 hours of instruction per year, and there are a few areas where major revisions using the ISD model are planned. However, at the school level we were frequently told that almost no new courses were being developed, and in all services we heard that the most frequent types of revisions were not major. In conclusion, it appears that TRAIDEX must be justified primarily on the basis of new course development and major course revision. Given the economy to be gained in delivery costs through the introduction of self-paced courses, the advent of Computer-Managed Instruction, the realignment of Military Occupation Specialty (MOS) categories, and the continual introduction of new weapon systems technologies, we should expect the development requirements to remain strong. Even if new development requirements only remain steady, a small percentage decrease in development cost should represent large dollar savings.

Hypothesis: *Course development efforts with a high degree of commonality exist among the services.*

In every service at every level we encountered doubts as to the degree of course commonality among the services. Of course, some people had strong convictions that this commonality does exist, especially at the level of the basic or introductory technical course. However, these basic courses were also assumed to be fairly stable. If this is in fact the case, TRAIDEX potential use will be less than assumed.

Hypothesis: *The areas of the course development process most relevant to TRAIDEX are the search for existing courses or materials, media selection, and actual learning material development.*

The phases of the instructional system development process to which TRAIDEX was originally thought to be most relevant were analysis of existing courses, development of objectives, test development, media selection, review–selection of existing materials, and development of instruction. The kind of TRAIDEX assistance expected in developing objectives was not actual reuse of previously developed objectives but rather the examination of well-constructed (and possibly unrelated) objectives for guidance by relatively inexperienced analysts. Through the interviews we sought feedback on these assumptions.

A nearly unanimous response to the question about the most difficult phases of the course development process (assuming use of a version of the instructional systems development model) was the conversion of job tasks to terminal learning objectives. Although this step is widely recognized as difficult and time-consuming, the only way that a TRAIDEX-like system could help is by offering samples of existing conversions for like tasks. Furthermore, searching for a similar set of job tasks associated with a course in another service appears to be very difficult, primarily because of service-specific terminology and function. The general feeling in the Army was that a large effort must be directed toward job and training task analysis before the resulting courses would have the quality necessary for beneficial sharing through TRAIDEX.

The TRAIDEX information system was designed to concentrate in areas where there was no question that productive assistance could be provided:

- Analysis of existing courses
- Display of learning objectives
- Review and selection of learning materials

These areas are common to all currently used development methodologies.

Hypothesis: *The potential for interchange of training development information is seldom achieved because current mechanisms are deficient.*

An important question concerns the degree of sharing that currently takes place relative to the existing potential and the adequacy of mechanisms currently available to assist the process. There exists a substantial body of opinion (particularly at higher staff and headquarters levels) that all possible sharing is currently done.

It was also claimed that there are a small number of schools dealing in any particular field, and that development personnel at these schools keep in touch to such a high degree that TRAIDEX would not be able to increase the level of communication substantially. Other currently available sharing mechanisms include service-specific catalogs or programmed instruction materials, videotapes, and audiovisual systems that include the scope, objectives, and student-entry level of the material as well as a description of the means of accessing it. Libraries and advisory services are used for information on training technology and in one service a TRAIDEX-like advisory service is provided at the training command headquarters level.

In spite of the existence of potential systems for courseware exchange, the majority of course developers felt that very little sharing is done. The problems that developers cited with regard to the currently available mechanisms for inter- and intraservice sharing of common development efforts may be summarized as follows:

- Current sources of information are inaccurate, usually because the time required to compile, print, and distribute hard-copy catalogs is long compared to the rate of change of the courseware involved. This leads to very rapid obsolescence of the catalogs.
- Current sources are incomplete because they do not usually contain enough information to allow the potential user to judge accurately either the relevance of the material to his own objectives or the quality of the instructional material in terms of its proven ability to achieve its own objectives.

Although the sharing of audiovisual and training aids is a partial solution to the problem that TRAIDEX addresses, there are no organized data bases of training courseware. The study concluded in relation to the interservice potential for sharing that there is a place for an effective, up-to-date, easily accessed data base of information on courseware with built-in relevancy and validation measures.

Hypothesis: *The TRAIDEX user will be the course developer or subject matter expert.*

When the TRAIDEX effort focused on the course development process, the course developer or subject matter expert clearly became the end user. However, the necessary perspective and incentive for improving course effectiveness and the motivation for reducing development time does not always exist at this level. The TRAIDEX study team concluded that the knowledge of TRAIDEX system use and the ability to monitor courseware exchange should reside at the level of the course development adviser or staff-level education or training specialist. The interviewing process demonstrated convincingly that it was at this particular level in the training hierarchy that the talented personnel with the most perspective on the training development problem coupled with daily contact with actual developers existed. Not only was the acceptance of the TRAIDEX concept greatest at this level, but the staff personnel in these positions generally have some type of review and approval rights over locally developed curricula.

Conclusions Based on Interviews

Based on the results of interviews, it appears likely that there is a need for an effective, timely method for the exchange of valid, relevant courseware. A system that implemented such a method would assist in new course development as well as facilitate the application of new types of training technology such as the ISD process. Such a system would reduce development time and increase the effectiveness and efficiency of the developer. The dollar cost savings or cost avoidance accomplished by this method depends upon

- Actual time savings
- Increase in developer efficiency
- Rate of new course development and revision
- Rate of TRAIDEX use
- Degree of interservice commonality

The TRAIDEX system feasibility is based on the assumption that some form of the ISD process will be used and that learning objectives exist in the form of action, condition, and standard.

The study team concluded that interservice sharing of relevant, validated courseware can significantly decrease the time and effort required to produce new technical training course modules. The effects of sharing will have the greatest leverage in situations where one or more of the following conditions is present:

- A new training requirement must be met.
- New instructional technology is being introduced.
- Course designer–developers are not subject matter experts.
- The production cost per delivery hour is high, as in self-paced programmed texts, CAI programs, or multimedia presentations.

This conclusion is based on a qualified evaluation of the interview responses, and upon the following observations:

- Personnel who agreed with the TRAIDEX concept were either currently involved or had previously been involved in situations similar to those described, and had or were attempting to share interservice information. In several cases, these developers had successfully shared another service's development experience and/or courseware.
- Personnel who disagreed with the TRAIDEX concept did so primarily for one of the following three reasons:
  —All potential sharing is already accomplished.
  —The developer will not use shared information.
  —Potentially sharable material cannot be identified short of actual examination of the product.

All three of these assumptions have proven to be erroneous. Developers are nearly unanimous in reporting that attempts to find sharable material are frustrated by the inadequate mechanisms available to them; only a few have developed the informal, "out of channels" contacts that allow them quick access to other developers. However, in the relatively few instances where interdeveloper contact has been made, the success of sharing similar development efforts has been significant. Finally, a substantial number of course developers, curriculum review and advisory personnel, and education and training spcialists in both military and civilian areas have agreed that a combination of the descriptors proposed for the TRAIDEX data base (learning objectives, sample test items, media, validation data) are adequate to give the inquirer confidence in the relevance of the courseware described.

TRAIDEX CONCEPTS OF OPERATION

During the course of the information needs analysis and system design tasks, it became clear that any feasible implementation of TRAIDEX would encompass the following fundamental concepts as part of its basic framework:

- There must exist a "data base" (whether computerized or manual) of course unit descriptions.
- There must exist some central organization whose function it is to control

and support the daily operation of the information exchange system.
- There must exist a trained "interface" person to whom the system's end user (the course developer) can turn for assistance with the details of system access and usage.

These concepts form the basic building blocks that are integrated into the final functional design.

Unit Description Data Base

The information needs analysis task established that in order to enable the course developer to locate and obtain reusable course material easily, the information that TRAIDEX manipulates must relate to a discrete unit within an entire course that can be determined by the developer to be relevant. Assuming that the development of learning objectives from training tasks leads to the development of separate and well-defined instructional units, the most useful indexable entity appears to be a course module that has been designed to achieve at least one major learning objective. This course module is referred to in the functional design as a course unit. It is important to note that, though course units are described in the TRAIDEX data base, all of the units of a course are selected for inclusion in TRAIDEX on the basis of the course-level subject and objectives, not the individual unit objectives. The contents of an entry in the TRAIDEX unit description data base are defined in Table 6.2. All of this information will be available to the course developer.

In order to select the mechanisms (computerized, manual, or a combination) that are required to implement TRAIDEX, certain critical system volume parameters were estimated. The TRAIDEX volume estimates fall into three key areas, as follows:

- Number of course-unit entries in the unit description catalog or data base. This number helps determine the mechanisms and associated cost to store the required data.
- Rate of change of the unit description catalog. This rate determines the mechanisms suitable for updating (and therefore storing) the catalog, and the associated cost.
- Rate of inquiry into the catalog. This estimate, coupled with the expected complexity of a typical inquiry and the required system response time, determines the nature of the required retrieval mechanism.

The estimated volume of this data base was determined by surveying the number of technical training courses in the category of interest that were listed in the service's formal (resident school) course catalogs and in the appropriate nonresident, correspondence, and career development course catalogs. The result

Table 6.2
TRAIDEX Data Base, Logical Record Contents

Field name	Contents	Source
Descriptor keys	Key words selected from thesaurus	Course title, block or module title, lesson title, equipment type, objective
Course unit identification	Code for service, course, unit, and subunit	POI, curriculum outline
Course title	Formal name of course	POI, curriculum outline
Developer	Name, address, telephone for cognizant developer	Local school screening committee
Learning objective	Full text of terminal objective for course unit	POI, curriculum outline
Learning action	Verb–object pairs	Same
Learning condition	Stimulus list	Same
Learning standard	Completion criteria	Same
Presentation time	Average or scheduled elapsed time to complete	POI, curriculum outline
Presentation method	Limited set of method-words	POI, curriculum outline
Development date	Initial development date	Developer
Source units	Course unit identifications of units that were used in the development of this unit	Developer
Personnel	Qualifications of support personnel required	POI
Test questions	Test questions selected from the unit test which further specify the unit content	Curriculum outline, local screening committee
Media	A group of one or more composite fields where each member of the group describes one particular type of available courseware	
Media code	One of a limited set of codes denoting the type of media (e.g., TV, PI text, sound–slide)	POI, curriculum
Media identification	Full text name or title of media package that contains the unit and by which it should be ordered, including National Stock Number, if one exists	POI, curriculum outline

(Continued)

Table 6.2 (*Continued*)

Field name	Contents	Source
Media source	Location from which media can be ordered	Development site
Media price	Price per package	Development site
Media package	Brief description of package of which unit is a part	Development site
Equipment	Support equipment required	Development site
Bibliography	References used to develop or as background-enrichment material	Developer
Validation method	Unit validation methodology used	Developer
Validation result	Current status of application of validation method	Developer
Entry requirement	Reading level, prerequisite courses, aptitudes, etc.	POI, curriculum outline, development site
Job task	Brief statement of task that is supported by the lesson	Course designer
Basic skill	Statement of basic skill that is supported	Course designer
Where-used list	Course unit identifications of other lessons that were developed using this material	Course reuse indicator

was the identification of 4200 technical courses with potential content for inclusion in TRAIDEX.

In order to estimate course unit volume, the study team examined course catalogs and course unit material from each service. The actual number of units for courses for which this number was available (from documents such as Plan of Instruction [POI] and curriculum outlines) was used to estimate the average number of units per course. Estimates across services were checked by consulting various members of the training community. The resulting total was 82,000 course units. This total appears to be reasonable; if a nominal 8 hours per course unit is assumed, the resulting 656,000 hours of instruction represents between half and two-thirds of all technical training presented, based upon informed estimates from within the training community.

It was impossible for the study team to obtain exact estimates for the rates at which new courses are created and old courses are revised. However, it is the policy in at least one service to review each course at least once every 3 years. The study team has, therefore, assumed that one-third of all course units will be examined for revision each year. This estimate, coupled with an estimated new course development rate of 10% of the revision effort, yields a total of 29,000 unit developments per year. Based upon an estimated 2000 person-years of course development per year and the nominal 8-hour unit, this yields an average development time per unit-hour of about 17 hours, which, although low, is in line with current experience. In any case, it indicates that the update volume (and associated cost) is conservatively large.

The inquiry volume is essentially driven by the estimated review and revision volume. The study team has assumed that each development will not generate a TRAIDEX inquiry, but rather that the average inquiry volume will equal about one-half of the unit development and review rate, or about 14,600 inquiries per year.

The projected volume of data in this data base, coupled with the requirement for rapid search and retrieval of unit descriptions, justifies the premise that a computer-oriented data base system connected to keyboard terminals located at the user (course development) site is needed. The use of a mechanical selection method, such as edge-punched cards, would require, at a minimum, one card per course unit. The preliminary estimate sets the number of course units to be considered at about 80,000. This would imply a possibility of having to search 80,000 cards, the equivalent in volume of 40 boxes of data processing punched cards. Further, unless the entire data base, in whatever form, is located at each development site, a printed copy telecommunication system will be needed to meet the overall response time requirement that was established in the information needs analysis to be on the order of a few hours to a day. The user's request to find relevant course units will usually consist of an iterative and interactive dialogue with the descriptive data base. A user will have to characterize his search criteria by more than one descriptive word in order to reduce the number of course units selected to a reasonable number, and may need to alter the content of his request based on what he finds in the system. This need for more than one selection criterion and the requirement for dynamic modification of the search process makes the use of preprinted "key word in context" lists or similar nonautomated methods cumbersome.

TRAIDEX Central

The study recommended the establishment of an organization, called TRAIDEX Central, that will have the primary responsibility for making the routine operation of TRAIDEX a success and will be responsible for the first level review and correction of TRAIDEX operation and policy. Specification of the required computer software will be a responsibility of TRAIDEX Central.

TRAIDEX Central owns the unit description data base. The actual course unit material is owned by TRAIDEX Central but remains the responsibility of the development site of the service where it was developed. This site will be responsible for distributing copies of the course material. During the course unit order and response cycle, the status of the order is maintained by TRAIDEX Central in order to assure that the development site ships the material to the requestor.

The TRAIDEX Interface

The TRAIDEX interface is one or more persons at the course development site who will help the course developer find and obtain relevant course units. The TRAIDEX interface will have access to a terminal through which he or she can interact with the course unit description data base. The primary function of the TRAIDEX interface is to make what help TRAIDEX can provide available to the developers, even if the developers are not motivated to seek out that help on their own.

Each TRAIDEX interface will be provided access to a terminal and instructions on how to connect the terminal to the computer holding the TRAIDEX data base. From time to time, these persons will receive from TRAIDEX Central updates and further information on TRAIDEX operation such as a list of new features added, notes on successful search strategies, and "alert reports" when descriptions of learning material with prespecified attributes have been modified or added.

A key part of the TRAIDEX interface job is to know how to form effective searches for relevant course units. This will require a good knowledge of the restrictive and descriptive words used to describe course units. A copy of the thesaurus of all descriptive words will be provided to each TRAIDEX interface by TRAIDEX Central.

Roles of Persons and Organizations Affected by TRAIDEX

The primary end user of TRAIDEX system information is the training course developer. It is the course developer who must identify an initial need for development information on a particular technical topic, a specific instructional strategy, or the use of a particular development methodology. Needs would then be discussed with the TRAIDEX interface person at the development site, and together they would decide on an appropriate set of descriptive information and an acceptable maximum volume of unit descriptions to be returned for examination by the developer. It should be noted that it is the TRAIDEX interface, trained by TRAIDEX Central, who possesses the detailed knowledge of how to use the inquiry terminal and query language and the thesaurus of technical descriptors, and how to develop successful search strategies. The only formal training that the developer will receive will be a brief (1-2 hour) seminar at which the information content, potential uses, and response times of TRAIDEX will be described, and the local TRAIDEX interface introduced and his duties discussed.

After a particular developer's request has been structured and entered by the TRAIDEX interface, the developer will be informed within (at most) a day whether or not material of potential interest exists within the system, and descriptive information about whatever learning materials have been catalogued will be provided. The developer may then decide on several options, including ordering specific items of material through the TRAIDEX interface, or contacting the developers of relevant material directly in order to resolve specific questions on such things as media selection, validation, and so on. If the developer decides to order specific learning materials, the TRAIDEX interface notifies TRAIDEX Central, and the developer receives a reply within 2 to 4 weeks.

The developers at a site will be asked by the TRAIDEX interface to evaluate the information received from the system and to indicate (in a brief questionnaire enclosed with learning materials that are shipped) whether or not the materials were used or modified to become part of a new course unit.

The local course development site must create the climate in which the TRAIDEX system can operate effectively. It must commit the resources of a trained, interested resource person as the local TRAIDEX interface, and it must support the TRAIDEX concept both directly by educating local curriculum design and development personnel, and indirectly by encouraging an atmosphere that lends prestige both to the use of TRAIDEX as a resource and to the contribution of potentially sharable material. Courses that contain units redeveloped from material obtained from TRAIDEX should be publicized, and other examples of TRAIDEX utility disseminated. The focus of much of this activity will be the TRAIDEX interface, and the development-site command must ensure that the TRAIDEX interface position is invested with sufficient prestige to make its operation effective. Based on both the nature of the curriculum review job and the characteristics of the personnel who occupy it, the study team concluded that the most appropriate location for TRAIDEX interface is in this review and advisory position, rather than at the lowest development or instructional level.

TRAIDEX cannot be successful in any of its phases if the development site personnel who are charged with screening, selecting describing, and searching for course units must be forced to do their job. TRAIDEX must be accepted on its merits by the end user (the TRAIDEX interface) as a viable means to reduce development costs and improve quality, or it will be bypassed. Interviews during the information needs analysis continually showed that the key to the introduction of any new training development technology has been the existence of a cadre of highly motivated and well-trained specialists in the area to be implemented. For example, the conversion of courseware from instructor-oriented to self-paced format or the introduction of formal ISD procedures has been most successful when the concept has been implemented by dedicated professionals at the course development and local curriculum review level. Where its installation has been legislated by headquarters or local school command without the support of trained and committed implementers, it has too frequently been allowed to become the object of paper exercises, and eventually to die out when upper command pressure shifted to other matters.

Fortunately, the same education and training specialists who have been acknowledged as the local leaders in the implementation of innovative training techniques have also shown the greatest interest in and support of the TRAIDEX concept. Our assumption is that each development site will contain a few of these individuals, that they will constitute the primary interface to the TRAIDEX system for the remaining course designers and developers, and that they will be in a suitable position to assist and monitor the screening, data base maintenance, description retrieval, and unit distribution process.

The commands will also have access to the TRAIDEX data base, since it will provide a considerable source of raw data about the state of training technology in a particular service. Although the focus of the data base design has been to provide descriptive information to the developer, much of this information, particularly in an aggregate form that could be extracted by computer programs for special reports, will be of interest to headquarters personnel. For example, statistical summaries on the utilization of certain types of media and instructional strategies, course unit length, validation techniques, and results can be readily collected.

TRAIDEX FUNCTIONAL DESIGN

The previous sections have described the conclusions from the information needs analysis and the TRAIDEX concepts of operation, but little emphasis has been placed on the role of computers in TRAIDEX. This lack of emphasis is in contrast to the initial belief in the three services that the principal problem to be overcome in developing TRAIDEX was the design and implementation of a complex computer software system. Our understanding of the "hard" problems involved in creating TRAIDEX was greatly facilitated by the use of the Structured Analysis and Design Technique (SADT®) to develop and specify the design (Ross & Schoman, 1977; SofTech, 1976a). The structured approach to analysis inherent in SADT helped focus attention on the importance of people-oriented procedures and roles such as the TRAIDEX interface and TRAIDEX Central. Without this focus the study would probably have neglected problems that would be critical to the success of the system, such as ensuring prompt shipment of requested material from the development site, and would have concentrated unduly on the computer-related issues.

The Structured Analysis and Design Technique is a method for helping people to understand complex *systems* (defined as any combination of computer hardware and software, people and things, structured together to perform a function). The system may be a new system to be built or an existing system and may be a combination of computers, people, and things, or it may consist only of people and things. In all cases, the result of applying SADT is a *model* that shows, by a series of diagrams, the understanding of the system that the analyst has gained as a result of its application. For new system building, SADT may be applied in planning, analysis, design, project management, or wherever a model is useful for system understanding.

On this project SADT was used to model all of the functions that made up the TRAIDEX system, including functions performed by TRAIDEX Central, the TRAIDEX interface, training command headquarters, course development sites (service schools), and the computer system to be used for storing and retrieving information. Analysts, after interviewing experts, used SADT to document their understanding of how the system might operate. The evolving model was described to the experts in the training commands to determine whether important aspects of the system would not work as proposed and to isolate issues that required more study. The SADT model in the final report describes how TRAIDEX would work. It provides a precise, blueprint-like description of the proposed system that can be used to answer detailed questions about the system.

Characteristics of an SADT Model

The diagrams in a model are organized in a hierarchic and modular fashion, often called *top-down*. That is, the scope of the system is established in a single overview diagram. The component parts shown in the overview are then detailed, each on another diagram. Each part shown on this detail diagram is again broken down, and so forth, until the system is described to any desired level of detail. This process is illustrated in Figure 6.1. Lower-level diagrams, then, are detailed breakdowns of higher-level diagrams. At each stage of breaking down the system, the higher-level diagram is said to a *parent*, or overview, of the lower-level *detail* diagram.

Figure 6.2 is the overview diagram representing the scope of the TRAIDEX system. The input data (on the left) are transformed into output data (on the right). Controls (on the top) govern the way the transformation is done.

SADT diagrams consist of boxes and arrows and text describing them. The notation is kept simple to permit easy reading with little special training. In SADT, boxes represent components in the breakdown, and arrows represent relationships between these components. Descriptive labels are written inside

STRUCTURED DECOMPOSITION

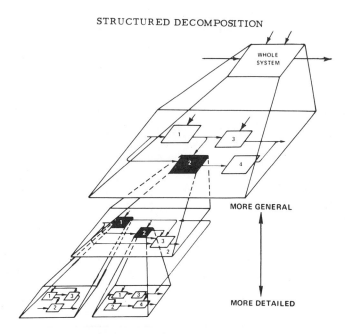

Figure 6.1 Structure of an SADT model.

each box and along each arrow to describe their meaning. Figure 6.3 is the diagram whose parent diagram is Figure 6.2. It shows the four functions that, when combined, constitute TRAIDEX. The boxes represent activities, and arrows represent data or things that are interfaces between those activities.

Functions in the SADT Model

The functions included in the SADT model are listed in Figure 6.4. Indentation is used to show how functions are composed of more detailed functions; for

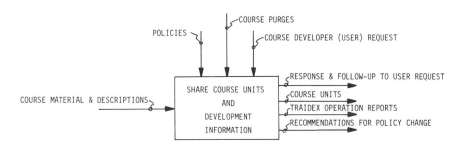

Figure 6.2 TRAIDEX scope diagram.

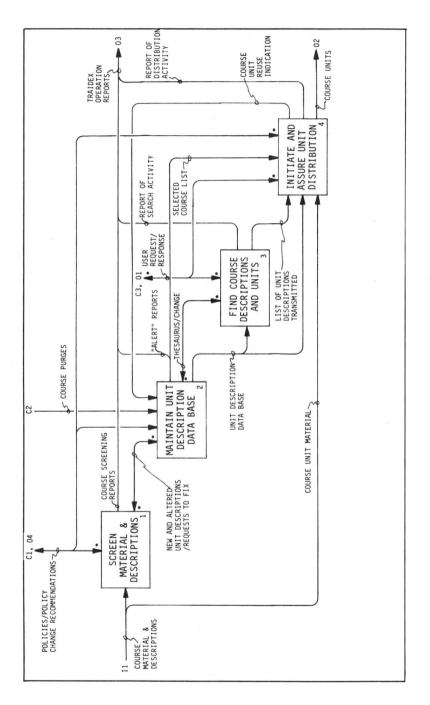

Figure 6.3 Diagram showing the four principal functions of TRAIDEX.

121

Share course descriptions and units

Screen material and descriptions
    Set course-selection rules
        Invent screening techniques
        Determine training command restrictions
        Look for missed courses
        Look for inappropriate courses
        Hold selection-criteria review

Maintain unit description data base
    Maintain thesaurus
    Format new unit descriptions
    Edit and alter existing descriptions
    Review changes
    Update data base

Find course descriptions and units
    Select restrictive factors
    Select and rank descriptive words
    Search data base
    Obtain full course unit description
    Monitor search activity

Initiate and assure unit distribution
    Log and route request
        Schedule required responses
        Cut, address, and mail paper work
        Record requests
        Follow up request actions
    Gather TRAIDEX material
    Assure training command response
    Ship course material
        Store and find course units
        Reproduce units
        Package units
        Ship and notify
        Track request

Figure 6.4 Functions contained in the TRAIDEX SADT model.

example, the figure indicates that "Set course-selection rules" is part of "Screen material and descriptions." The relationships between these functions are shown in the complete SADT model included in the project final report (SofTech, 1976a). The eight diagrams provide a comprehensive and precise description of TRAIDEX in much less space than a text description at the same level of detail would require.

The italicized functions indicate those functions that require computer support. Most functions of TRAIDEX will be created by specifying new roles for people and developing new manual procedures, not by developing computer software.

TRAIDEX COSTS AND BENEFITS

Following the completion of the functional design using SADT and reviews with key service personnel, the study team selected the best computer configuration, estimated the costs to build and operate that configuration, and estimated the amount of courseware development cost that would have to be saved in order for TRAIDEX to pay back all development and operational costs by its fifth year of operation. Five years was selected, since the study team recommended that the data base of unit descriptions for the selected courses be loaded incrementally during the normal process of course review and revision at each course development site. This should result in the loading of about one-third of the basic inventory of course units in the second, third, and fourth year after TRAIDEX development begins. Although this approach eases the data entry burden on the local development sites (it is probably necessary to ensure their cooperation and should raise the overall quality of the available descriptive learning objectives), it does mean that the full potential benefits of TRAIDEX will not be realizable until 5 years after development begins. However, the development plan recommended that a kernel of very high-quality descriptions of broadly applicable courseware developed using the ISD process be entered into the data base by TRAIDEX Central personnel in parallel with the installation of TRAIDEX capability at the local development sites. The reason for this approach is to provide early system users with a general base of high-quality unit descriptions both for inquiry and as a model for their own data entry.

TRAIDEX Central Hardware and Software

In order to avoid the necessity of procuring computer hardware and/or developing new data base software to support such a system, the study team investigated various currently available information storage and retrieval systems to determine the feasibility of selecting one of them for the TRAIDEX data base host site. In view of the above rather demanding functional requirements and the parallel and competing requirement to keep costs at a minimum, the study team recommended that the TRAIDEX unit description data base be implemented on the INFOCEN information storage and retrieval system currently being operated by the U.S. Air Force Aeronautical Systems Division at Wright–Patternson Air Force Base, Dayton, Ohio.

The INFOCEN facility is a particularly attractive site for TRAIDEX because it is already a host for two complementary training-related systems:

- The Defense Audio Visual Archive (DAVA) is a catalog of audiovisual media and equipment covering all services.
- The Automated Data on Instructional Technology (ADIT) is a (currently) experimental collection of several thousand carefully indexed and evaluated ab-

stracts of research articles in the field of instructional systems design and development.

The use of the INFOCEN system will require little, if any, new software to be written. By fully understanding the functions to be performed by SADT, the study team was able to nearly eliminate new hardware and software acquisitions.

TRAIDEX Cost Estimation

Development and operational costs for the TRAIDEX system have been divided into three major categories. The costs that have been estimated are those required to support the actual operation of the system. Because no additional development site personnel are expected to be required with the introduction of the TRAIDEX system, no local site labor costs have been included.

The categories into which TRAIDEX operational costs have been divided are as follows:

- TRAIDEX Central labor and travel costs. These costs include the salaries and benefits of the TRAIDEX Central director, the service representatives, clerical personnel, and a computer-system analyst to assist in the initial system setup. Travel costs include both TRAIDEX Central staff requirements and invitational orders for members of the three services covering policy-planning meetings.
- TRAIDEX Central nonlabor costs. These costs include all other TRAIDEX Central costs except for computer and telecommunications items, and are primarily restricted to costs for office space and equipment.
- Computer and telecommunications costs. These costs include INFOCEN charges for setup and maintenance (updating) of the unit description data base, access charges for TRAIDEX inquiries, and the costs for purchasing terminals and for using the packet-switching communication network.

The estimated total cost over a 5-year period is $1,900,000, of which approximately $1,000,000 represents computer and telecommunications costs.

TRAIDEX Benefit Analysis

Given the lack of explicit course development cost data on which to base projected cost savings from TRAIDEX use, the final justification of the system must be based on a judgment of the percentage of course development cost that would be saved by sharing relevant courseware. Therefore, we have developed an estimate of the total cost reduction for course development that must occur over the first 5 years of TRAIDEX operation in order for the system to pay for its own development and operational costs. This total cost saving, or "break-even point," is then expressed as a percentage of the total development cost for technical training courses whose subject area is covered by the TRAIDEX data base, and it is the judgment of whether or not this percentage reduction is attainable that should determine the economic feasibility of TRAIDEX. The total cost reduction, or break-even point, is defined as follows:

*When the sum of all costs for startup and operation of TRAIDEX in each of the first 5 years **equals** the sum of the cost savings realized in each of the first 5 years, then TRAIDEX is said to break even.*

In order to calculate the percentage of course development costs that must be saved for TRAIDEX to break even over the first 5 years of operation, the following formula was used:

Percentage of development costs that must be saved by TRAIDEX over a 5-year period for break-even to occur equals sum of annual costs to develop and operate TRAIDEX during the 5-year period divided by sum of annual costs of course review, revision, and development in areas impacted by TRAIDEX over the 5-year period.

Once the costs of TRAIDEX development and operation have been calculated, the break-even percentage can be calculated if the annual costs of course review, revision, and development in TRAIDEX-relevant areas can be estimated.

In order to estimate the percentage of development costs that must be saved for TRAIDEX to break even, the key value is the total annual cost of course review, revision, and development in TRAIDEX-relevant areas. The study team believes this total value can be estimated with the required accuracy, even though data on individual development projects was not available. Knowledgeable people from the training community in the three services were asked to help in estimating the yearly course development costs of interest to TRAIDEX. This estimate was the product of two factors. First, it was determined that 2000 person-years per year of course-development time for courses in the categories of interest to TRAIDEX was a reasonable, and, in fact, conservative estimate for the three services. Second, it was determined by this group that an overall cost of one person-year of development effort was about $20,000 (FY 1975 dollars). This was confirmed later as the number being used by the Army in its own studies. In addition, the group agreed that the product of these two factors (2000 person-years $\times$ $20,000 per person-year) produced an estimate of the total yearly cost of technical course revision and new development — $40 million — that was determined to be reasonable.

When these development costs are used in the formula to calculate the percentage of development costs that must be saved by TRAIDEX over a 5-year period for break-even to occur, the percentage calculated is approximately 2% (based upon the $1.9 million, 5-year cost of developing and operating the TRAIDEX system).

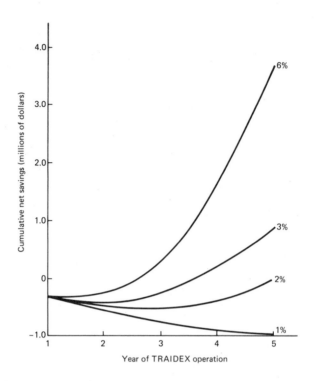

Figure 6.5 Cumulative net cost savings versus year of operation.

Figure 6.5 has been prepared by assuming different values for the percentage of development costs that will be saved by TRAIDEX. The exhibit shows the cumulative savings achieved by the use of TRAIDEX after all development costs have been deducted for four values of the percentage of course development costs to be saved (1, 2, 3, and 6%). For example, it shows that if the saving in development costs by using TRAIDEX should be 3%, TRAIDEX will break even by the end of the fourth year of operation and will have a cumulative net savings of nearly $900,000 by the end of 5 years. If one believes a larger percentage of savings will be realized, the cumulative net savings can be quite substantial; for example, a savings of 6% will result in a break-even period of under 3 years and will achieve a total savings of $3.6 million in the first 5 years of TRAIDEX operation. In summary, a cost reduction of over 2% produces very high net savings when viewed against the risk and costs of implementing TRAIDEX.

STUDY CONCLUSIONS

The estimated costs of TRAIDEX development and operation over the first 5 years of system use total less than $2 million. If the recommended development plan is followed, by the end of the third year a majority of the potential TRAIDEX developers will have access to the system and it will contain approximately half the potential data base. The study recommended that an in-depth evaluation of the utility of TRAIDEX to its intended audience, the course developers, be conducted at that time before a commitment is made to operate TRAIDEX on a permanent basis. To reach the point where this evaluation is carried out, based upon significant developer experience with the system, approximately $1 million will have been invested in initial development and operation of TRAIDEX.

The study recommended that the Interservice Training Review Organization (ITRO) proceed with the development of TRAIDEX up to the point of the evaluation if the ITRO is confident that

- The reduction in course development costs required for net savings to accrue is achievable, given the TRAIDEX capabilities described in previous sections of this report. A key issue in assessing the projected savings is the ITRO's confidence in the estimate of total course development costs ($40 million per year).
- The training commands will **actively** support the TRAIDEX concept, especially in regard to the establishment of the TRAIDEX interface positions as described in the integration plan.

The study team believes other benefits, especially higher-quality courses, will result from the development of TRAIDEX. However, these other benefits are not quantifiable and have not been included in the cost-benefit calculations, but they do provide significant further justification for developing TRAIDEX if the above conditions are met.

STUDY DISPOSITION

The Interservice Training Review Organization decided, late in 1976, not to proceed with the implementation of TRAIDEX. The following factors are believed to have influenced that decision, although the importance of each factor is not known:

- No strong champion for TRAIDEX existed at a command level to answer key questions about the concept and its rationale.
- The general enthusiasm for interservice exchange through TRAIDEX was mild at best, especially if lack of participation in interservice exchange could then be monitored quantitatively by the Department of Defense and by Congress.
- The belief at the command level that
  —All potential sharing is already accomplished, or
  —The developer will not use shared information, or
  —Potentially sharable material cannot be identified short of actual examination of the product.

The lack of a champion having contacts with the type of developers interviewed during the study made it difficult to change this opinion.

- The payoff period appeared too long, especially in the face of tight training budgets for the fiscal year in which development was to begin. As is the case with nearly all Department of Defense programs, the initiators of the project will not be in the same position when the benefits of the program begin to be reaped, thereby eliminating their incentive to undertake the program in the face of the three reasons cited above.

The study team is confident that the TRAIDEX approach is a viable, cost-effective concept that will eventually be implemented in a form not significantly different from that presented here. The increasing investment in each service in materials developed using the ISD process greatly increases the amount of potentially sharable material. When this study was done in 1975, the amount of validated material developed with the ISD process was much smaller than it is projected to be in the mid-1980s. Therefore, the economic incentives to reconsider the TRAIDEX concept will be much higher within a few years. A start on a program that could lead to a TRAIDEX-like capability has been made in the Army, as described in the next section.

ARMY TASK DESCRIPTION DATA BASE PROJECT

The use of SADT on the TRAIDEX project was sufficiently successful that DARPA and the U.S. Army Training and Doctrine Command (TRADOC) undertook a jointly funded project to demonstrate and evaluate SADT in the TRADOC environment (SofTech, 1977). The principal objectives of this project were to

- Identify charges in Army training required to increase combat effectiveness significantly
- Describe how Army training, testing, and evaluation programs will operate after the proposed changes are accomplished

The project also included an independent evaluation (Borich & Jemelka, 1977) that was designed to provide ARPA with

- An assessment of the utility and effectiveness of the SADT methodology in the TRADOC environment
- An evaluation of the impact of the project on TRADOC's ability to identify and understand the changes required in ARMY training

Early in this project, it became apparent that the new training innovations would be difficult to implement without a mechnaism for managing task descriptions (conditions, standards, and measures) Army-wide. Also, based on the results of the TRAIDEX study, it was believed that access by TRADOC schools to task descriptions would be useful in sharing course and task analysis material.

Each Army job, which will be called duty position, is broken down into tasks from which the Army selects those it believes to be critical to the Army's mission. These tasks are not necessarily simple but are small in that a soldier can usually demonstrate his ability to perform the task in 20 minutes or less and can usually learn to perform the task in from 1 to 3 days. Each task has conditions, standards and measures, and what must be learned to perform the task. Each task is equivalent to one or at most a few learning objectives in the ISD sense.

Duty positions are grouped into Military Occupational Specialties (MOS). An MOS defines an environment in which a soldier is expected to function; for example, MOS 11 E is for an armor crewman; MOS 11 B is for an infrantryman. Each soldier has one primary MOS.

The list of tasks that are critical to soldier performance is different for each duty position (tank driver versus tank gunner for the armor crewman [MOS 11 E]) and for each hardware type (heavy antitank weapons versus anti-aircraft guided missile for infantryman [MOS 11 B]) to which the soldier is assigned, even though these assignments are all within a single MOS.

Each MOS is also divided into skill levels. The skill level may determine allowable job assignments, as in the case of infantry (11 B), where Skill Level 2 is required for assignment to the HAW (Heavy Antitank Weapon). However, even when allowable assignments do not change with skill level, as for track vehicle mechanic, soldiers at higher skill levels must be proficient in more tasks than soldiers at lower skill levels.

The problem is to manage the task descriptions and to cluster and recluster the descriptions when needed by MOS, by duty position within MOS, and by other attributes such as the weapon system to which the task is related.

The task descriptions are now managed within each MOS and are identified within MOS — that is, numbered using an MOS prefix. The average number of tasks to be described for one MOS is estimated to be more than 1000. The number of Army MOSs is more than 400 and the total number of task descriptions has been estimated at over 400,000. These task descriptions represent a large source of training knowledge. Better managing of these descriptions appears to offer a rich opportunity for both training-effectiveness improvement and training-cost reduction. The training-effectiveness improvements are expected to come from making the task conditions and standards clearer and more consistent. The cost reduction is expected to come from the discovery of common tasks that can use common training material.

A prototype task description data base system has been implemented with SofTech assistance, to meet the following objectives:

- To assign Army-wide task identifiers
- To establish links or pointers to associated MOS, duty position, hardware type, weapon systems, skill level, and proponent school.
- To find common or near-common tasks within and across MOS

- To find incremental lists of tasks to be learned when changing duty position, MOS, or hardware type
- To provide a means to monitor and encourage the use of common descriptive terms across all Army MOSs
- To improve the writing of task descriptions by providing the writer with immediate access to other well-written task descriptions

The task description data base will be designed to facilitate enhancements so the Army will be able to key course material to the one or more tasks that it teaches.

By confining the task description data base system to a single service, a significantly different approach to sharing common material can be taken than was feasible in the TRAIDEX triservice environment. The sharing approach is based upon the following assumptions:

- Course material development for a task is assigned to only one school even when common to more than one MOS
- For each task, regardless of MOS, there will be only
  —One set of learning materials
  —One set of standards, conditions, measures, and actions
  —One performance test

Therefore, the search for sharable course material in the TRAIDEX sense is equivalent to the Army's search for common tasks. Once a common task has been identified, the Army plans to assign the common task to a school. The school will than have responsibility for learning material development.

Whether this approach to handling the hundreds of thousands of tasks in the Army is managerially feasible and will prevent the duplication of learning materials has yet to be demonstrated. The prototype task description data base system is a required adjunct to this management approach and will use the computer to assist with the most difficult parts of the process, identifying common tasks and retrieving the identification of the school to which a common task has been assigned.

Differences in terminology and in training approaches make infeasible identifying common tasks and assigning those tasks to schools on a DOD-wide basis. The study team is confident that the TRAIDEX approach is the required one to facilitate sharing of learning materials among the three services. When the economic payoff of interservice sharing becomes better established, the TRAIDEX concept is likely to reappear. By the mid-1980s the costs of *not* having a TRAIDEX-like system will be obvious.

REFERENCES

Borich, G., & Jemelka, R. *An evaluation of an advanced system analysis technique for modeling a DOD training environment* (ARPA Order No. 3230, Contract No. MDA 903-76-C-0249). Washington, D.C.: Active Technical Information Service, 1977.

Ross, D. T., & Schoman, K. Structured analysis for requirements definition. *IEEE Transactions on Software Engineering,* 1977, *SE-3* (1),

SofTech. *An introduction to SADT* (Document 9022-78R). Waltham, Mass.: Author, 1976. (a)

SofTech. *TRAIDEX needs and implementation study* (Final report). Waltham, Mass.: Author, 1976.(b) (Document 1020, ERIC Document Reproduction Service No. ED 129 244.

SofTech. *The Army training and evaluation system* (ARPA Order No. 3230, Contract No. MDA 903-76-C-0249). Waltham, Mass.: Author, 1977.

SofTech. *Demonstration of a prototype task description database* (Document 1026-9, NTIS ADB 026-111-L [restricted]). Waltham, Mass.: Author, February 1978.

7

Production of Computer-Based Instructional Materials[1]

R. A. AVNER

Production of instructional materials is the most labor-intensive part of instructional systems development. While the costs of hardware used in presentation and control of the most sophisticated forms of instruction have shown continued decreases over the past few years, the costs of skilled human labor have continually increased.

Although instructional design may be based on scientifically derived principles of learning, in application it remains an intensely private and almost artistic venture. Quality and quantity of production are often controlled by variables other than the relatively well-documented factors that enter logical analyses of instructional needs and resources. Clearly it is of supreme practical importance that all these variables be considered by designers of instructional systems if their systems are to survive the demands of any but experimental situations. Yet, until recently, the manner in which instructional material production was carried out minimized motivation for study of correlates of productivity.

[1]The work reported here was made possible by the direct or indirect support of the following agencies: Defense Advanced Research Projects Agency (contracts DA-28-043-AMC-0073 (E), ONR Nonr 3985(08), and DAAC-15-73-C-0077), U.S. Office of Education (OE-6-10-184), National Science Foundation (NSF GJ81, NSF GJ 974, NSF 65 29981, and NSF C-723), Ford Foundation (710-0293), U.S. Department of Health, Education and Welfare (NPG-188), Illinois Department of Education. Conclusions stated in this chapter are the responsibility of the author alone and do not necessarily reflect the policies or views of these agencies.

Some of the recent advances in instructional systems (such as computer-based education) have now both motivated further study of variables affecting quality and quantity of production and, at the same time, made such studies feasible. This chapter describes the results of two studies of individual instructional designers working either independently or as members of teams. The studies were selected from a larger longitudinal study conducted by the author that made use of the demands and capabilities of computer-based educational systems to quantify and track production efforts under a wide variety of situations. These particular studies are intended to indicate factors present at each end of the continuum of experience seen in implementation of a complete instructional system: from start-up with instructional designers new to the system to steady-state production with an experienced staff.

PRODUCING INSTRUCTIONAL MATERIALS

The past decade has seen a growing scholarly interest in the practical process of designing instruction (Bruner, 1968; Frase, 1975; Gagné & Rohwer, 1969; Glaser & Resnick, 1972; Merrill & Boutwell, 1973) that has strengthened the foundation set by an abundant literature on techniques of use of specific instructional media (Baker, 1973; Briggs, Campeau, Gagné, & May, 1967; Hicks & Hunka, 1972; Hubbell, 1960; Kemp, 1968; Spottiswood, 1957). As a result, there has been no lack of information on potentially promising techniques for design of instructional materials. Unfortunately, this increased attention has not yet ameliorated what has been described by the Carnegie Commission on Higher Education (1972) as "a grossly inadequate supply of good quality instructional materials [p. 48]." A possible reason for this lag may be the paucity of detailed information on the process of production itself — the laborious creative effort that converts plans and instructional design approaches into effective instructional products ready for dissemination.

Practical Issues

In the few instances where it is available at all, information on resource requirements for production of instructional materials is usually stated in broad, undifferentiated terms of total time or money expended (Godfrey, 1967). Explicit costs and detailed analysis of effects of designer characteristics such as training, background, and work methods on production are seldom reported. Thus, the inexperienced person setting out to create effective instructional materials is often in uncharted waters as soon as efforts reach the stage of converting plans to reality.

The limited availability of information on the production process is most likely the result of both the sheer difficulty of collecting appropriate data and a lack of strong interest in the support of such efforts. The creative stage of production of instructional materials is largely a private effort performed by an individual or a small group. Collection of accurate information about such covert processes requires either conscientious self-reporting by those carrying out the process or close interaction with an outside observer. Unless great care is taken, both of these techniques can lead to distortion of the process being described. Valid measures are seldom possible if those being observed wish to be perceived in a fashion other than that which would be conveyed by their normal activities or if the data gathering takes up significant amounts of production staff time. In either case, collection of detailed process data can be exceedingly costly in terms of both time and effort (House, 1973). It is therefore not surprising that the few production process studies that have been made tend to concentrate on easily collected and quantified data (e.g., test scores and employment time) and to be limited to single projects (Grimes, 1975; M. E. Ward, 1972) or to groups working for short periods under experimental conditions (Lysaught & Pierleoni, 1970).

Motivation for Production Studies

Until recently, support for such costly studies was limited because the production process was perceived to be of little practical concern to the educational community. The vast majority of instructional materials consisted either of books distributed by publishing houses for a mass market or teacher-made study aids designed for use by the producer's own classes. Despite the large expenditure of time and creative effort often involved for each of these types of materials, production was usually seen as a spare-time or at least a private effort by an individual who was compensated only for the final result of his or her labors. The author of a book was paid on the basis of sales rather than on the time spent in preparing the manuscript. The classroom teacher was paid for presenting instruction rather than for preparing it.

Only with the advent of media such as film did there come a need for specialized media personnel who were a necessary part of creative production but who were not, at least initially, supported on a full-time basis by educational institutions. Since these specialists were customarily paid directly for their efforts rather than for a finished product, heretofore "invisible" costs of production had to be considered along with more visible dissemination costs. Film and video tape are, however, media with potentially low presentation costs. Where a low presentation cost makes mass marketing possible, even relatively high production costs may be distributed across many users, again reducing the perceived importance of studies of the production process. As an example, $6,500,000 was spent during 1970 to produce a 130-hour series of *Sesame Street* programs viewed on television by about 7,000,000 children (Grayson, 1972). The large audience reduced shared production costs to less than 1 cent per child per hour during initial use of the materials. Subsequent reuse of these television programs reduced the impact of production costs on total cost per user for the series to an even lower level. Hence, although production costs for film and video tended to bring the production process into more public view, motivation for detailed study of the production process was still limited.

Interest in reduction of preparation costs through the identification and use of efficient production techniques does arise when production costs are high both in absolute terms and in relation to total instructional costs. Where a specific medium must be used for presentation of materials and when potential audiences for materials in that medium are restricted by limited availability or high presentation costs of the medium, there is no chance for production costs to be shared by an audience large enough to reduce per-student costs substantially. Under such conditions, production costs may have sufficient impact to justify support of studies that might lead to more efficient production techniques.

Currently, computer-based education (CBE) is the only widely used medium that has problems both of limited availability (Wang, 1976) and high presentation costs (Hunter, Kastner, Rubin, & Seidel, 1975). Fortuitously, computer-based education also possesses certain characteristics that facilitate the study of the production efforts of instructional designers.

Computer-Based Education

Computer-based education is, despite its title, more a medium for communication of information than a coherent instructional plan or approach. Thus, the fact that the computer is used in a given instance tells little about the instructional design philosophy followed. The term *computer-based education* (or the alternative *computer-assisted instruction*) has in common usage come to connote simply some form of instruction in which students interact in real time with materials presented under direct control of an electronic computer (Wang, 1976). Examination of the history of development of computer usage in education suggests that this outcome was probably not entirely intentional.

Computer-based education is essentially an offspring of the extensive "teaching machine" design efforts of the 1950s. These teaching machines each automated a specific instructional approach (usually some form of drill) in an attempt to reduce the observed discrepancies between learning research and practice (Pressey, 1926; Skinner, 1968). By providing an automatic means of immediate and appropriate feedback to students as individuals, the teaching machine was expected to produce more effective learning than classroom methods at a cost lower than individual human tutoring (Galanter, 1959; Lumsdaine & Glaser, 1960; Stolurow, 1961). The computer was initially perceived as simply a means by which selection and pacing of prestored instructional materials could be pro-

TABLE 7.1
Effects of Design Tools on Productivity of CBE Authors

Condition	Active authors	Hours per author-month
Authoring in FORTRAN	38	.07
CBE language added	43	.26
On-line editing added	47	1.06

Note. Data are for the PLATO III system at the University of Illinois at Urbana-Champaign from June 1966 to June 1969. Production rates under each condition were essentially constant after the first few months. Hours per author-month are the estimated number of student hours of material produced, adjusted for the number of active authors present during the period.

vided in a manner that was more adaptive to student differences than was possible by the electromechanical devices then available (Stolurow, 1961). The development of procedures in the late 1950s and early 1960s for time-sharing of a single computer by many simultaneous users promised an economical means by which early experiments in computerization of instruction could be extended to practical applications (Bitzer, Braunfeld, & Lichtenberger, 1961; Pask, 1957; Rath, Anderson, & Brainerd, 1959).

As might be expected, the actual use of the computer as an active element in the instructional process revealed applications and techniques that could not have been completely anticipated during early planning (Alpert & Bitzer, 1970). Far from remaining simply a means of controlling access to prestored materials, the computer permitted the automatic generation of materials following designer-specified rules (e.g., drills matched to the demonstrated skill level of each student) and even controllable by the student (e.g., simulations that permit the student to develop problem-solving skills through realistic practice).

The fact that the computer follows rules specified by the instructional designer rather than by the hardware designer also makes it possible for each instructional designer to specify a pedagogical approach or combination of approaches suitable for each situation rather than being forced to follow the Procrustean lead of a device that relies on a single, unchangeable approach. Development of inexpensive mass storage devices for computers, flexible automated text-editing features, and special instructionally oriented computer languages (Avner & Tenczar, 1969; Zinn, 1971) additionally permitted use of the interactive capabilities of the computer to ease the preparation as well as the presentation of instruction.

Table 7.1 suggests the effects of such technological innovations on rates of production of instructional materials for one heavily used CBE system. During the period in which a flexible, instructionally oriented computer language was introduced and an on-line editing capability was initiated on the University of Illinois PLATO III system, the population and productivity of instructional authors was monitored. Prior to July 1967 a modified version of a formula-oriented computer language (FORTRAN) was used for the majority of materials. Prior to October 1968, most materials had to be prepared off-line on punched paper tape, with only limited on-line magnetic tape editing features available during hours when the computer was not used for instruction. After introduction of the on-line editing capability, instructional authors could write, edit, and make trial use of instructional materials at any time the system was operating and terminals and computer space were available. Some of the total gain in productivity during the period was undoubtedly due to influences such as increased administrative and planning experience by the author population. Yet it would be difficult to explain the step-function increase that followed introduction of the language and editing features as resulting solely from such long-term effects.

Inexpensive mass storage, coupled with the computational power inherent in the computer, also provided the instructional designer with the possibility of collecting and analyzing data from student interactions within a matter of seconds after the interactions occurred. Together with the capabilities provided by an *author language* and on-line editing, this feature gives the instructional designer the basic tools required for effective learning of pedagogical techniques. If it is true that learning in students is hampered by the lock-step of classroom instruction and by delayed or inappropriate feedback, then the same must be said of the teacher trying to learn effective instructional approaches. By the mid-1960s the instructional use of the computer thus offered the possibility of superior learning for both student and instructional designer.

Since instructional materials designed for a computer may require use of the system during production as well as during presentation, the production process itself becomes directly accessible to the data-gathering capabilitites of the computer. Thus computer-based education itself provides tools that strongly facilitate the study of the instructional production process.

Conditions for Study of Production of
Computer-Based Materials

Not all of the 222 instructional computer centers now existing (Wang, 1976) would be equally likely to provide fruitful settings for a study of the production process. As suggested by Table 7.1, technological aids may have an enormous effect on rates of productivity. Unless one is specifically interested in the effects of such aids, data should originate from a single center or group of centers with identical equipment. At the same time, standardized equipment would not be an advantage if it were a type that restricted the range of possible instructional approaches. Nor would a center with a small number of workers or a center dedicated to use of a single instructional design and production process be as likely to serve as a source of generalizable data. To be generalizable, a study of the production process for computer-based instructional materials demands a setting or settings where a relatively large number of independent instructional production projects interact with equivalent equipment that minimally limits the range of possible instructional approaches.

At the time the studies reported here were begun (1966) and for many years following, only one CBE center satisfied all of these requirements. Only the PLATO CBE system at the University of Illinois combined the presence of a relatively large number of independent instructional production efforts with equipment that provided full graphics capability and the computational power necessary for sophisticated real-time simulations and computations. By the early 1970s this center had produced more material in more subject matter areas than any other single center and accounted for over 912 of the 6962 hours of documented computer-based instructional materials in the world (Lekan, 1971). The difficulty in finding alternative sources of generalizable data is suggested by the fact that even by 1970 most of the 137 centers identified by Lekan (1971) used a variety of nonequivalent equipment and had very limited experience in production of CBE materials. Based on data reported by Lekan, the 10 most active centers had produced more than 60% of the existing CBE material. Unfortunately, none of these 10 centers used equivalent equipment, and the most productive ones (aside from the PLATO system) used a very limited number of design groups or used equipment that restricted the range of instructional approaches possible.

The presence of a large number of independent instructional designers on a single computer system was obviously not typical during the 1960s and early 1970s. Most systems simply did not have adequate resources to support large numbers of users of any type. Many, in fact, shared equipment with other computer applications. Centers that had equipment dedicated to education frequently had instructional research programs that dictated either production of limited amounts of material used in experimental situations or the production of large amounts of material by a few teams following specific instructional models. The University of Illinois PLATO system differed in that it was supported by a laboratory that had design of computer-based educational systems as a primary goal. The realistic test and development of the experimental system designs produced by this laboratory demanded heavy use by real students using the widest possible range of potential applications. For this reason the laboratory strongly encouraged production and use of materials by all individuals or groups who expressed an interest in the medium.

There was good reason to believe that the resulting applications were representative of the full range of approaches used by instructional computer systems. Included were research programs that followed tightly controlled experimental conditions (e.g., Avner, 1964; Montague & Wearing, 1967; Schwartz, 1966), naturalistic investigations of the medium (e.g., Dennis, 1968; Rothbart & Steinberg, 1971; Smith, 1970), programs directed toward replacement of substantial amounts of standard instruction with computer-based materials (e.g., Axeen, 1967; Bitzer, Boudreau, & Avner, 1973; Curtin, Clayton, Finch, Moor, & Woodruff, 1972; Scanlan, 1970). and explorations of innovative applications of the medium (e.g., Hicks, 1965; Neal & Meller, 1971; Umpleby, 1971). Materials were programmed both by persons who had never seen a computer before and by persons with years of computer experience. Instruction was designed by highly qualified staff members of major curriculum projects as well as by persons who had never attempted to teach before. Some efforts were well organized with clearly specified goals and standardized procedures for attaining those goals. Others followed an "artistic" approach of seeking inspiration while exploring the medium.

Organization of the Studies

The most visible skill required in effective use of any medium is the ability to interact with the medium. Unless one can translate materials to a form directly usable by the medium, the medium is not truly available. Thus, the potential producer of materials for a computer must either learn to produce materials in a language interpretable by the computer or work through a person who already possesses this skill.

There are, however, at least two other necessary skills. If possession of skills in the subject area being taught and facility with the natural language (e.g., English) in which the instruction is to be given are assumed, there remains a need for (a) pedagogical skills in order to ensure that the subject matter is structured in a manner that will maximize learning in students, and (b) organizational skills in order to ensure that time, funding, and other resources are used efficiently.

Skills in medium, pedagogy, and organization may be possessed by a single individual or by a team of specialists in each area. This individual or team would also possess the assumed subject matter and communication skills or support other individuals who did. Whatever the situation, the three skills of interest in these studies may be seen to form a hierarchy of accessibility to the medium in question. Primary are the medium skills. Without such skills, even the crudest application of the medium is not possible. Second are the pedagogical skills. Without these skills, application of the medium for effective instruction is not possible. Third are organizational and planning skills. Without these last skills, use of the medium for anything but limited exploration is likely to be so inefficient as to be impractical.

The need for inclusion of pedagogical and organizational skills in a study of the production of materials for a specific medium may not be readily apparent. They were, in fact, not considered when the studies were begun. Only after early

data were collected did the extent of the effect of interactions of the use of CBE
with these skills become apparent. The nature of the effects will be described in
some detail later in this chapter; however, they can be briefly indicated here. Instructional computing permits, above all, an approach to individualized instruction. The training and experience of most educators in the past, however, were
of necessity in the area of group instruction. Effective use of CBE thus required
a shift in pedagogical approach for the majority of new authors of CBE materials. This shift took an appreciable amount of time, which, in many cases, exceed-
ed the amount of time needed to acquire basic skills in the medium. Finally, the
details of production and maintenance of CBE materials differ sufficiently from
those of other media that changes were also needed in the area of organization and planning. Most notable is the fact that revision of CBE materials is so
greatly facilitated by features of a computer system that the discrete steps required in production and revision of materials for most other media are virtually
eliminated.

In practice, skills in each of these three areas were often acquired simultaneously by a new CBE author or by members of authoring teams. For clarity, however, data on acquisition or application of each skill will be presented separately
and interactions will be indicated only to the extent that they affected the skill
being described at the moment. In addition, all the basic skills are not necessarily
held by a single individual. Although some production efforts did in fact consist
of a single all-purpose member, this was not always the case, nor is there any evidence that there are clear advantages to teams made up of such prodigies.

ACQUISITION OF CBE LANGUAGE SKILLS

Computer Languages

A computer is basically a device that carries out instructions. Unlike a human,
a computer requires that all instructions given it be absolutely complete and explicit. Each instruction to a computer is interpreted in an unquestioningly literal
fashion. Instructions containing obvious errors or logical ambiguities that would
be corrected or questioned by a human are blindly carried out by a computer.
As a result, communication with computers must be done by unambiguous
methods applied with meticulous care. This communication must also be in languages understandable by both humans and computers. Such languages are, unfortunately, always compromises between the conflicting goals of generality and
simplicity.

A general computer language allows direct access to the full capabilities of the
computer. Such direct access requires complete responsibility for most computer functions and hence may demand that exceedingly detailed instructions be

given even for trivial operations. Humans generally find that requirements for such detail increase both the difficulty of use of the language and the chance that errors will occur.

Simplicity in a computer language is usually obtained by restricting frequently used procedures to a subset of possible approaches. Though such restricted procedures also require that detailed instructions be given the computer, the instructions need be only written once (as a part of the language itself). These detailed instructions are never seen by the average user of the language, who needs only to specify values for a limited set of parameters. When a limited range of options is permitted for a procedure, it becomes feasible to build internal checks into the language to ensure that only valid parameters are accepted. A computer language with a limited number of standardized procedures thus makes use of the computer both easier and more reliable in exchage for a loss in flexibility.

Compromise approaches in CBE languages additionally tend to reflect factors such as restrictions of hardware and desired instructional approaches. Great generality is not, for example, demanded of a CBE language restricted to use with a single type of teleprinter or intended solely for use with a specific form of drill and practice.

PLATO CBE Language

The TUTOR language (Avner & Tenczar, 1969; Sherwood, 1977) used by the University of Illinois PLATO system, though not a general computer language, is one of the most general languages for instructional purposes in wide use (Lower, 1976). Since it is designed solely for use in education, frequently used basic procedures such as text presentation, student-response processing, record keeping and computation are made available with minimal effort. However, since no particular pedagogical approaches are universally accepable to all designers of instructional materials, the language does not offer the simplifications possible by standardizing procedures for specific pedagogical approaches. In this area, TUTOR departs from other languages that provide extreme ease in production of instructional material at the cost of restricting designers to a single pedagogical approach. Users of such limited CBE languages can modify the standard pedagogical approach provided by the language only by modifying the language itself – usually a difficult task. The lack of standardized pedagogical procedures within the TUTOR language itself makes it a very useful vehicle for the general study of CBE language acquisition. The range and type of features that TUTOR does provide permit each instructional designer to develop or modify his or her own pedagogical procedure if desired. Thus, an instructional designer who feels a particular pedagogical approach is most efficient may program a procedure in TUTOR that automates use of that pedagogical approach in a manner that mimics more restricted languages (e.g., Schulz & Volk, 1974; Stull, Cohen, & Hody, 1976) without sacrificing the ability to easily modify the approach selected. This facility allows one to study the acquisition and use of both a highly general CBE language (the basic TUTOR language) and more restricted special-purpose languages (macroscopic procedures programmed in TUTOR) without the problems attendant to comparisons between languages used for greatly differing systems or pedagogical applications.

Learning CBE Languages

Acquisition of CBE language skills is a sufficiently protracted venture that it is rarely the sole activity of the learner. Most persons learn such a language in order to produce instructional materials, and most begin that production early in the process of learning the language. This mingling of learning and application makes explication of the process of learning the language itself difficult. On the other hand, since the learner is engaged at an early point in producing actual instructional materials, early and direct measures of the ultimate application of successful learning become available.

Another potentially troublesome issue arises because many experienced teachers have relatively limited knowledge of individualized instruction. Early efforts of such persons might thus be concerned with learning new pedagogical techniques as well as the language. This potential source of confusion for studies of language learning has in practice been found to have negligible impact during the first year of learning. Comments made during interviews with new workers in CBE suggest three possible reasons for an absence of effects. First, most people seem to perceive the process of instruction as something that they already know all about from their experience as students. Those who have actually taught in classrooms usually assume that such experience is sufficient for effective use of any medium. Second, the problems encountered by new CBE instructional designers during their first year tend to be seen as relating more to the technical aspects of the medium than to pedagogy. Finally, the immediate feedback provided by a computer for those learning the language and applying it to produce materials seems to make such programming so attractive that time for other pursuits is limited.

Productivity and Retention of New CBE Authors

During the period between October 1969 and August 1971, the PLATO III system was able to support interested instructional designers in a relatively open manner. Sufficient documentation on the operation of the system and the language was available (Avner & Tenczar, 1969) to permit reasonably independent functioning by workers who were learning to program instructional sequences. System resources, although heavily used, were also sufficient to permit production and experimental use of materials by such people (although no formal training in use of the language was provided). Thus, during this period it was possible to permit access to PLATO to essentially every person who indicated a reasonable educational application. Since computer file space necessary for permanent storage of materials developed for PLATO was at that time of fixed length, it was also possible to monitor productivity of these new workers simply by noting the date at which each additional file space was allocated. This rough measure of productivity, combined with biographical, interview, and observational data, provided the basis for a study of factors relating to the productivity and retention of unselected new authors. The term *author* rather than *instructional designer* will be used to describe subjects of this study. This usage is intended to indicate that these individuals were involved not only in the design but also in the production of the materials. As implied above, *instructional design* for these new authors often entailed little more than application of previously known pedagogical techniques to the CBE medium. Efforts of these authors seemed directed toward learning how to ensure that the materials were functional in a mechanical rather than an educational sense.

Method

To provide a reasonable period for learning of the new skills needed for successful use of PLATO, the 12 months following the first acquisition of a file space were arbitrarily defined as the period of study for each individual involved. Since all new authors worked in academic settings (the University of Illinois or Parkland Community College), a 1-year period had the advantage that 1 complete academic-year cycle would be completed, thus providing all authors equal opportunity for working during academic vacation periods despite different starting times. Data beyond August 1971 could not be used because of influences of severely reduced storage space and major shifts in interest of all users to the PLATO IV system. Thus, to ensure a full year of effort, data are reported here only for the 27 authors who were given their first computer file space in the 11-month period from October 1969 to August 1970. New authors were interviewed shortly after receiving their first file space and again at the end of the 12 months (or at the end of their PLATO effort, if earlier). Initial interviews sought to identify differences in approaches and backgrounds of the new authors that might be expected to affect their productivity. In addition, new authors were asked to indicate their reason for wanting to use PLATO and their expectations. The final interview sought to identify critical factors that the authors considered as having major importance in effective use of the medium. In most cases it was also possible to interact informally with each of these authors frequently during the intervening months.

During the course of the study a number of factors were identified as having possible effects on productivity. Five factors were identified during the initial interview.

1. *Academic status.* Authors were classified as either *student* or *staff*. All

students were university graduate students with teaching experience. All staff were full-time employees of a university or a community college. The majority of the authors from both groups had from 1 to 3 years of classroom teaching experience, although 4 of the 15 staff authors each had over 10 years of classroom experience. Since staff authors seemed better able to articulate expected benefits of computer-based education during the initial interview and since two of the student members desired to use the computer system solely as a means of gathering experimental data for a thesis, higher productivity was hypothesized for the staff group.

2. *Affiliation.* The two authors affiliated with the community college reported much heavier instructional loads than did those affiliated with the university. It was hypothesized that authors under such a workload would generally not be able to produce as much as those who had more discretionary time available.

3. *Support for production.* Nine of the authors were supported through grants, salary, or released time specifically for production of instructional materials. All other authors used PLATO during their own free time without support. It was hypothesized that specific support for production of materials would significantly facilitate productivity.

4. *Stated intention.* Eighteen of the authors indicated an intention to produce substantial amounts of material, whereas the remainder indicated either limited goals (e.g., the two students using PLATO for thesis research) or simply a desire to explore the possibilities of using the computer for instruction. It was hypothesized that those who expressed an intention to produce large quantities of material would in fact produce more than those who expressed limited goals.

5. *Computer experience.* Those who had had significant past experience with computer programming (i.e., those who had written and executed at least two computer programs on any computer) generally reported during initial interviews that this experience was useful in helping them learn to use the author language. Several without such experience expressed concern over lack of computer experience. It was hypothesized that past computer experience would aid in at least early production.

During the course of the study, four additional factors were identified as potential predictors of CBE productivity.

6. *Group membership.* Ten of the authors were members of groups of two or more who worked jointly on production of materials in a subject area. Most of these authors reported that aid from other members of their group contributed considerably to their progress. Most new authors receive aid voluntarily from more experienced persons. Since members of a group would be expected to have a special interest in enhancing productivity of persons in their own group, an experienced group member would probably be willing to give more aid to a new author who was a member of the same group than to a nonmember. For

this reason, group membership was hypothesized as contributing to higher individual productivity during early production. It should be noted that because of technical difficulties in coordinating work within a single file space, production of a group most often consists of a collection of files, each of which is the responsibility of an individual author. Thus, a count of files completed generally remains a valid measure of individual productivity even for members of groups.

7. *Content orientation.* Several authors mentioned that they thought certain subject matter areas were inherently easier to adapt to computer based learning than others. These observations were made most often in the course of attempting approaches used by more experienced authors. In general, it was thought that more concrete and quantitatively oriented materials (such as those that occur in introductory mathematics or physical science courses) were easier to adapt than were the more abstract or qualitative materials of the arts. A test of this hypothesis was attempted by categorizing each author's materials as being predominantly *quantitative* (dealing with concrete or easily quantifiable concepts) or *qualitative* (dealing with abstract concepts or with concepts that are not simply definable). Although some subject matter areas such as the physical sciences lend themselves to almost automatic classification, others require careful examination of specific instructional material. For example, a course in psychology might cover extremely quantitative material in the area of statistical techniques or highly abstract material in the area of personality theory. Based on opinions of most authors, it was hypothesized that quantitatively oriented content would be most easily produced.

8. *Working time.* Obviously, those who spend a good deal of time at a task are likely to produce more than those who devote less time (all other things being equal). In addition, however, observations of this group of authors suggested that those who spend relatively little time working at production of lessons were also less efficient than those who spent larger amounts of time. Thus, the trivial hypothesis relating total productivity to total effort needs to be supplemented. Two additional hypotheses seemed to offer plausible explanations for the perceived differences in efficiency. Most authors reported lowered efficiency at the start of each period of work because of the time required to organize materials, identify the point at which work from the previous period had left off, and determine the direction in which work for the current period was to proceed. This warm-up period would occupy a relatively larger proportion of the total work time for those who spent less total time per work session. A second possibility is suggested by authors who reported that until they had reached a minimal level of proficiency with the programming language, they seemed to progress at an exceedingly slow pace. Fortunately, these two hypotheses yield somewhat different predictions. A "warm-up" effect would be expected to be present for all production, whereas a "learning" effect would be expected to cause a shift in

productivity after the time needed to attain minimal proficiency had passed.

The measure of working time had to be based on reports from the authors. To make this estimate as accurate as possible, these figures were developed during the course of interviews in which the authors described their experiences on a week-by-week basis with the aid of a calendar. Wherever possible, the reports were verified by interviews with coworkers and supervisors and by reference to notes made by the observer during the course of the study. All independent estimates for the same period of time for a given author agreed to within 10%, and most agreed to within better then 5%.

9. *Facility with authoring language.* Since all of the authors performed their own coding of instructional material, facility with the authoring language was necessary to production. The required degree of proficiency and the extent of knowledge were not, however, the same for all authors. Few authors needed to use all features of the language, and several were satisfied with the simpler applications even of such a selected subset. Thus, the "required" level of proficiency was a highly individual matter. Several times during the study authors were asked about the extent to which they felt that they had identified those aspects of the language that were required for their own application, and the degree to which they felt that they could use these features to meet their own instructional goals. Understandably, reports were rather vague as to the precise moment at which they felt they had reached this level of competency. Nevertheless, all but four authors eventually indicated an approximate date at which they judged themselves to be adequately proficient in those portions of the language required for their own needs. In order to produce a measure in which early proficiency would be indicated by a larger value than delayed proficiency, *facility* was defined as the number of months remaining in the first year after the reported date of competency. Thus, authors reporting proficiency by the third month would have nine months left in the year during which problems related to learning the language should have been minimal.

Productivity, the dependent variable in this study, was based largely on various facets of a single index. "Number of files completed" served as the major measure of productivity. File completion was initially defined as occurring on the date an additional file space was requested. As a matter of administrative policy, new authors were required to justify acquisition of additional file space by demonstrating that all prior file spaces had been utilized in some reasonable fashion. This policy tended, however, to be generously interpreted once a second file space had been justified, and subsequent requests were usually granted almost automatically. As a result, it was necessary to determine file completion more directly. Fortunately, most new authors were eager to show their work to anyone willing to look. It was also common practice for all users of the system to view each other's files as "students" during work sessions when an author was

TABLE 7.2
Characteristics of New Author Group

Author	Status	Supported	Group or individual	Course production intended	Computer experience	Content orientation
1	Student	y	g	y	n	Qualitative
2	Staff	n	i	n	y	Quantitative
3	Staff	y	g	y	y	Quantitative
4	Staff	n	i	y	y	Qualitative
5	Staff	n	i	y	n	Qualitative
6	Staff	y	g	y	y	Qualitative
7	Staff	y	i	y	y	Quantitative
8	Staff	n	i	n	y	Quantitative
9	Staff	n	i	y	y	Quantitative
10	Student	y	i	n	y	Quantitative
11	Student	n	i	y	n	Quantitative
12	Student	n	i	y	y	Quantitative
13	Staff	n	i	y	y	Qualitative
14	Student	n	i	n	y	Qualitative
15	Student	n	g	y	y	Quantitative
16	Staff	n	i	y	n	Qualitative
17	Staff	n	i	n	n	Qualitative
18	Student	y	g	y	n	Qualitative
19	Student	n	i	n	n	Qualitative
20	Student	n	i	n	y	Qualitative
21	Staff	n	g	n	y	Quantitative
22	Student	y	g	y	y	Quantitative
23	Staff	n	g	y	y	Quantitative
24	Staff	y	g	y	y	Quantitative
25	Student	n	i	y	n	Qualitative
26	Staff	n	i	n	y	Quantitative
27	Student	y	g	y	n	Quantitative

Note. Authors 14 and 20 used PLATO solely for collection of research data. Authors 13 and 17 were affiliated with a community college rather than a university.

testing a new lesson. Thus, it was possible to monitor progress of all the authors in this study almost constantly. This form of monitoring also permitted the investigator to exclude several files used for storage of duplicate or trial material from the study.

Results

General characteristics of the group are summarized in Table 7.2. A wide variety of subject matter specialties was represented by the group. The largest departmental concentrations were three authors in electrical engineering and three authors in psychology (the latter included both students who were using PLATO solely as a means of gathering data for a dissertation). The other authors provided a diverse selection of disciplines from the academic community with representatives from languages, biological and social sciences, fine arts, engineering, the physical sciences, education, and mathematics. An analysis comparing sample and population proportions of full-time versus graduate-student instructors and computer-experienced versus inexperienced persons indicated no evidence of sampling bias. Although an instructor population predominantly from a major university is certainly atypical of most instructor populations, it can be argued that such a select population is probably quite similar to the select population of creators of mass instructional materials such as textbooks or instructional films.

Table 7.3 presents a summary of all major outcomes of the study. During the course of the study two major departures from the expected sequence of events were discoveed. First, three of the authors (1, 3, and 9) acquired one file space that was used solely for testing or storage of material to be subsequently placed in another file. These *work spaces* were not counted as part of the productivity of these authors. Second, seven of the authors worked simultaneously on two or more file spaces. Virtually every author who had more than one file space did additional work on *completed* files (files reported as ready for class use by the author and so verified by the observer) while working on new files. However, seven authors also began work on a new file well before a previous one was completed. Estimates of working hours required for this simultaneous effort were based both on reports given informally by the authors during the period when such dual work was carried out and on direct observations. Time spent on files subsequent to their completion was added to the original completion times. Although some new authors have been observed to make radical changes to early lessons (even to the point of totally rewriting them), changes to completed files made by this group during the period of this study were relatively minor. In no case did the total amount of time spent subsequent to completion exceed 3% of the original time.

In all, 71 files were completed by 22 of the 27 new authors during their first year of use of PLATO. When completion times for individual files were averaged across all of the authors, the first few files appeared to take significantly longer to be completed than later files. For example, examination of data for the first seven files (only two authors completed more than seven) showed a significant difference in completion times for different ordinal file numbers [$F(6,60) = 5.596$; $p = .0001$; 35.9% of sample variance was accounted for by this effect]. This effect was almost entirely the result of differences in mean completion time for Files 1 and 2 in comparison with completion times for all subsequent files ($p < .0005$ by Scheffé's test). Since only three new authors had completed seven files, it is quite possible that this significant trend might be an artifact produced by combining data from inefficient authors who completed only a few files with data from very efficient authors who completed many files. Comparison of completion times for the first file in fact shows that the seven authors

TABLE 7.3
Productivity of New Authors during Their First Year

Author	Working[a] hours	Skilled[b] months	Five years[c] later	Hours to complete each file[d]										Total files	Mean time
				1	2	3	4	5	6	7	8	9	10		
1	1012	6	A	159	535	186	36	20	24					6	160
2	220	8	A	192										1	192
3	1932	10	A	160	160	104	220	304	296	160	320	142	54	10	192
4	104	6	N	–										0	–
5	282	6	N	240										1	240
6	418	9	I	208	204									2	206
7	1064	11	I	270	312	246	86	142						5	211
8	480	9	N	312	168									2	240
9	1115	9	I	160	225	280	175	120	46	48				7	151
10	522	11	A	484										1	484
11	144	10	N	–										0	–
12	1280	10	A	230	184	192	134	80	152	120	108			8	150
13	96	0	N	–										0	–
14	624	0	N	570										1	570
15	906	11	A	360	360									2	360
16	450	6	N	384										1	384

17	278	6	N	—	212	152	180	56	0	—
18	1092	10	N	360	414				5	192
19	844	6	A	370					2	392
20	761	4	N	620					1	620
21	256	11	I	196					1	196
22	1100	6	A	420	496	156			3	357
23	1134	10	A	355	348	305			3	336
24	1031	9	A	312	224	184	240		4	240
25	1021	0	N	295	320	184	380		3	332
26	190	0	N	—					0	—
27	662	6	N	215	361				2	288

[a]Includes time spent on files not completed.

[b]Number of months in first year after date author reported feeling competent in use of TUTOR.

[c]A = active author; N = PLATO inaccessible to author; I = inactive author (PLATO accessible).

[d]Work was done concurrently in files that have entries connected by the same underline.

TABLE 7.4
Mean File Completion Times for Six Authors Who Completed at least Five Files

File	1	2	3	4	5
Mean hours	223.2	271.3	193.3	138.5	120.3
SD	81.3	139.2	63.3	67.8	100.0

who completed only one file took an average of 147.85 hours longer to complete that file than did the seven authors who completed at least four files [$t(12)$ = 1.985; p = .07; 24.7% of sample variance accounted for by this effect]. This possible ambiguity can be reduced by making comparisons for individual authors rather than for grouped data. A Monte Carlo analysis of completion times for each of the 15 authors who completed at least two files showed that the probability that the observed trend toward shorter completion times for later files was due to chance alone was about .003 (10 random orderings in 33,000 showed an equal or greater trend). Thus, the hypothesis that individual authors become more proficient with time appears to be supported.

It is not surprising that experience would have such effects, but the length of time required for the effect to reach an asymptote is quite surprising. In fact, there is no clear evidence that an asymptote was reached by any of these authors in their first year. The six authors who completed at least five files (spending an average of over 900 hours) showed evidence only of a continued trend toward reduced mean time per file completion at their fifth file (Table 7.4) and very high individual variability. Almost 22% of sample variance was accounted for by linear regression between file numbers and total hours spent on the file [$r(28)$ = −.468]. As might be expected, a somewhat better fit was provided by nonlinear regression (eta = .539), but the improvement over linear regression was insignificant [$F(3,25)$ = .85; p = .482].

Interviews with the authors suggested that a major part of the variability in completion times could be ascribed to idiosyncratic exploration of instructional and programming techniques. A common practice for the more prolific authors, for example, included extensive experimentation with a new technique in a single file followed by highly efficient application of the technique in several subsequent files. In most cases the file in which the major development efforts were concentrated required noticeably longer times for completion.

File 2 followed by 3 through 6 for author 1 (see Table 7.3) provides an ideal example of such a development–exploitation pattern. Most authors tended to experiment with several new approaches at the same time or to experiment with one new approach while applying a recently perfected one, thus obscuring possible evidence of increased efficiency. Author 3, for example, developed and applied four distinctly different instructional or programming techniques in the course of completing Files 4 through 8. Only Files 9 and 10 could be considered as examples of application of already learned techniques for this author. All authors who completed more than two files reported that they felt that efficiency in producing materials was only partially a function of knowledge of TUTOR (although it was, of course, a necessary condition). All indicated that ultimately the development of a repertoire of proven programming techniques appropriate to the subject matter and the student population was of equal or greater importance. Acquisition of such a repertoire can be an exceedingly time-consuming operation, as demonstrated by the time spent by this group of authors. One of the most time-consuming and important components of such learning, as reported by these authors, was the extensive use of test and revision by the author at a PLATO terminal. It was not unusual for an author to make a dozen revisions of a portion of a display or instructional segment within an hour. After each revision, the author would cause a new student version of the material to be produced, view the result as a student would, and then shift back to operation as an author — often within a matter of seconds.

Since it had been assumed that 1 year would be sufficient time for major learning in use of CBE to be accomplished, the lack of evidence for an asymptote in the trend to reduced time for completion of files during the duration of this study is disappointing. It had been hoped that identification of such a point would permit tentative specification of a basic level of experience required for effective use of the author language. Interviews indicated that most of the authors felt relatively competent in the use of TUTOR and the equipment well before the end of the year (after an average of 2.7 months for the six authors who completed at least five files), but independent supporting evidence for such beliefs is difficult to find.

Twelve authors began and completed at least one file after reporting a feeling of competence in the language. If there is a point at which a distinct shift in facility with the language exists, it should be visible as an increased rate of production. Detection of such a shift is made difficult by the wide variation in completion times (resulting partially from the development–exploitation cycle already described) and by the general trend toward shorter completion times with increased experience. The average reduction in completion times for successive files by the 12 authors was 32 hours (based on 45 comparisons, SD = 118.9). The difference between completion times for the file being worked on at the time of reporting competence and the immediately succeeding file was 90.4 hours (N = 12; SD = 134.8). The mean difference for the remaining 33 comparisons was only 10.8 hours (SD = 107). The difference between these values is significant [$t(43)$ = 2.06; p = .046; alpha = .05], although only 9% of the total sample variance is accounted for by this effect. The mean hours of experience at the time of reporting competence for the 12 authors was approximately 240 hours (SD = 155). If this self-estimate is accepted as an indicator of minimal proficiency, then one would estimate (with 90% confidence) that 75% of the members of a similar group would attain a like level in 424 hours or less.

An alternative measure is suggested by the fact that minimal facility with the author language is a necessary (but not sufficient) requirement for completion of the first file. The mean time for completion of the first file to a point where it was deemed (by an independent judge, a member of the PLATO administrative staff) to be a potentially useful application was 312.4 hours (SD = 129) for the 22 authors who completed at least one file. These last data suggest that one could be 90% confident that at least 75% of the members of a similar group of authors would reach the same level in 444 hours or less of work. Taken together, these measures and the information in Table 7.4 seem to imply that a minimum initial effort of 300–500 hours may be required for effective use of a general CBE language and that continued experience beyond that minimum leads to continued improvement in rate of production during the first year. Thus, there appears to be evidence in support of the "learning" effect mentioned by some of the authors in this group.

Interviews with authors during their first year indicated that some authors tended to spend several hours during a typical session, whereas others tended to limit their sessions to 1 hour or less. It was hypothesized that the relatively high proportion of warm-up time for those who worked in shorter sessions might make them less productive. This view is supported by the fact that all five of the authors who failed to complete any files reported that, as a result of limited free time, they usually could only work with PLATO for periods of about an hour. In addition, Authors 7, 8, 12, 18, and 22 reported that they had initially attempted to work for such short periods on their first file but had found it to be so inefficient that they had shifted to longer work sessions when working on subsequent files. Despite the presence in the short-session group of the five non-productive authors (who spent the least total amount of time working on CBE materials), there was no evidence of a relationship between total time spent and work style, either when the five authors who shifted work style were included [$r_{pb}(25)$ = .0058; p = .977] or when they were omitted [$r_{pb}(20)$ = .0355; p = .875]. Comparison of total time spent by authors using short or long work sessions on their first file showed a significant advantage for those (Authors 1, 2, 3, 5, 9, 15, 25, and 27) using longer work sessions [$t(20)$ = 2.857; p = .0097; 29% of sample variance accounted for by group membership]. Those authors using long work sessions spent an average of 141 hours less to complete their first file than those using short sessions (95% confidence interval for this difference is 38 hours to 244 hours).

Table 7.5 shows the relationship between predictors and various aspects of the criterion. Total files produced (TF) is of major interest. One predictor (institutional affiliation) was dropped because most of the authors in the study were

TABLE 7.5
Intercorrelations between Predictors and Indexes of Productivity for 27 New
Instructional Authors

	St	Sp	Pr	Cp	Gp	Qn	Wh	Lg	TF	H/F
St	1.00	.16	.00	−.32	.09	−.10	.25	−.09	.07	−.16
Sp		1.00	.33	.00	.60	.16	.44	.33	.43	−.37
Pr			1.00	.17	.38	.00	.38	.19	.44	−.14
Cp				1.00	.05	.47	.10	.16	.11	−.06
Gp					1.00	.22	.43	.38	.35	−.41
Qn						1.00	.25	.54	.27	−.20
Wh							1.00	.30	.89	−.60
Lg								1.00	.39	−.42
TF									1.00	−.56
H/F										1.00

Note. Dichotomous variables were scored as follows: St (Academic status): staff = 0, student = 1; Sp (Supported effort): no = 0, yes = 1; Pr (Production intent): no = 0, yes = 1; Cp (Computer background): no = 0, yes = 1; Gp (Group effort): no = 0, yes = 1; Qn (Quantitative materials): no = 0, yes = 1. The last four variables, Wh (Total working hours), Lg (Language competence), TF (Total files completed), and H/F (Hours per complete file), are continuous. For those who had completed no files, H/F was arbitrarily set to 2000 hours (one working year). Correlations involving H/F should thus be interpreted with caution.

affiliated with a university. The two authors affiliated with a community college completed no files and were both unsupported staff members who worked as individuals and had qualitative subject matter orientations. This confounding of variables and the small sample size thus reduced the potential utility of institutional affiliation as a useful predictor in this study.

None of the individual predictors account for major portions of sample file-production variance. Production support, production intention, and reported language facility show the most evidence of representing nonrandom relationships (alpha = .05), whereas academic status, computer experience, group membership, and subject matter orientation show insignificant effects. Some of the strongest relationships seen in Table 7.5 appear between different aspects of the criterion, as would be expected. Thus, almost 80% of sample variance in total files produced is accounted for by information on the total number of hours spent in producing materials. The mean number of hours spent per file provides a measure of efficiency of the authors. In view of the findings suggesting increased productivity as a function of increased CBE experience with the system, it is not too surprising to find that 32% of the sample variance in this measure is accounted for by knowing the total number of files produced by an author, and 36% is accounted for by knowing the total hours spent by the author. The normal cautions necessary when interpreting correlations between indexes and their components must obviously be heeded in these comparisons.

Of somewhat more interest are the relationships among predictors and between the predictors and different aspects of the criterion. Almost 36% of sample variance is accounted for by the positive relationship between production support and group membership. It appears that the presence of production support tended either to demand or to permit group (rather than individual) efforts. Interviews with authors who were members of supported groups did indicate that support generally preceded organization of a group effort. Presence or absence of support also accounted for 19% os sample variance in total hours spent and almost 19% of sample variance in total files produced. Every author who was supported produced at least one file, whereas five of the 18 unsupported authors failed to complete any files during their first year.

A stated intention to produce extensive amounts of computer-based material was positively related to number of files produced (accounting for almost 20% of sample variance)' and was the only predictor showing such a high relationship that did not also show an equally strong relationship with mean time per file (less than 2% of the sample variance was accounted for by that measure).

Computer experience shows an understandably strong relationship with quantitative subject matter orientation (accounting for 22% of sample variance) but shows virtually no relationship with either total files produced or mean time per file (accounting for 1% and 0% of sample variance, respectively). Even more surprising is the small relationship between computer experience and stated time before attaining competence in the language. Interviews suggested that this apparent lack of relationship was probably because of the limited range of the predictor. Past computer experience was most useful in design of quantitative materials. Since all but 2 of the 15 authors with a quantitative orientation had prior computer experience, the restricted variance for this measure may have obscured evidence of a relationship.

Those authors who worked as a part of a group effort rather than as individuals tended both to spend more total working hours and to produce files in less time (the association between group membership and these last measures accounted for 19% and 17% of sample variance, respectively). Interview data suggested that these relationships might result partly from the increased time available to supported groups. The partial correlation between total hours and group membership (holding support constant) was in fact only .23, accounting for about 5% of sample variance. The need for group coordination also required working time beyond that needed for individual authors. Group members commonly complained about the amount of time spent in meetings or individual conferences. The increase in efficiency for group members, on the other hand, appears to have been a joint result of increased practice in production, ready access to guidance from other group members, and availability of procedures written by others that could be easily adapted to the needs of the new author. It should be emphasized that even those group members who modified routines

TABLE 7.6
Long-Term Productivity of 27 New Authors

	End of first year	End of fifth year
Productive (two or more files per year)	15	11[a]
Nonproductive (less than two files per year)	10[b]	3
Inactive (no access to PLATO)	2[b]	13

[a]Includes Author 9, who was on sabbatical during fifth year but produced more than one file in the fourth and sixth years, and two authors who had produced less than two files in their first year.
[b]Includes one author who used PLATO solely for gathering thesis data.

written by others did the major part of work independently rather than simply serving as clerical aides to more experienced authors. Reported time before competence with the language was also lower for group members $[t(25) = 2.064; p = .049]$. Interview data here suggested that this may have been the result of a more realistic perception by group members of the limited subset of the language that was actually required for their needs.

The small total sample size and the large number of variables involved in this study unfortunately limit the potential value of multivariate approaches to analysis of these data. Multiple correlations between relevant predictors and total files produced or mean production time were not significant $(R = .61, p = .102;$ $R = .68, p = .085$, respectively). Nor did an attempt to apply discriminant analysis techniques to determination of a prediction formula to distinguish between productive and nonproductive authors yield significant results [Wilks' lambda = $.652; F(10,36) = .860; p = .577]$.

The foregoing suggests that a substantial amount of effort is required of a potential CBE author before he or she is capable of using the full flexibility of computer-based instruction for materials in a given area. Given the costs in time or money of such preliminary learning, it is important to know how many potential authors ultimately produce computer-based materials and how long they maintain this activity.

If one classifies those who produced less than two files during their first year as nonproductive, we find that 12 of the 27, or 44.4%, must be so judged. If the two students who used PLATO solely for thesis data collection are excluded, the proportion drops to 10 of 25, or 40%. This 40% of authors accounted for only 14.4% of the total working hours expended by the reduced group of 25, for an average of 254.2 hours per nonproductive author as opposed to 1006.1 hours per productive author. Thus, whether as cause or effect, resources actually expended by nonproductive authors were a fraction of those used by productive authors. Table 7.6 summarizes the status of the entire group at the end of the first year and at the end of their fifth year. Unfortunately, modifications in the structure of files for the PLATO IV system prevent direct comparisons of PLATO III productivity during the first year with subsequent productivity. A PLATO III file space was of a fixed length that, when filled with instructional material, typically occupied a student for slightly less than an hour (although individual files produced by this group required from 30 minutes to over 3 hours for average students). A PLATO IV file space is of variable length, and the range of possible completion times and extent of content are so great that comparisons based on file counts are quite misleading. It is, however, possible to determine gross measures of activity such as indicated in Table 7.6. The number of productive authors after 5 years is rather impressive considering the high proportion of graduate students in the original group together with the mobility of university and college personnel. Although those who were still active after 5 years tended to have completed more files in their first year, the difference was not significant $[t(12) = .851; p = .412; 5.7\%$ of sample variance accounted for by this effect]. In fact, two of those active after 5 years were classified as nonproductive during their first year. Both had become PLATO staff members as a result of interest generated by their early experience.

A significant relationship did exist between the number of files produced in the first year and access to PLATO (even if not used) in the fifth year. The 14 authors still in the community at the end of 5 years produced significantly more files their first year than the 13 authors who left $[t(25) = 3.034; p = .0056; 26.9\%$ of sample variance accounted for by this effect]. Interview data indicated that many of the graduate students and several staff members who stated that they had found PLATO to be a rewarding experience (a group with relatively high productivity) made special efforts to find employment or support that permitted continued use of PLATO. Even the three former authors who had access to PLATO but who were not active indicated a continued interest. In each case these individuals indicated that lack of support (financial or professional) or pressure of other duties was the only deterrent to their continued work with PLATO.

Comparability of Data

Summary estimates of production efforts for new authors under similar conditions but in different settings are generally in accord with the findings of this study. In the Kansas City School System experienced teachers learned to use the IBM Coursewriter language to produce sophisticated individualized materials. A. F. O'Neal found that they required an estimated 300 hours to prepare a student-hour of material during the first year of a new project (personal communication, May 5, 1970). A group of eight new military authors using the PLATO IV system averaged 292 hours to produce material designed to replace an hour of class instruction during a production effort that lasted somewhat less than 1 year (Dare, 1975). It should be emphasized that these estimates (and the data for the study described in this section) hold for creative efforts that demand the full flexibility of CBE and apply to relatively inexperienced authors. Translation of programmed text to computer-based material requires minor amounts of effort. For example, D. D. Redfield (personal communication, April 14, 1970) at Florida State observed an instance in which such material was translated at a rate of about 6.9 hours per hour. Material can also easily be generated to fit a fixed pedagogical model. O'Neal reports an average of 25-50 hours per hour for a "straight drill and practice" model, whereas T. Cooper (personal communication, June 11, 1975) reports 15-20 hours per hour for a branching programmed-text model used in commercial settings. Author 1 of the present study used such a fixed approach for his fifth and sixth files, which averaged 22 hours per hour. The approach, a language vocabulary drill, had been developed while producing his second and third files.

Highly experienced teams working in established programs are able to produce materials that provide full access to the capabilities of CBE in substantially less time than was required for the new authors in this study. Examples range from 21 hours per hour (S. G. Smith, personal communication, July 28, 1973) to 80 hours per hour (Grimes, 1975) in university settings. The productivity of experienced instructional designers will be discussed in more detail in the next study.

Informal interviews were conducted with 25 of the authors in the present study as they reached the end of their first 12 months. Authors 4 and 20 left the community after 11 and 9 months of PLATO experience, respectively, and were interviewed shortly before their departures. During initial interviews most authors had indicated that they had begun work in computer-based education because they considered that it had great potential for improving the instruction possible in classroom settings. At the end, all indicated that they still felt there was great potential. Eight felt that they had demonstrated this improvement to their own satisfaction, although none had collected data. All were emphatic in stating that the computer demanded just as much as or more effort than other media on the part of the instructional designer. Several indicated that, although they were glad they had gone through the experience, they might not have begun if they had realized how much work was involved (one author suggested a parallel to graduate study). The three major factors seen by this group as limiting production were (a) lack of access to the system for editing and testing materials; (b) lack of time to devote to development; and (c) lack of access to information about new or esoteric features of the system and language. In addition, several indicated a growing interest in learning better instructional approaches. This last point was mentioned in particular by those who had used their materials for several groups of students. Only a few of this group had actually made efforts to learn instructional techniques other than those they had been acquainted with at the time they began. Nine had read books on instructional design and expressed universal disappointment with what was then available. Two graduate students were attending a course on instructional design that they believed would prove helpful in their future efforts.

Observations made in the course of the study supported all of the above reports. Heavy student use of the PLATO system forced most of these authors to work in evenings and on weekends if they wanted to program or test new materials. Aside from the two students completing theses, all of the authors worked on PLATO in addition to carrying out other duties. Those who were supported in their PLATO work generally were released from their regular duties for only a quarter or half of the time, and many put in far more hours than this support provided. Access to information on the language was hindered by changes in the language and system that often happened at a pace that could not be followed by printed documentation. At the time of this study most of the authors reported that they relied on word-of-mouth information to keep abreast of new developments. Finally, concern with the technical details of communicating with the medium did seem to occupy these authors to the point of excluding experimentation with pedagogical techniques that could allow full instructional use of the medium. This appears to be a common observation. When instructional design is taught together with use of the computer language, novice authors frequently exhibit impatience at spending time on material that does not contribute directly toward facilitating their use of the system (Francis, 1976; House, 1974).

Efficiency of Production

In addition to verification of author reports, observations suggest two other factors that seemed to affect efficiency. These factors were the degree to which the new authors sought an appropriate level of understanding of the language and the degree to which they used an appropriate level of planning and organization of efforts.

Two extremes of understanding TUTOR were observed in less productive authors or during unproductive periods of an author's development. At one extreme was the blind use of language features with minimal effort to understand their logical basis. Such an approach was frequently seen in individuals who had not learned to experiment systematically with newly encountered features as a way of acquiring proficiency in their use. The result was blind trial-and-error effort that was exceedingly inefficient and usually ineffective. At the other extreme was the individual who sought to understand the entire language completely before producing his or her first instructional material. Since the language was continually expanding, this approach could easily become a full-time occupation. Fortunately, only a small portion of the language is needed for a given application. This portion, like any natural language, is best learned by actual practice. The most effective authors struck a balance between the extremes by orienting their language acquisition to those parts of the language required to produce the effects desired in their current instructional effort. As each new term was acquired, careful experimentation aided in learning its accurate use. As new instructional effects were needed, new terms were added to the vocabularies of these effective authors. Thus, language acquisition followed a "growing edge" based on need and reinforced by usage.

Similarly, two extremes of planning and organization were seen in less productive design efforts. Underorganized individuals tended to plunge into production without clear goals or attempts to set priorities for efforts. Work was performed in a haphazard manner that increased chances for errors. For example, rather than planning use of resources such as information storage space, the individual would assign space as needed during the programming without any effort at documentation. As a result, the same area might be unwittingly assigned to two conflicting uses. Frequently these disorganized efforts would lead to materials that made interesting uses of computer capabilities but, unfortunately, did not meet known instructional needs — a case of a cure seeking a disease. At the other extreme, overly organized efforts led to premature investment of large amounts of planning time. Thus, before an individual had determined effective instructional approaches for a student population (or had even produced materials for the group), complex routing and testing structures might be designed. In addition, great amounts of off-line preparation of materials following a specific instructional approach might be performed before any attempt had been made to verify that the approach was instructionally effective or technically feasible. More effective authors again struck a balance between these extremes. Depending on their philosophy of instruction, they set general or highly specific goals and priorities before beginning production and used this structure to determine the starting point of their on-line work. Actual production followed a "lean" programming technique in which only known deficiencies of students were addressed in early drafts of the material. These draft materials were then used as soon as possible on students or student-surrogates to determine what, if anything, needed to be added to produce effective learning. Programming itself was marked by more extensive use of documentation within files (although few authors during their first year made use of documentation that was sufficient to allow subsequent modifications to be easily performed). The effective author also tended to follow an organized approach to testing code at each stage of development so that potential errors would be easily identified and corrected rather than become hidden within a substantial amount of untested material.

Summary and Discussion

The study just described was designed to determine factors involved in learning use of a general CBE language for production of materials requiring direct access to the full capabilities of an instructional computing system. Data from such a study should provide a conservative estimate of requirements for production of any computer-based material. Materials can be prepared to fit a fixed, preplanned pedagogical approach with substantially less effort than is required for preparation of materials that require special programming design such as those used for most of the files in this study. In addition, highly experienced CBE programmers are generally more efficient than persons who, like the participants in the study described, are just learning the techniques required.

As is typical of those who develop course materials at the college or university level, all authors in the study were qualified in the subject matter area being taught, had experience in classroom instruction, and were largely self-selected. None received formal training in the TUTOR language, although all had access to a manual that permitted a degree of self-instruction.

Few authors need all features of a general language, and individual needs vary greatly. Hence, it is likely that the inefficiency of self-instruction in basic elements of the language was offset by the efficiency gained in limiting learning to aspects that were necessary to the unique needs of each individual. The data on performance of a group of new military authors mentioned earlier (Dare, 1975) were derived from a group that did undergo formal TUTOR instruction. The productivity of that group did not vary significantly from that of the self-trained group just described. Interviews with participants in this study and with persons in other settings who learned a general CBE language with the aid of formal courses suggest that whichever method is used, a substantial part of actual learning depends on the learner's being able to experiment with the language and interact with experienced users of the language.

During their first year most authors relied on instructional techniques they had formerly used. Acquisition of programming skills tended to be given highest priority. Only near the end of the first year did interest in pedagogical techniques appropriate to the new medium increase noticeably, and then mainly among those authors who were using computer-based materials extensively for instruction in accredited courses. Other authors became so involved in use of TUTOR that production of impressive sequences of animation or simulation became almost an end in itself. Although facility with the language is necessary for preparation of most innovative materials, the observed extended interest in experimenting with the medium could not be entirely justified on the basis of a need to acquire basic skills. Reports from interviews as well as direct observations suggested that the immediate feedback for an author who designed a program and was able to see it function (or nearly function) within a matter of minutes was a far stronger reinforcement for many than the delayed gratification of observing successful student use hours, days, or weeks later.

Attainment of minimal proficiency with a general CBE language was not found to be a rapid process even when the major part of a new author's efforts were directed toward that goal. Two methods of estimating the point of minimal proficiency led to predictions (with 90% confidence) that about 430 hours would be required for 75% of a similar group to attain that level. Beyond the basic skill level, added practice resulted in continued gains in proficiency for at least a year following first efforts.

Wide ranges in rates of productivity were evident for different efforts by a single individual (e.g., a factor of over 26:1 for preparation of two different files of equivalent length by Author 1) as well as between individuals (e.g., a factor of over 2:1 for overall mean rates between Authors 1 and 22). Possibly because the authors in the group studied were representatives of a highly select population (i.e., persons qualified to instruct at the college or university level), the only factors that discriminated between success and failure were those related to obvious physical constraints on initial learning and later productivity. Primary among these was the factor of time. Every author who had support that permitted released time for work with the CBE system completed at least two files, whereas 5 of the 18 who had no released time failed to complete even a single file. In addition, there was evidence of great inefficiency for efforts that had to be scattered over many brief periods of available time rather than performed in blocks of several contiguous hours.

A stated intention to produce a substantial amount of material was, as might be expected, also positively related to total production, as was an early facility with the language. Additional predictors for success might possibly be based on perceptions of appropriate techniques for learning the language and for planning or organizing initial production efforts.

In summary, facility with a general CBE language, a skill necessary for production of instructional materials that make full use of the capabilities of a flexible system, can be gained only through a substantial investment of time and effort. At the college or university level, it appears that almost any instructor sufficiently well motivated and provided with enough free time can gain a minimal level of competence. The wide range of production rates and the variations seen in efficiency of learning and in planning, however, indicate a need for effective predictors of these factors for staffing of instructional design efforts.

PRODUCTION EFFORTS BY EXPERIENCED CBE AUTHORS

As the previous study indicated, access to the full capabilities of computer-based education requires knowledge of both a CBE language and a repertoire of techniques for using this language. However, even this preparation is not sufficient to ensure efficient production of effective instructional materials. The study described here suggests that the design of effective instruction for a computer also requires learning yet another repertoire: one consisting of special techniques for individualized instruction. It also describes effects of manipulation of a major management tool — the setting of work deadlines.

Nonlinear Effects of Deadline Stress

In an exploratory study, 18 designers who worked as individuals preparing computer-based materials for university students were found to have rates of production that were negatively correlated with amount of time available for production. Materials that had to be prepared for student use at short notice were produced with greater efficiency than materials for which more adequate time was available. Since very high or very low stress has been found to limit performance in a variety of situations (Miller, 1955), data for individual members of this group were examined in an attempt to find evidence for an optimal level of deadline stress that might yield maximum productivity. Unexpectedly, the relationship between deadline stress and individual performance was neither the smooth unimodal function suggested by Miller nor the gradual increase of productivity with increased stress suggested by the original grouped data.

Designers appeared to be split into two groups. One group showed no significant reaction to a wide range of deadlines; the other group showed an abrupt increase in productivity when deadlines of less than about 2 weeks were set for production of about an hour of material. Interviews with members of the two groups and examination of their techniques suggested two distinct work orientations. One group seemed more concerned with efficient production of material, whereas the other group seemed more concerned with the effectiveness of the materials produced. Interestingly, it was the group oriented toward efficient production that appeared least affected by deadlines. Idealized characteristics of designers with either a *production* or *effectiveness* orientation are outlined in Table 7.7. The term *effectiveness orientation* should not be construed as implying that those with a *production orientation* were not concerned with effectiveness of the instructional materials. Rather, the distinction is that members of the production group seemed to feel that effectiveness was an easily identifiable (if not automatic) attribute of materials produced by the particular technique they used. Those in the effectiveness group, on the other hand, seemed to feel that empirical process of test and revision formed the only reliable basis for production of effective materials. Both groups were composed of individuals who were proficient in use of the language and who had prior teaching experience but who had just begun serious production of CBE materials. In order to verify effects of the two orientations on production rates, a controlled comparison study was conducted.

Method

Subjects were drawn from the population of instructional designers who were planning, producing, and implementing computer-based materials for accredited courses at the University of Illinois. All had teaching experience and a good working knowledge of the TUTOR language, but limited experience in designing CBE materials without close supervision. To ensure an independent replication

TABLE 7.7
Characteristics of Two CBE Designer Orientations

Aspect	Production orientation	Effectiveness orientation
Perceived purpose of instructional design process	Efficient implementation of known techniques	Discovery and application of effective instructional techniques
Most used remedy for ineffective material	Extensive polishing of current approach	Change to alternative approach
Purpose of review of material	Detecting typographical errors	Checking for pedagogical effectiveness
Purpose of formative evaluation	Certification for administrators	Providing data for revision
Most important reviewer	Instructional designer	Potential student
Point at which effectiveness of material should be tested	After completion of production	During production
Point at which students should first see material	After completion of production	During production
Method of using students during early design	Using full class on first student use	Using individual students on first student use

of the previous findings, no members of the initial study were included. Unfortunately, this restriction severely limited the potential subject pool. Four subjects were judged to meet requirements for inclusion in the effectiveness group by having had at least 1 year of TUTOR experience and by indicating approaches to design that coincided substantially with the profile given in Table 7.7. Seven subjects were judged to meet similar requirements for inclusion in the production group. All four candidates for the effectiveness group and six of the candidates for the production group agreed to participate. Two members of the potential production group who were faculty members were eliminated in order to provide better comparability between groups (all members of the effectiveness group were graduate teaching assistants). Mean years of language experience was then 1.19 for both groups, and mean years of teaching experience was 2.06 for the effectiveness group and 2 for the production group. Five subject matter areas were represented, with four of the authors (two in each group) belonging to the same basic subject area.

Production assignments that were completed by entry of text into a preprogrammed instructional logic were not included in the study since such assignments did not require use of design skills. Each production assignment that required actual design efforts by the author was given a demand score based on the number of weeks between the assignment and the first scheduled class use of the material. All assignments made 8 or more weeks prior to first use received a demand score of 8. Assignments with shorter work periods were given scores that represented the nearest integral number of weeks available. During production of materials, informal observations were made to determine the orientation actually followed and to verify designer reports of the amount of effort expended. The first class use of the material was monitored, where possible, in order to obtain an estimate of quality based on student acceptance and performance. Each completed instructional sequence was also reviewed by the investigator when ready for use by a class and was rated for instructional and design quality. Finally, each designer was informally interviewed and asked to estimate the amount of time spent in producing the material and to describe the design approach used. Flaws found during the quality review were shown to the designer, and designer responses were noted. Each author was followed until his or her employment ended (generally as a result of completion of degree requirements) or until four semesters of work had been completed.

Quality Rating

Instructional materials can seldom be accurately rated on internal standards alone. The language skills, motivation, study habits, and past learning of each student must be considered as part of the instructional situation. Roderick and Anderson (1968) describe one case in which a programmed text was compared to a summary of the same material. A group of high school students learned best from the programmed text, whereas a group of college students learned equally well from either (but required five times longer to go through the programmed text). In a startling case observed by the author, students who were unintentionally assigned a programmed text containing gross factual errors showed better learning than another group that used a corrected version of the text. The group using the faulty text spent several hours gleefully documenting the errors and, in the course of using outside references for this purpose, learned the correct material quite well. Use of materials containing factual errors might, of course, not have had such a fortuitous outcome had the students been less able or the errors more subtle.

The scale used to rate quality of instructional design in the present study was developed with recognition of the importance of the interaction of members of the student population with the rated materials. The scale is heavily dependent on subjective judgments of the characteristics of the intended student population, accuracy of subject matter content, and appropriateness of instructional design. Such subjectivity restricts the exportability of the measure and makes it imperative that independent measures of quality be used wherever possible as a cross-check for the validity of ratings.

Ratings were made on a five-point scale scored as follows:

1. Student is unable to interact with a major portion of the required material (e.g., because of a logical blunder in routing).
2. Student interacts with desired material in an inappropriate manner (e.g., insufficient interaction to ensure learning or a basis for mislearning exists).
3. Student interacts with desired material in an inefficient manner (e.g., ambiguities or awkward structures make it likely that some students may not learn the intended objectives).
4. Student interacts appropriately with desired material but minor flaws exist (e.g., misspelled words, awkward routing).
5. Student interacts appropriately with desired materials (no flaws or hindrances to effective learning found).

Results

Fifty-five CBE lessons were designed by the authors, 34 by the effectiveness group and 21 by the production group. No conclusions should be drawn from this difference in productivity since members of the production group worked for projects that had planned production of less new material. Reports of total efforts required and the design approach used for each assignment were consistent with the independent observations. Student ratings of perceived helpfulness of 23 lessons were obtained from the three courses in which all CBE materials were used by all students. Counts of inclass announcements required to clarify problem areas of 21 lessons (including 5 lessons for which helpfulness ratings were available) were also collected. Together, these measures provided independent indicators of design effectiveness for 39 lessons produced by five of the eight authors.

Use of materials by students varied greatly. For some classes materials were used on a voluntary basis only, with no performance measures made. Off-line performance measures could not be used since students in all cases had access to supplementary materials that would alleviate deficiencies in the lessons. Accurate observation of all student problems was not possible in large classes, so student performance or in-class reaction was also not usable as a general measure of design quality. Only the ratings made by the investigator provided a uniform basis for judging quality of the materials. Since the investigator was aware of which group produced each lesson, there was clear danger of bias in the ratings. The quality ratings are, however, strongly related to the independent measures of helpfulness and clarity gathered for a subset of the lessons. Thus, there appears to be little evidence that ratings were in fact biased by extraneous factors. The correlation between quality and helpfulness ratings was $r(21) = .923$ (.95

confidence range for this value is $r = .825$ to $r = .967$). Because instructors tended to have different base rates of in-class comments, the correlation across the three observed instructors between number of corrective in-class comments and the quality rating was lower than the average of correlations for individual instructors. The combined correlation between quality rating and number of in-class comments was $r(19) = -.720$ (.95 confidence range for this value is $r = -.878$ to $r = -.417$). The individual correlations for the three instructors observed were $r(7) = -.832$, $r(5) = -.830$, and $r(3) = -.918$.

Another estimate of the accuracy of the quality ratings is provided by the responses of authors when shown the problems identified by the investigator in making the ratings. A total of 515 problems were noted for the 55 lessons involved. For all but 8 problems in three lessons, the authors agreed with the investigator's opinion that an error existed or that an incorrect or inappropriate approach had been used. In each of the eight exceptions, the investigator believed that an ineffectual pedagogical approach was used, but the authors did not concur. The rather impressive 98.45% agreement suggested by these figures was somewhat tarnished, however, by subsequent review of the materials, which showed that only 447 (86.80%) of the identified problems were actually corrected by the author after the conference with the investigator. In some cases (including obvious errors, such as overwriting of lesson displays and one case in which there was no possible way for a student to proceed beyond the first half of the lesson), corrections were probably not made because the material was not to be used again until the next year, and other problems were more pressing. However, it is possible that in other cases an author may have concurred with the investigator merely to be polite. Thus, the more conservative figure of 86.80% agreement should probably be used as an indicator of concurrence between the views of the investigator and those of the authors.

The overall relationship between rate of production and deadline stress was found to be significant for the combined groups $[r(53) = .496; p = .00012]$. This same relationship held for those in the effectiveness group $[r(32) = .722; p < .0005]$ but was absent for those in the production group $[r(19) = .270; p = .2366]$. Though all members of the production group consistently followed a production orientation, members of the effectiveness group seemed to use both orientations with equal frequency. Table 7.8 summarizes mean productivity and quality measures for materials produced under the above conditions

Overall comparisons showed that the production group took a shorter mean time for production [17.05 hours per hour compared to 32.09 hours per hour for the effectiveness group; $t(53) = 3.616; p = .0008; p$ approximated by Welch's method since group variances could not be considered equal]. Overall comparisons for rated quality were in favor of the effectiveness group but at an insignificant level $[t(53) = 1.697; p = .0955]$. When the comparison for rated quality was limited to those instances where the effectiveness group was judged to have

TABLE 7.8
Source and Characteristics of 55 Instructional Files

Source[a]	N	Mean (SD) hours per hour to produce	Mean (SD) quality[b]
P	21	17.048 (8.034)	3.095 (.944)
E	34	32.088 (21.991)	3.588 (1.104)
EE	15	50.067 (22.170)	4.467 (.516)
EP	19	17.895 (4.725)	2.895 (.937)

[a]P = Production group, E = Effectiveness group; EE = Effectiveness group when operating in effectiveness mode; EP = Effectiveness group when operating in production mode.
[b]Quality rating on scale from 1 (low) to 5 (high).

operated in effectiveness mode, a significant advantage was seen whether the comparison was to themselves when operating in production mode $[t(32) = 5.827; p < .00005]$ or to the production group $[t(34) = 5.098; p < .00005]$. The effectiveness group when functioning in production mode was not distinguishable from the production group in either mean time for production $[t(38) = .401; p = .6908]$ or in quality $[t(38) = .671; p = .5060]$.

An abrupt shift in rate of productivity for assignments with deadlines of less than 2-3 weeks was seen in the effectiveness group. This shift was significantly correlated with a shift to production orientation [point biserial $r(32) = .737; p < .00005$]. Table 7.9 shows the distribution of work orientation with deadline stress. The difference in productivity between the two modes of operation in the effectivenss group was quite pronounced $[t(32) = 5.522; p = .0001$, where p is estimated by Welch's method because of gross differences in variances] and was estimated to account for some 63% of population variance in rate of production.

Examination of data for individuals in the effectiveness group additionally suggests that a sort of inertia or hysteresis effect is present at the points of shift in mode of operation. Rather than a fixed demand threshold marking the boundary between modes, there was a tendency for designers to persist in whatever mode had been used in the preceding assignment. Figure 7.1 shows an idealized representation of such a hysteresis effect. The amount of production time spent on a task under Stress Level B in Figure 7.1 would be indicated by a point on

TABLE 7.9
Work Orientation of Effectiveness Group at Different Deadlines

Deadline (weeks)	1	2	3	4	5	6	7	8
Observations	10	6	5	7	0	4	0	2
Proportion in production mode	.90	.83	.40	.43	.00	.00	.00	.00

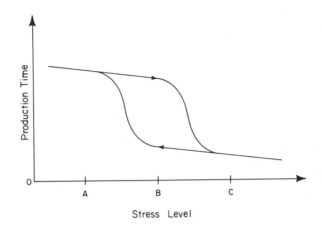

Figure 7.1 Idealized hysteresis loop for effectiveness group at point where mode of operation shifted. Production time for a task under Stress Level B is dependent on whether the immediately preceding task was performed at Stress Level A or C.

the upper leg of the hysteresis curve if the prior task were performed under Stress Level A, and by a point on the lower leg of the curve if the prior task had been performed under Stress Level C.

Thus, the shift point in deadline stress (estimated by taking the average of the assignment deadlines immediately before and after a shift in mode of operation) was lower for the entire group when shifting from effectiveness to production mode than when shifting from production to effectiveness mode $[t(7) = 2.278; p = .0568]$. Effects of individual differences in this shift point can be reduced by examining assignments for which a single designer had the same deadline but used different modes of operation. If these differing modes under equal stress were simply the result of chance variations near a fixed threshold, no particular relationship would be expected between the mode used on that assignment and the mode used on the immediately preceding assignment. Table 7.10 shows the 15 assignments that meet the above requirement along with the requirement of having a preceding assignment. In every one of these 15 assignments the mode of beginning work was the same as the mode used in completing the preceding assignment. If all assignments for each individual are examined in sequence, the proportion of successive pairs showing the pattern of identical completion-start-up mode is found to be .7333. The probability that a random sample of 15 pairs taken from this population would all show this same pattern is thus $.7333^{15}$, or .0095. In a more stringent analysis in which assignments where the mode of design shifted during work (e.g., Assignment 3 of Designer A) were excluded, the probability becomes $.6923^{12}$, or .0121.

TABLE 7.10
Deadlines and Work Orientation for Individual Assignments for Effectiveness Group

Designer	Assignment									
	1	2	3	4	5	6	7	8	9	10
A	6e	3e	2ep	1p	1p	2p	4e	4e		
B	4e	1ep	1p	6e	3e	2p	1p	3p	4p	
C	8e	1e	3p	2p	1p	4p	4p	8e	6e	4e
D	6e	2e	1p	1p	3e	1p	2p			

Note. Numbers in the assignment code indicate weeks available betwen assignment and first planned use. Mode of work is shown by letters: e = effectiveness; p = production; ep = shift in mode during assignment. Underlines indicate comparisons used to test the hysteresis hypothesis.

Discussion

Production efficiency for this group of authors was distinctly higher than that observed for authors who have not become proficient in use of the TUTOR language. Authors in the current study required an average of 26.4 hours to produce an hour of instructional material. The 22 new authors who created at least one file in the study described in the previous section required an average of 295.1 hours per hour of instructional material. This tremendous difference in efficiency probably results only in part from increased experience in use of the language. It may also be the result of loss of interest in computer-based instruction by less proficient authors, thus increasing the average efficiency of those remaining. An even stronger possibility is the influence exerted by the work situation of these more experienced authors. All were employed to produce materials covering specific topics under a stated deadline and, quite frequently, following a specified general instructional approach. Hence, even though they were responsible for creating pedagogical approaches, they usually had a clear idea of what the finished product should cover and, in many cases, what it should look like. Nevertheless, most of these authors did not have extensive experience in independently designing individualized instruction. It appears that they responded under production pressure in two ways to this lack of design experience. The effectiveness group empirically sought further knowledge by use of student data. The production group seemed to assume (correctly, it appears, in one case) that prior experience as classroom teacher, student, and CBE programmer was sufficient to ensure that any material they produced would be effective.

This behavioral dichotomy has many parallels in the literature. Cronbach (1946) had distinguished between *speed* and *accuracy* response sets in test-taking activities. Persons with a speed set seem to act as if completion of the test is the primary goal, whereas those with an accuracy set may leave items unattempted in a quest for correctness of items completed. Piaget (1954) has distinguished between *assimilation* and *accommodation* in problem solving and learning. The assimilator forces all new events into an available classification scheme, whereas the accommodator develops new approaches where old ones seem inappropriate. Finally, Platt (1964) has distinguished between *method-oriented* scientists who apply a fixed approach to all problems and *problem-oriented* scientists who use strong inferential processes to identify and eliminate potential but improper alternative approaches. In each of these cases it should be noted that there are situations where the less flexible behavior may be the more effective. If a problem is known to be solvable by application of a well-practiced procedure, it would be inapropriate to treat is as if it were a novel situation requiring a complete examination and development of new techniques. Thus, in this situation, it is not necessarily the case that a production approach is maladaptive — the person using a production approach may actually have sufficient appropriate experience not to require full-scale developmental efforts to solve a particular problem. Although the effectiveness group as a whole had the highest mean quality rating, the highest average individual rating was held by a member of the production group who had done most of his teaching in individualized settings. Assumption of the production approach was, however, not always warranted. The average quality ratings of the three remaining members of the production group were the lowest of the study (except for the ratings of members of the effectiveness group when operating in production mode). Students in a section taught by one of these other members of the production group reported the least positive attitudes for computer-based education at the college level ever observed by the investigator.

Given that most members of both groups lacked experience in design of individualized instructional materials (despite their experience with a programming language), explanation of the radical differences in productivity and quality between the two approaches seems straightforward. Early use of data from students was time-consuming but permitted corrections to be made before the first classroom use. The resulting product thus did not contain many of the problems present in first-draft attempts. Eliminating student input from the design process cut development time by better than half for the designers in this study but also cut mean quality ratings drastically (from 4.5 to 2.9). The hysteresis effect seen in shifts between the two approaches seems equally understandable. It is not surprising that a designer committed to production of quality materials might be reluctant to give up insurance against poor materials, but, once having given it up, be equally reluctant to regain it at the cost of a return to a heavier workload.

Although the study extended over a substantial period of time (2 academic years for most participants), the wide variation in design assignments makes it

TABLE 7.11
Production Rate and Quality Ratings for Early and Late Efforts under Production Mode by Effectiveness and Production Groups

Source[a]	Files	Mean hours per hour to produce	Mean (SD) quality[b]
Early effectiveness	9	17.22 (4.06)	2.33 (.71)
Late effectiveness	9	18.33 (5.70)	3.67 (.87)
Early production	10	18.20 (10.27)	3.00 (1.05)
Late production	10	18.90 (6.59)	3.10 (.88)

[a]The first and last $N/2$ files produced by an individual in production mode were defined respectively as *early* and *late*. In the two cases where N for an individual was odd, data for the middle file were not used.
[b]Quality rating from 1 (low) to 5 (high).

difficult to detect evidence for increased proficiency in design. Table 7.11 compares mean production rates and quality ratings for files produced by the two groups in production mode both early and late in the study period. The measure of production rate showed no difference for any of the groups [$F(3, 34) = .089$; $p = .9654$; .8% of sample variance accounted for by group membership]. Possible gains in efficiency might well have been obscured by an observed tendency for the authors to use more sophisticated approaches during later periods of the study.

Quality ratings did show a significant difference between groups [$F(3, 34) = 3.403$; $p = .0286$; 23.1% of sample variance accounted for by group membership]. The only pairwise difference that was significant by post hoc measures was the contrast between early and late efforts by the effectiveness group ($p = .029$ by Scheffé's test; all other comparisons had $p \geqslant .33$). It is tempting to ascribe this significant gain in quality to superior learning in the effectiveness group resulting from their use of student data. Fairness suggests, however, that a large part of the gain accrued from the very poor initial production-mode efforts of the effectiveness group (although they were not significantly poorer than those of the production group; $p = .457$ by Scheffé's test).

Both interviews and observation of these authors indicated a growing sophistication in pedagogical approaches during the time of the study. Though they continued to sharpen their skills in use of the language and to add programming techniques to their earlier repertoire, their main effort during the last portion of this study was clearly directed toward developing techniques that were instructionally effective. Members of the production group often seemed to avoid systematic attempts to validate their intuitive feelings of how students ought to learn. Members of the effectiveness group, however, tended to spend substantial amounts of time in collection and analysis of student performance measures.

Interviews with more experienced CBE designers indicate that when materials in a single subject area are designed over a period of years for the same student population, a repertoire of instructional approaches can be built up. This collection of approaches permits the majority of materials to be designed by combining or slightly modifying well-tried techniques. Development of the repertoire of pedagogical approaches is similar, but not identical, to development of a repertoire of programming approaches. A repertoire of programming approaches permits flexible use of the medium. This flexible use does not necessarily imply that the results will be instructionally effective — only that the medium will be used in a technically competent manner. A full repertoire of instructional approaches, on the other hand, makes it more likely that the resources of a CBE system will be applied in a pedagogically effective manner.

A person possessing a full repertoire of CBE instructional approaches would be expected to use a production orientation for generation of all CBE materials. Probably no person ever possesses a "full repertoire" even in a limited application of computer-based instruction. However, even if they are constantly devising new techniques, instructional designers with over 4 years of active CBE experience do tend to follow a production orientation in the majority of cases and to create materials far more efficiently than less experienced designers do.

Observations of CBE authors by the investigator over the past 15 years suggest that the working conditions of those in the study just described may have been nearly ideal for generation of an instructional design repertoire. All authors worked with or for experienced authors who set assignment deadlines that were generally realistic. The fact that the deadlines were actually achieved meant that these authors rarely approached the highest levels of stress considered by Miller (1955). Such is not always the case. In another group observed by the investigator, a relatively inexperienced author who was given an assignment with a 2-week deadline submitted his resignation after an unsuccessful 10 days of frantic effort. In several projects, unrealistic production deadlines were "solved" by reducing project goals at the last minute.

At the other extreme, authors who have never been exposed to the demands of several years of meeting frequent, short production deadlines seldom seem to develop repertoires of either programming or pedagogical approaches that permit the efficient levels of production observed in this study. Such skills would seem to be best produced in a situation in which repeated deadlines provide both the motivation for their generation and the opportunity for their continued development.

The effectiveness orientation appears to be a potent factor in development of the instructional design repertoire. In addition to a possible impact on ultimate effectiveness of the repertoire, as suggested by the data shown in Table 7.11, the strength of the effectiveness orientation appears to interact with deadline stress. In several projects staffed by personnel with strong effectiveness ori-

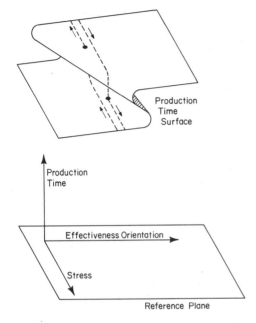

Figure 7.2 Cusp-form catastrophe model of production time as a function of deadline stress and level of effectiveness orientation. The upper fold of the time surface represents operations in effectiveness mode. The paths indicate changing production behavior when deadline stress is varied for authors with given levels of effectiveness orientation.

entations, deadlines were simply ignored if staff members did not feel that materials of high quality could be produced in time for a scheduled class or test session. Rather than prematurely shift to production mode in order to meet the deadline, authors would be allowed to continue production at a slower rate in effectiveness mode, and the planned use would be postponed or dropped. Authors who only rarely resorted to such practices did not seem to be hindered in development of instructional design repertoires. Authors who frequently ignored deadlines were often deficient in programming skills and seldom developed repertoires in either of these areas.

The complex interactions among stress, strength of effectiveness orientation, and production rate for authors who have not yet developed production-orientation procedures for a given type of material seem to fit one of the basic models of *catastrophe theory* (Sussman, 1975), a recently developed framework for permitting the description of phenomena that exhibit discontinuous behavior. Figure 7.2 shows a form of the cusp catastrophe (Thom, 1969) that concisely describes most of the observations discussed above.

Figure 7.2 is based on an assumption that the production-effectiveness dichotomy described earlier is in fact a continuum with a production orientation forming one bound, the total absence of effectiveness orientation. At the lowest level of effectiveness orientation, increased stress causes a moderate decrease in production time, but all production remains on the lower fold of the time surface (the production-mode level). For higher effectiveness orientation, production under low stress is on the upper fold of the time surface (the effectiveness-mode level), and increased levels of stress ultimately lead to a sudden shift to the production-mode level. The shift point between modes is higher for higher levels of effectivenss orientation. The time surface of Figure 7.2 can be interpreted as defining a family of hysteresis curves such as that shown in Figure 7.1. The path shown in Figure 7.2 represents one such curve. Data collected in other studies do generally support evidence for the relationship between deadline stress, effectiveness orientation, and production rate described graphically by Figure 7.2. Individual variability, however, is too great to warrant current practical application of a quantitative version of the model.

SOME GENERALIZATIONS

The economics of instructional media have made it possible, until recently, to ignore much of the cost of preparation of instructional materials. Recent advances in educational technology that permit increased individualization of instruction are, however, also forcing an end to the hidden subsidization of the costs of preparation. At the same time, this new technology has provided an economical means of making longitudinal studies of producer behavior. Such studies provide one of the few realistic means for predicting start-up and steady-state costs of generating instructional materials for the new media.

The two studies described in this chapter present the sort of data that are now clarifying misconceptions that arose from past reliance on cross-sectional studies. The detailed findings of the two studies will not be repeated here but it is worth noting three major sources of past confusion.

Start-Up versus Steady-State Costs. Workers new to the emerging individualized instructional technologies commonly underestimate both the extent and the nature of the specialized learning that precedes efficient and effective use of the media. Learning to control a medium is both an obvious and a necessary skill, but it is often also the least difficult of a series of skills required before the medium can be used effectively. Much of the published data on production costs for CBE, for example, are based on groups with only about a year of working experience with the medium. Such data may grossly overestimate production costs possible in steady-state operations by experienced design teams and underestimate start-up costs.

Media versus Method Costs. Though the physical structure of an educational computer system and the CBE language used have undoubted effects on the range of pedagogical approaches possible and the ease with which these approaches can be implemented, medium effects are commonly overemphasized. The degree of prestructuring in the pedagogical approach used often has a larger total effect on productive effort required. Table 7.12 indicates the tenth to ninetieth decile ranges of production times seen for 590 files. These files were produced by instructional design teams and individuals with differing levels of ex-

TABLE 7.12
Effect of Team Experience and Pedagogical Structure on Production Rates

	Team experience	
Pedagogy	Low	High
Existing	8 to 63 hours per hour	6 to 39 hours per hour
	(126 files by 47 teams)	(134 files by 35 teams)
Generated	165 to 610 hours per hour	27 to 180 hours per hour
	(199 files by 52 teams)	(131 files by 29 teams)

Note. Ranges are the .1 and .9 points on the distribution of mean production rates for individuals and teams in the indicated categories.

perience (less than 1 year or greater than 2 years) using either existing pedagogical structures or structures generated as a part of the file design. Although all data were from users of PLATO systems, the ranges are close to those observed on other CBE systems used for extensive production efforts. Thus, where major differences in production ratios are observed for equally experienced design teams on different systems, the differences may be as much a function of availability of a standardized pedagogical structure as of differences in the systems.

Premature Application of Systems Approaches. Wholesale adoption of a restricted set of standardized pedagogical approaches for all materials is a tempting shortcut to cutting production costs. A systems approach to design is predicated on the existence of standard production techniques of proven effectiveness that permit relatively close control of production scheduling. All too frequently the management portion of such a system is adopted before the production team in fact possesses a repertoire of proven production techniques. The result is efficient production of poor-quality material.

REFERENCES

Alpert, D., & Bitzer, D. L. Advances in computer-based education. *Science,* 1970, *167,* 1582–1590.

Avner, R. A. *Heart rate correlates of insight* (CSL Report R-198). Urbana: Coordinated Sciences Laboratory, University of Illinois, 1964.

Avner, R. A., & Tenczar, P. *The TUTOR manual* (CERL Report X-4). Urbana: Computer-based Education Research Laboratory, University of Illinois, 1969. (ERIC Document Reproduction Service No. ED 050 583)

Axeen, M. *Teaching the use of the library to undergraduates: An experimental comparison of computer-based instruction and the conventional lecture method* (CSL Report R-361). Urbana: Coordinated Sciences Laboratory, University of Illinois, 1967. (ERIC Document Reproduction Service No. ED 014 316)

Baker, E. L. The technology of instructional development. In R. M. W. Travers (Ed.), *Second handbook of research on teaching.* Chicago: Rand-McNally, 1973.

Bitzer, D. L., Braunfeld, P., & Lichtenberger, W. *PLATO: An automatic teaching device. IRE Transactions on Education,* December 1961, *E-4,* 157–161.

Bitzer, M. D., Boudreau, M., & Avner, R. A. *Computer-based instruction of basic nursing utilizing inquiry approach* (CERL Report X-40). Urbana: Computer-based Education Research Laboratory, University of Illinois, 1973.

Briggs, L. J., Campeau, P. L., Gagné, R. M., & May, M. A. *Instructional media: A procedure for the design of multiple-media instruction.* Pittsburgh: American Institutes for Research, 1967.

Bruner, J. S. *Toward a theory of instruction.* New York: W. W. Norton, 1968.

Carnegie Commission on Higher Education. *The fourth revolution: instructional technology in higher education – A report and recommendations.* New York: McGraw-Hill, 1972.

Cronbach, L. J. Response sets and test validity. *Educational and Psychological Measurement,* 1946, *6,* 475–494.

Curtin, C., Clayton, D., Finch, C., Moor, D., & Woodruff, L. Teaching the translation of Russian by computer. *Modern Language Journal,* October 1972, *56,* 354–360.

Dare, F. C. *Evaluation of the PLATO IV system in a military training environment* (Final Report). Aberdeen Proving Ground,: U.S. Army Ordnance Center and School, 1975.

Dennis, J. R. *Teaching selected geometry topics via a computer system* (CERL Report X-3). Urbana: Computer-based Education Research Laboratory, University of Illinois, 1968.

Francis, L. *The TUTOR training course: Lessons learned* (MTC Report 7). Urbana: Computer-based Education Research Laboratory, University of Illinois, 1976.

Frase, L. T. Advances in research and theory in instructional technology. In *Review of research in education* (Vol. 3). Itasca, Ill.: F. E. Peacock, 1975.

Gagné, R. M., & Rohwer, W. D., Jr. Instructional psychology. *Annual Review of Psychology,* 1969, *20,* 381–418.

Galanter, E. H. (Ed.). *Automatic teaching.* New York: John Wiley and Sons, 1959.

Glaser, R., & Resnick, L. B. Instructional psychology. *Annual Review of Psychology,* 1972, *23,* 207–276.

Godfrey, E. P. *The state of audiovisual technology: 1961–1966.* (Department of Audiovisual Instruction Monograph No. 3). Washington, D.C.: National Education Association, 1967.

Grayson, L. P. Costs, benefits, effectiveness: Challenge to educational technology. *Science,* 1972, *175,* 1216–1222.

Grimes, G. M. Cost of initial development of PLATO instruction in veterinary medicine. *Journal of Biomedical Communications,* 1975, *2*(2), 9–15.

Hicks, B. L. *PLATO program: VERBOSE* (CSL Report I-129). Urbana: Coordinated Sciences Laboratory, University of Illinois, 1965.

Hicks, B. L., & Hunka, S. *The teacher and the computer.* Philadelphia: W. B. Saunders, 1972.

House, E. R. The relevance of evaluation. In R. M. Rippey (Ed.), *Studies in transactional evaluation.* Berkeley, Calif.: McCutchan, 1973.

House, E. R. *The politics of educational innovation.* Berkeley, Calif.: McCutchan, 1974.

Hubbell, S. *Television programming and production* (3rd ed.). New York: Holt, Rinehart and Winston, 1960.

Hunter, B., Kastner, C. S., Rubin, M. L., & Seidel, R. J. *Learning alternatives in U.S. education: Where student and computer meet.* Englewood Cliffs, N.J.: Educational Technology Publications, 1975.

Kemp, J. E. *Planning and producing audiovisual materials* (2nd ed.). San Francisco: Chandler, 1968.

Lekan, H. A. (Ed.). *Index to computer assisted instruction* (3rd ed.). New York: Harcourt Brace Jovanovich, 1971.

Lower, S. K. Authoring languages and the evolution of CAI. *Proceedings of the Association for the Development of Computer-based Instruction Systems,* Summer 1976, 105–116.

Lumsdaine, A. A. & Glaser, R. (Eds.). *Teaching machines and programmed learning.* Washington, D.C.: National Education Association, 1960.

Lysaught, J. P., & Pierleoni, R. G. Predicting individual success in programming self-instructional materials. *A V Communication Review,* 1970, *18*(1), 5–24.

Merrill, M. D., & Boutwell, R. C. Instructional development: Methodology and research. In *Review of research in education* (Vol. 1). Itasca, Ill.: F. E. Peacock, 1973.

Miller, J. G. Toward a general theory for the behavioral sciences. *The American Psychologist,* 1955, *10,* 513–531.

Montague, W. E., & Wearing, A. J. The complexity of natural language mediators and its relation to paired-associate learning. *Psychonomic Science,* 1967, *7*(4), 135–136.

Neal, J. P., & Meller, D. V. *Computer-guided experimentation – A new system for laboratory instruction* (CERL Report X-30). Urbana: Computer-based Education Laboratory, University of Illinois, 1971. (ERIC Document Reproduction Service No. ED 078 677)

Pask, G. A teaching machine for radar training. *Automation Progress,* 1957, *2,* 214–217.

Piaget, J. *The construction of reality in the child.* New York: Basic Books, 1954.

Platt, J. R. Strong inference. *Science,* 1964, *146,* 347–353.

Pressey, S. L. A simple apparatus which gives tests and scores – and teaches. *Schools and Society,* 1926, *23,* 373–376.

Rath, G., Anderson, N. S., & Brainerd, R. C. The IBM research center teaching machine project. In E. H. Galanter (Ed.), *Automated teaching,* New York: John Wiley and Sons, 1959.

Roderick, M., & Anderson, R. C. A programed introduction to psychology versus a textbook-style summary of the same lesson. *Journal of Educational Psychology,* 1968, *59,* 381–387.

Rothbart, A., & Steinberg, E. Some observations of children's reactions to computer-assisted instruction. *Arithmetic Teacher,* January 1971, pp. 19–22.

Scanlan, R. T. Computer-assisted instruction in the humanities. *Illinois Journal of Education,* February 1970, pp. 33–36.

Schulz, R. E., & Volk, J. *HumRRO authoring aids for PLATO users.* Alexandria, Va.: Human Resources Research Organization, August 1974.

Schwartz, S. H. *A paradigm for the investigation processes in concept attainment* (CSL Report R-321). Urbana: Coordinated Sciences Laboratory, University of Illinois, 1966.

Sherwood, B. A. *The TUTOR language.* Minneapolis: Control Data Education Company, 1977.

Skinner, B. F. *The technology of teaching.* New York: Appleton-Century-Crofts, 1968.

Smith, S. G. The use of computers in the teaching of organic chemistry. *Journal of Chemical Education,* September 1970, *47,* 608–611.

Spottiswood, R. *Film and its techniques.* Berkeley: University of California Press, 1957.

Stolurow, L. M. *Teaching by machine.* Washington, D.C.: Office of Education, 1961.

Stull, P. E., Cohen, B., & Hody, G. L. QWRITER: An automatic lesson programmer. *Proceedings of the Association for the Development of Computer-based Instructional Systems,* Summer 1976, 217–219.

Sussmann, H. J. Catastrophe theory, *Synthese,* 1975, *31,* 229–270.

Thom, R. Topological models in biology. *Topology,* 1969, *8,* 313–335.

Umpleby, S. The teaching computer as a gaming laboratory. *Simulation and Games,* March 1971, *2*(1), 5–25.

Wang, A. *Index to computer based learning.* Milwaukee: Instructional Media Laboratory, University of Wisconsin, 1976.

Ward, M. E. *Examination and application of formative evaluation for author utilization during the preparation of a cai course.* Unpublished doctoral dissertation, University of Pittsburgh, 1972. (ERIC Document Reproduction Service No. ED 076 056)

Zinn, K. L. *Requirements for programming languages in computer based instructional systems* (Technical Report). Ann Arbor, Mich.: Center for Educational Research and Innovation, Organization for Economic Cooperation and Development, March 1971.

8

Implementation Issues in Instructional Systems Development: Three Case Studies

ROBERT K. BRANSON

One of the principal purposes of this book is to provide specific data and discussion about the state of the art in instructional systems development (ISD) This chapter treats the general area of implementing ISD through different change strategies. Those who are concerned with implementation of technology generally accept the notion that there exists a large body of research and development knowledge that is potentially of immense social value but that has not been widely adopted.

The Center for Educational Technology at Florida State University has been concerned with educational technology implementation and institutionalization problems since the 1960s. The approach to this effort has been the creation of change models and change strategies, implementing these designed changes, and studying the results. This process is captured in the Korean Model, which will be described in sufficient detail to relate that model to the subsequent case studies.

Here, case studies will be described in which alternative approaches were taken to the implementation of an ISD solution in three military settings. This author views the military as a giant socio-bureaucratic organization in which all change strategies and implementation research are equally as applicable as in any other large social institution. The color of the uniform does not change the nature of organizational criteria.

Based on inferences from the case studies, a number of conclusions will be drawn that are believed to be generalizable to other settings. Then suggested areas for future research and development will be discussed.

ISSUES IN INSTRUCTIONAL SYSTEMS DEVELOPMENT

CHANGE AND RESISTANCE

Those who attempt to substitute systematic, data-based, or research-based decision-making techniques for more traditional and power-based methods in established institutions soon find that they are dealing with a political problem of immense proportions.

A complete power-based method is one in which all decisions are made personally by the king. Approaches to management by principle or law are often strongly opposed by those in power, because they often view the delegation of authority as a reduction in personal power. The larger the institution, the greater the size of its budget, and the more people potentially affected by those decisions, the more likely it is that powerful forces will coalesce in an attempt to maintain the status quo. Sometimes vast sums of money are involved.

For example, when states attempt to change the methods by which they select their school textbooks, those who have grown accustomed to doing business in the traditional way frequently resist the attempt by whatever legal or illegal means they deem necessary in order to have their views prevail. In 1974 the chief state school officer in Florida was convicted on charges stemming from illegal activities involved in school book selection. A way of doing business had evolved through the years and when the legislature changed the law, many people were faced with drastic alterations of their traditional procurement practices. Thus, in order to maintain the power-based status quo a number of risks were taken that ultimately led to jail.

How is it, then, that one can go about engaging those in power to join the change-making effort? There may be no set of absolute principles, but Morgan and Chadwick (1971) presented an approach that has been used successfully by the Korean government. The description of the Korean model identifies some aspects of this approach.

THE KOREAN MODEL

Morgan and Chadwick were involved in one of the more ambitious and far-reaching of implementation efforts that outlined a plan for systematic educational change in the Republic of Korea. By studying the Korean economy, society, and educational sector, they were able to plan reallocation of public school resources so that schooling could be made available to all children. This change involved an intensive application of the systems approach and substantial efforts in institution building to permit sufficient technology transfer to occur according to the scheduled plan.

When the government of Korea requested technical assistance from the U.S. Agency for International Development, they were aware of the general nature of their educational problems. Historically, the government of Korea had become accustomed to the nature of their problems. Only by having these real problems documented by an outside agency could they obtain a clearly objective look at them – and at potential solution alternatives.

Korea had recognized a clear gap between the status quo and what they wanted for their children. Their economy depended on a reliable supply of intermediate school graduates to perform the mounting backlog of technical work that advanced the nation's economy. At a time of severe technical manpower shortages, there were more than a million children for whom there were no schools. Having accepted the reality of the problem, the government was amenable to suggested solution alternatives.

The Korean Educational Development Institute was created as an institution that would serve both as the government's chief change agent for the school system and also as a research organization to acquire knowledge and technology from elsewhere that could be usefully applied in the Korean setting.

Patterns can often be identified in change strategies that give one hope that if sufficient study of these patterns is conducted, principles of implementing change, particularly implementing technology, should be made more predictable in the future. The search for an application of these strategies was a constant part of the Korean study.

One general pattern of implementing change in an organization appears to occur when a comprehensive study is undertaken that has sponsorship at a high level and also credibility to members of the power groups. Typically, from such studies, a clear-cut outcome gap between **what is** and **what ought to be** can be inferred. Obviously, such gaps are institution-specific and may be discovered only by knowing what the goals of the institution are and comparing the results of prior efforts to plans based on those goals. For example, if free universal primary education is a national goal and one documents, as in the case of Korea, that a million children are unable to attend school, then the outcome gap can be defined. Having acknowledged and quantified the outcome gap, it is then possible to consider alternative strategies that will provide incremental positive change. The first step, documenting the outcome gap, is followed by the consideration and selection of solution strategies. The third step then becomes one of design and implementation of the solution strategy in either a pilot effort or on a broad scale phased through time. Then if – and only if – there is sufficient time for the solution strategy to be fully executed, *institutional* change has a chance to occur. When all of these necessary conditions are not met, major changes cannot be expected.

The approach in Korea was to obtain sponsorship from key government officials, funds from acceptable sources, and sufficient technical expertise to assess national needs. Then presentation of the needs as defined problems was made to key decision makers who chose alternative solutions acceptable to them. These solutions are now being implemented. Thus, the key decision makers became a part of the **solution** rather than continuing to debate the **problem**.

An attempt was made, beginning in 1973, to apply this approach in a military setting. The sponsor was the Army's Combat Arms Training Board.

U.S. MILITARY TRAINING

The Combat Arms Training Board

In 1971, the results of a study undertaken by an Army project group, the Board for Dynamic Training, were released. That board made a careful analysis of the results of Army training and concluded that there was clearly an outcome gap between the results they were obtaining through training and the required level of expertise on the job. The board presented formal recommendations and then dissolved itself. Perhaps the most significant recommendation was to establish the Combat Arms Training Board as a continuing entity to implement other recommendations.

The latter board can be viewed as the Army's internal change agent to improve training. It consisted of some 40 highly selected officers and the necessary support personnel. Their mission was sufficiently broad to permit consideration of a variety of solution alternatives and their budget was adequate to permit them to have a serious impact. Two important reports documenting some of the efforts of the board may be found in Roberts, Lawson, and Neal (1975) and Roberts (1977).

In May of 1973, the Center for Educational Technology at Florida State University contracted to assist the board in applying educational technology to Army training problems wherever such applications appeared feasible. An initial study (Branson, Stone, Hannum, & Rayner, 1973) had outlined opportunities for comprehensive initial applications of educational technology in the school system operated by the U.S. Army Training and Doctrine Command. Based on that report, a second task became that of developing and updating the Army's regulations and guidance on planning and conduct of training. The center and the board agreed that what was required was a model for the development of training and sufficient procedural guidance to permit those assigned the training responsibility to follow and perform the prescribed activities. This model and procedures would replace existing regulations.

Subsequent to this agreement between the center and the board, a committee including members from all of the military services was formed. This interservice committee, established originally to achieve consensus on military training terminology, became aware of the board's contract with the center. Following discussions about the potential mutual interest of the two organizations, the Army agreed to include this interservice committee (subsequently titled the Interservice Committee for Instructional Systems Development) in its review process.

The committee ultimately served as the principal reviewing authority for all contractor-developed products. From July 1973 through December 1975 a series of products was developed and then revised several times based on critique and test results (Branson, Rayner, Cox, Furman, King, & Hannum, 1975).

The Model and Materials

It was decided that a package of materials was required containing as its major component an instructional systems development model usable in the Army as well as in interservice training. The model would specify the steps necessary to produce, control, and evaluate acceptable training in those environments.

It was stated that there would be interservice agreement on the model prior to the undertaking of further content development. Then a set of procedural guidance manuals would be produced that specified the technical approach to be taken in order to accomplish each of the steps included in the model. For example, among many topics covered, a method for job analysis, techniques for the development of learning objectives, and procedures for conducting formative evaluation were included. The model is presented as Figure 1.1 in Chapter 1 of this volume. Workshops would be empirically developed to train those who would actually perform the work specified in the model.

Because it had been well established in the literature that management support was critical, it was decided that two levels of managers' workshops would be required to familiarize managers with the procedures and model. Further, in the managers' workshops basic principles of training management would also be addressed. First-line supervisors would be trained to schedule, inspect, critique, and approve those products developed by the technical staff. Additional workshops would be developed for senior managers at the level required to serve the needs of school commandants and others with major command responsibility.

Finally, specifications for adapting the model and procedures to the peculiar training requirements of each of the services were given. Because of the past literature available on the implementation of change, it became clear that if materials were to be institutionalized, those responsible for implementation would have to take steps to adapt them to the **specific** requirements of training for different services and jobs. It was intended that this process of implementation and adaptation would constitute the *transfer of ownership* necessary for the general acceptance of the procedures. The Navy, for example, has begun replacing Army examples and procedures with Navy examples and procedures.

During the development process, each chapter or related group of chapters was printed in sufficient quantity to circulate throughout each of the services for professional staffing. This elaborate procedure of seeking feedback was used in an attempt to get the widest possible visibility and identification with the procedures in each of the services and to solicit useful revision suggestions.

Such staffing procedures are not without their difficulty, in that it is not possible to follow everyone's advice. Some reviewers who believe their advice should be accepted without question are often offended when they find that the requesting author has selected a different point of view. For the most part, though, reasonable and competent people at least appreciate the opportunity to express their views even though they may not always prevail.

The Trainers' Workshop

As the materials were repeatedly tried out on members of the target populations provided by the Army and Navy it became apparent that an important aspect of successful implementation would be that of producing enough people who could train trainers within their own service. Further, to be sure that this training was consistent with the philosophy and intent of the interservice package, it was decided that those selected to do the training within the Army and Navy should first receive workshop "trainer training" to ensure consistency from one service to another. Based on that general rule, an intensive 4-week workshop was conducted at Florida State University during the fall of 1975 for Army and Navy implementation personnel.

The Army participants were selected as three-member teams, each representing an Army school. These teams were mixed with the Navy representatives in order to get as much between-service transfer of skill and information as could be achieved. Their assignment was to go through the interservice technical-level workshop first and then the managers' workshop, then to receive instruction on how to conduct both of those workshops, and finally to lay out an implementation plan to follow when they returned to their respective jobs. The instruction was relatively straightforward and modeled the instruction they were to give when they returned.

One-fourth of the time was spent in developing their implementation plans. There were important differences between the Army and Navy plans. From the U.S. Army Training and Doctrine Command, those attending were in groups of three from selected schools (the U.S. Army Infantry School, the Signal School, and the Aviation School) chosen from the total of 23 schools. Those who came from the Navy had been assigned to a variety of commands, but they were being transferred or reorganized into a centralized training development command (Scanland, in press). Though the Navy had a complete and detailed plan for implementation throughout the training command headed by the chief of Naval Education and Training, the Army's plans were all school-specific. There was not, at the time, an Army-wide implementation plan for the materials.

Two distinct purposes were served by the development of these implementation plans during the workshop. First, people who return from a training exercise conducted for the purpose of transferring technology back to their school or command often find themselves in the position of being missionaries. If the individuals are of sufficiently high rank, much more can be immediately accomplished on the basis of an order from a high-ranking officer. However, if those high-ranking officers or executives are not experts on the **specific techniques**, their orders can be faithfully carried out only if subordinates have the necessary skills or are trained to have them.

On the other hand, if the people returning are at lower rank and are charged with the technical work, they must conduct their missionary work through their ability to convince the higher ranks of the value of their ideas. Having plans prepared by at least three lower-ranking individuals provides the basis for social interaction and mutual support once they have returned to their organization. The development and presentation of implementation plans was made a part of the workshop in order to ensure that each member was familiar with the technical aspects of the material and also had practiced briefing the plan.

THREE CASE STUDIES

In order to illustrate the problems, results, and successes of various implementation strategies, three separate case studies have been selected. The basis for their selection is that they illustrate various approaches to the implementation and adoption of new techniques (i.e., ISD). The first case to be described occurred in the Navy, the second in the Army signal school, and the third in the Army infantry school.

The Navy Plan

In 1972 the chief of Naval Education and Training made a careful analysis of the necessary skills and resources required to design and implement high-quality training programs. One result of that analysis was the conclusion that the skills required to perform the high-level functions of training analysis and design were sufficiently rare that Navy schools would have little access to such expertise. (Montemerlo and Tennyson [1976] have elaborated on this problem.) The Navy's solution was to centralize the instructional development function by assigning to central locations in San Diego, Great Lakes, and Pensacola those individuals who had sufficient expertise to design effective and efficient instruction. The first of these Instructional Program Development Centers was established in San Diego in 1976, and the second was established in January 1977 at Great Lakes.

Immediately following the fall 1975 workshop, the staff of the San Diego Instructional Program Development Center began to conduct the same workshops for other Navy staff members. Their plan was to get enough people trained in the interservice procedures and techniques to provide trained people as the work demanded. Their strategy was based on a cascading approach: That is, the first group of senior individuals who were trained at the Center for Educational Technology subsequently trained others of lower rank to conduct the workshops. These subordinates then continued to conduct the workshops, enabling the senior staff to concentrate their efforts on analysis and design. The trainers were able to guarantee a supply of trained people to the program development centers and also to the schools where the instruction would be implemented.

It would be naive to expect this amount of change to occur in the Navy without a great deal of turbulence. It became clear in 1973 that there were strong points of resistance within the Navy, where, for whatever reasons, some senior and influential commanders chose to oppose the implementation plan. When resistance occurs from people at that level of authority, time and resources must be expended toward overcoming it by all available means. Because of the strong dedication of the chief of Naval Education and Training to this centralized development plan, the program development centers finally became functional, but a year or more was lost in the changeover.

Since the San Diego group was the first one formed, it was charged with the responsibility of applying the new technology to the pilot effort in the Navy's radioman rating. The revised radioman's course was implemented in late 1977, just 2 years after the date of the initial 1975 workshops. All of the effort thus far has been concerned solely with getting the procedures implemented and used in the Navy. It will be some time before an evaluation can be made to establish the degree to which the practices employed match the stated specifications. Then it will be possible to evaluate outcomes of the instruction as developed.

In the case of the implementation plan approved by the chief of Naval Education and Training, several important and notable features should be identified. First, there was elaborate advance preparation and a clear-cut plan of action with milestones already in place before the interservice materials were distributed. The Navy was prepared for the implementation effort, and command dedication was apparent from the beginning. This preparation was due in large part to the technical expertise applied by Worth Scanland, chairman of the Interservice Committee. Further, resources had been identified to make the plan occur even though these resources had to be reallocated from existing budgets. This reallocation process did not increase the willingness of other commanders to participate, since in a fixed-budget (zero-sum game), if one command gains resources, another loses. Finally, a clear-cut institution-building effort had been undertaken to transfer the technology into the Navy and to allow for its perpetuation. People had been prepared to receive the program and to act with purpose and deliberation.

The Signal School

A second case study is based on experience at the Army's signal school. Here, well before the interservice materials became available, members of the Combat Arms Training Board met with officials of the signal school to propose a plan for implementation. The board agreed to fund contractor support to assist the school in making the transition and implementation effort more productive. After extensive briefings of the proper authorities, agreement was reached between the school and the board to begin work on the implementation effort in August 1975.

The plan approved by the school required the contractor (i.e., Center for Educational Technology) to place a full-time resident consultant at the school to train staff, assist with planning and design efforts, and arrange for additional expert help when technical problems occurred. The support schedule involved a series of workshops conducted by the contractor and a programmed series of conferences that would yield plans and decisions. The first of these decisions to be reached was the selection of the military occupational speciality in which the interservice procedures work effort would be undertaken. To demonstrate the interservice model, the following activities were planned:

1. The selection of an existing course offered by the signal school that would be revised according to interservice procedures
2. A new course in the selected speciality that would be developed completely by using interservice procedures
3. A job or duty position within the selected occupation for which a formal on-the-job training program would be developed
4. A task or series of tasks in the occupation that would be accomplished through the use of newly developed job-performance aids

In order to avoid the perception that this effort was something imposed by outside authority, the responsibility for the origination of all documents and decisions was vested within the school. The first item called for was a plan of action to be undertaken through the entire life of the project, including selection of the target occupation and assignments of project staff.

During the time that the initial planning and discussions were taking place at the school, a number of consequential staff changes occurred. First, the project officer for the board who originated the plan was assigned to other duty overseas. He was a lieutenant colonel and was replaced by an officer of considerably lower rank. Second, the chief civilian education adviser to the school commandant, who had been present during all of the prior discussions, retired and was replaced through the normal seniority selection procedures of the Civil Service. The replacement, lacking both interest and expertise, found the project considerably more ambitious than had his predecessor. Third, a substantial change occurred within the structure of the board when some of its important elements began the process of relocating to a different base. These status and personnel moves created the opportunity for changes in priority among the board, the contractor, and the school.

There was a substantial difference between the signal school and the Navy with regard to the project's origin. In the Navy all initiatives came from within the same command. Further, it was clearly the intention of the chief of Naval Education and Training to implement the plan. On the other hand, at the signal school the commandant and his associates agreed only to "participate" in the implementation effort. The project was brought to the signal school by an outside entity; it was not originated there.

It became apparent soon after the project began that it was not a top priority of senior managers at the school. The impact of this lessened priority permeated the entire staff. As a result, planned deadlines slipped by without being met and without any significant consequences or increased effort to get back on schedule. In addition, many of the people assigned to attend the training workshops were people who were not primarily concerned with the selected occupation or with the various parts of the contracted effort. Some attended simply because they could be spared from their jobs. Further, the internal direction of the project was passed around from person to person as other internal organizational changes were made and priorities were shifted.

The contractor was unable to facilitate the technology-transfer process at the school principally because of the lack of infrastructure within the school to accept the transfer. Partly because of the changes in the personnel, the "ownership" of the project was not successfully transferred either. During this period of confusion, opposition to continuing the project increased significantly. It was later abandoned at the request of the local commander.

The Infantry School

In 1973, the U.S. Army Infantry School at Fort Benning assembled a plan for revising its staff- and faculty-training functions. The school had been aware that the instructor-training plan then being used was effective in training only for the delivery of live lecture instruction. Although that course was effective in training people to deliver regular platform instruction, it was not so effective in the more important aspects of instructional design, development, and evaluation.

During the 1973–1974 academic year, the infantry school in cooperation with its contractor put together the framework, objectives, and model for the Trainer Development Program (Insgroup, Inc., 1973). The distinguishing characteristic of the new trainer program in contrast to the traditional instructor training course was that the instruction provided varied considerably depending on one's job assignment. Some noncommissioned officers going through instructor training were assigned to spend their time taking troops to the field. There was no benefit in making them into polished classroom lecturers. Others who were going through the course were assigned to job analysis, instructional development, and assistant instructor roles in which they would be doing a variety of tasks to support instruction.

Instead of treating all individuals alike and sending them to the same 3-week instructor-training course, the trainer program allowed for vast ranges of individual differences in past experience and in future assignments. Further, the previous course was lock-step, where everyone received the same instruction in the same time period, while the trainer program allowed for self-paced progress in each of its special-purpose *routes*. When students entered the trainer program, they were assigned to one of the seven routes designed to prepare them for the job they would be doing.

Each route is composed of a series of self-contained and often self-instructional modules that include the objectives, sample test items, a description of where to obtain the instructional materials, and other information useful to the student. The content of these modules is decided solely on the basis of the individual's future assignment. Further, there is no limit to the number of modules that any student can be required to complete. This last feature is critical in that it permits expansion or contraction of any of the routes as organizational changes are made within the school. When duties are added or moved from one department to another, the modules can simply be moved back and forth across the various routes until the appropriate mix is achieved.

Another important aspect is that as new subject matter or new doctrine becomes available, it can be converted to the modules and added to the course wherever it is appropriate. Because the management framework and scheme have been well established, a minimum of disruption occurs when it is necessary to make even substantial revisions in the content of the course.

Using the Interservice Materials

In anticipation of the availability of the interservice procedures, members of the staff- and faculty-training department at the infantry school were sent to various training workshops sponsored by the Army. The school sent three key staff members to the fall 1975 workshop. It was during this period that these staff members drafted the interservice implementation plan for the infantry school (Begland, 1977). The key elements of the 1975 plan can be seen in Table 8.1.

One of the more difficult changes the Army undertook was that of attempting to reorganize the schools under the guidance of a new organizational document (Department of the Army, 1976). When the interservice model and materials became available in 1975, the Army's resource management group devised

TABLE 8.1
Key Elements of U.S. Army Infantry School Implementation Plan for Instructional Systems Development

Title of activity	Purpose	Major milestones	
Communication plan (internal and external)	Designed to provide the appropriate information at the correct time	First month:	Initial persuasion efforts
		First month:	Workshops
		Fifth month:	Exportable modules
		Eighth month:	News releases
		Eleventh month:	Audiovisual programs
Resister identification	Designed to identify through various strategies the relative resistance of members within the organization	First month:	Identify resistance
		Second month:	Provide for early involvement in analysis of problem finding and solution, pilot course selection, regulation production, etc.
Approval and institutionalization	Designed to achieve 1) Acceptance 2) Organizational support 3) Ultimate institutionalization of procedures	First month:	Form ad hoc committee
		Third month:	Begin planning for school reorganization
		Sixth month:	Begin school reorganization
		Seventh month:	Prepare draft school ISD regulation
		Ninth month:	Finalize regulation and validate it on pilot course

Category	Description	Month	Activity
		Twelfth month:	Terminate ad hoc committee
Personnel training	Designed to develop and conduct training to insure trained staff	First month:	Develop workshop materials
		Second month:	Begin training
		Third month:	Train middle managers
		Fourth month:	Put self-paced course into operation
Institutional credibility	Designed to facilitate attitude change and develop internal philosophy of change	First month:	Develop internal instructional advisory teams
		Second month:	Hold first workshop: "Why a System and how it Will Help Me"
		Fourth month:	Hold second workshop: "From Occupational Analysis to Development"
		Seventh month:	Discuss the why and wherefore of evaluation
		Tenth month:	Discuss how instructional systems development fits external to U.S. Army infantry school
		Thirteenth month:	Ask where we go from here

Note: The original plan from which this table was extracted covered 11 major implementation activities and was descriptive of a 15-month program. The items selected represent only a sample of the categories and activities. Activities in the seventh, tenth, and thirteenth months consisted of seminars.

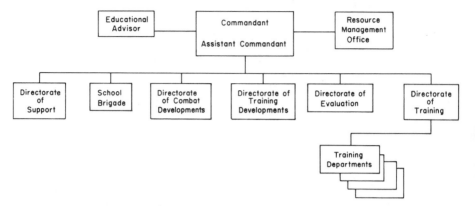

Figure 8.1 School model 1976, as presented in revised draft DA PAM 570-558, August 2, 1976.

an organizational chart for each of the Army schools based on the functions called for in the interservice model. The reorganization was totally consistent with the requirements spelled out in the model, including a separation of the *analysis* and *design* functions from the *development* and *implementation* functions. The quality-control function was also assigned to a separate division. Such an organization provides for checks and balances within the system and helps to maintain clear lines of responsibility. Since the infantry school had planned ahead and implemented the trainer program they were well ahead of the other schools.

The approximate organizational chart for the infantry school is presented in Figure 8.1. The critical aspects of the chart include three major phases of the interservice model. The Directorate of Training Developments is responsible for the analysis, design, and development phases of the model. This group decides what is to be trained and then designs and develops instruction to achieve that end. The Directorate of Training conducts the training that has been developed by the Directorate of Training Developments. The Directorate of Evaluation evaluates the quality of the outputs of the Directorate of Training Developments as well as their processes, the conduct of training by the Directorate of Training, the progress of the students, and the follow-up studies in the field to ascertain the quality of the school's output.

In addition to the fall 1975 workshop cosponsored by the board, the infantry school arranged to have training for an additional 25 staff members conducted at the school during the fall of 1976. This 1976 workshop was a part of a larger plan where the training was based on an analysis of the most significant issues confronting the Staff and and Faculty Development Division, the organization responsible to conduct the Trainer Development Program. Further, in addition to that analysis and training program, a follow-up evaluation of the Trainer Development Program was included.

This evaluation documented what had been known intuitively for a long period of time: that individuals who do the technical work are frequently trained as required, whereas the managers often do not receive adequate training. At the infantry school, for example, at the time the evaluation was made, 75% of the technical staff had gone through an appropriate trainer-development route during that calendar year, while only 8% of those who supervised or managed this technical work had attended a trainer-development route during that period. Such results are often indicative of a potential conflict situation in which there are vast differences in understanding of the work by those who are doing it and those who are supervising it (Branson & Rayner, 1977).

Organizational Turbulence

The time period 1973-1976 was one of considerable turbulence in the Army school system, particularly because of the continuing cutbacks in the military population and budget. In the context of consolidation and the cutbacks in population, other change factors intervened to make the implementation of new training programs more difficult.

For example, the heads of these directorates are all at the top level (colonel) and report to the assistant commandant of the school (see Figure 8.1). Ideally, the organizational structure accomodates various needs, levels of staffing, and numbers of trainees by establishing clear lines of authority and a means of follow-up to check results against plans. However, the system does reach a saturation level when it must accommodate many kinds of change at the same time. Budget reduction and major changes in organization make implementing new training systems unusually complex.

The infantry school had planned sufficiently far ahead to contract for the Trainer Development Program, putting it at a clear advantage when the inter-service package became available. By continuing to assign a priority to the new approach to training, they were able to sustain the momentum. Accordingly, they sent trained competent officers to the fall 1975 workshop and arranged for the 1976 follow-up training and evaluation. In all, they have made a strong commitment to change.

CONCLUSIONS:
REQUIREMENTS FOR SUCCESSFUL
IMPLEMENTATION

None of the efforts reported can as yet be classified as a total success or a total failure in implementation of a new technology. Although there is some reason to believe that success is more likely in the Navy and at the infantry school, dramatic changes have often been brought about by external events, changes in command, and other factors. However, there do appear to be some factors lead-ing to success that could be identified and, one hopes, exploited in future activities. These requirements are detailed in the next section and will be related to the case studies.

Availability of the Technology

One important consideration in the successful implementation of a new technology is the *availability of the technology* itself. On the surface this seems obvious, but there is often a great confusion in the minds of research and development personnel as to what constitutes the availability of the technology. Perhaps an example would clarify this issue. A number of years ago an astute student of scientific management and production techniques conceived the notion to develop a production line for ships. The idea behind it all was to establish a regular production line in order to increase the productivity and reduce the unit cost, as had been done successfully in many other industries but never in shipbuilding. Analogies were made and often cited to the production lines on which aircraft and automobiles are assembled.

Having created this notion and worked out some of the more esoteric equations in his head, he then put the idea before the company's management. Seizing the potential opportunity to win large contracts and impressive profits, while at the same time beating the competition through lowering prices, the corporate managment proceeded with the large-scale proposal. It was then that the original ideas were passed on to the engineering department to fill in all the necessary details. What became too soon apparent was that while the concept appeared to be sound, the technology lagged considerably. The originator of the plan lamented the fact that incompetent designers had managed to implement the original big picture so ineptly that any hope for a useful technology was lost. True to form, the implementers responded that they were only human — they could not implement what was not well designed or planned. In this instance it was clear that the power of the idea swept people ahead on a wave of optimism long before the technology gap was closed. (Will the videodisc be next?)

Thus, to implement a successful innovation one must first be sure that the full range of problems has been addressed and certainly that pilot programs or other trial efforts have provided a clear basis for projecting actual results. When the interservice materials were produced, ample time was available to fill in the details and complete the first operation with developed technology.

Necessary Resources

A second consideration in the implementaton of a technology is the *necessary resources* assigned to that effort. These resources come in all sizes and shapes: personnel competence, facilities, equipment, and expense. If any or all of these resource requirements go unmet, it is unlikely that sufficient thrust can be given to the implementation effort.

When the interservice project was originally planned, the resource requirements were spelled out and plans were made by the board to acquire them. In application, the resources were adequately provided by the Navy and the infantry school, whereas the priority was never high at the signal school.

Acceptance of an Outcome Gap

The third important consideration in making a successful implementation is the degree to which the important decision makers have accepted a *documented outcome gap* as representing the true state of affairs. The more satisfied the chief decision makers are with the status quo in the organization, the less likely they are to accept any major change strategy. It is only through careful study and documentation that outcome gaps can be used in a positive way to implement change. One approach to a decline in quantity or quality of output occurs when one simply attempts to do more and more vigorously that which has not worked in the past. Nowhere is this approach perpetuated more vigorously than in the more than 20,000 public school districts.

Acceptance of an outcome gap by the chief executives creates large-scale difficulties. If the executive has been the manager for a while and then discovers the gap, it is often necessary to seek a public relations answer instead of a realistic solution. Here, a public relations answer refers to the technical process of changing the public's **perception** of a problem without changing its potential magnitude. A perfect illustration of this approach occurred in 1974–1978 in relations between the U.S. government and the international oil companies, concerning the problem of decreased fuel supplies and high prices. There, the questions of who was to blame for the problem and what the problem actually was became hopelessly confused. The government pointed to dramatically increased profits as evidence that the oil companies were creating a fuel crisis. The oil companies countered with charges of massive government regulation hampering normal development and supply efforts. The thoughtful citizen was torn between the powerful logic of both arguments, but the problem was not solved.

In dealing with an outcome gap, two historic approaches are then possible. The first and perhaps the most common is the political approach to find a scapegoat, blame the scapegoat for the discrepancy, fire the person in charge, and then sweep the matter under the rug.

The second and more promising approach is to make a systematic analysis of the problem, try to locate its cause, and then select realistic alternative solution strategies to eliminate the problem. It is only under the second of these two approaches that it is likely an important *innovation* would be used in solving problems.

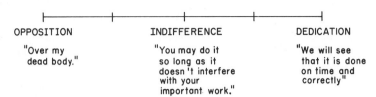

OPPOSITION   INDIFFERENCE   DEDICATION

"Over my   "You may do it   "We will see
dead body."   so long as it   that it is done
                        doesn't interfere   on time and
                        with your   correctly"
                        important work."

Figure 8.2 Hypothetical rating scale illustrating "command support."

The credibility of the person or method used to establish the potential outcome gap is of importance. Some problems, as well as some people, are far more credible than others. Commonly one hears, "We tried that technology but *it* didn't work." It is rare to hear, "That is a good approach, but we have not been able to learn how to use it."

In an organization with a long history of successful process implementations, such a criticism is well worth taking seriously. In organizations with severe limitations in executive ability, the quality of the process is often in doubt. Further, the emotional impact of process failure can be highly disruptive. Change agents must plan carefully to avoid situations that permit a confrontation between new and old approaches in organizations with limited talent.

In the Army projects described here, there was clearly a documented outcome gap that was originally revealed by the Board for Dynamic Training. This gap was accepted by the infantry school as evidenced by their moving ahead on action program. It was also true that the chief of Naval Education and Training had accepted a similar conclusion in that service. No evidence of this concern was found at the signal school.

Command Dedication

An important consideration in the success of implementing a new technology is *command dedication*. Figure 8.2 depicts the range of attitudes a command or chief executive might exhibit toward a new approach. On the extreme right is the notion of command dedication and on the extreme left is the notion of command opposition. The farther one is able to move to the right on this scale of enlisting command support or dedication for an effort, the more likely is the success of the effort. Certainly one could not expect to make much of an impact on a large bureaucratic organization by starting out with indifference on the part of the chief executive officer.

It might be pointed out that one element of command dedication to a particular approach or innovation can be measured by the quality of the people assigned to implement it. If one consistently assigns top-notch people to important tasks to ensure that the tasks will be done correctly, that is good evidence that those tasks are receiving the attention they ought to receive. On the other hand, if one assigns second-rate staff to the implementation, it is not likely that it will gain the attention it deserves or that it will succeed.

Another important consideration in testing the degree to which command dedication exists is the quality and realism displayed in the plan of action with milestones. Because of the peculiar nature in which resources are often committed, the ceremonial approval or signing of the finally negotiated plan of action is an important indicator of the degree to which command dedication has occurred. Thus, the very existence of an approved plan and consistent monitoring of that plan by the appropriate commander indicates that results are expected and are expected in a realistic time.

If, on the other hand, the reports of delays and missed deadlines are not given serious attention, this act in itself indicates that the program is not among the highest priorities. In those organizations where the typical approach is one of "management by crisis" rather than management by plan, it is often difficult to know what the priorities are. Real-world problems often do occur and may rightfully preempt assigned priorities. Patching a badly damaged wall to prevent heat loss may suddenly be less of a priority when flood waters begin to rise.

In the studies, command support was clearly apparent in the Navy when the entire school system was reorganized to achieve better results through a new technology. At the infantry school the chief executive officer regularly attended briefings, openings of training programs, and graduations. At the signal school senior people were not assigned to the project and no direct action was taken when the project got off schedule. On the basis of the projects reported here and those contained in the references, several generalizations have been made that could represent important research and development opportunities. Although some appear to be obvious, systematic research has yet to offer solution alternatives.

"OPPORTUNITIES" FOR FUTURE RESEARCH AND DEVELOPMENT

The example given earlier of a concept for the development of a production line to produce warships occurred in one of the highly visible corporations of the 1960s. At that time the nation's economy was often said to be "overheated." The war in Viet Nam was causing large-scale government spending, and, at the same time, $25 billion or so was invested in the Apollo program, which was attempting to send a man to the moon.

Emerging during that period were a large number of hot "go-go" management approaches. A common element of those approaches was the "buzz phrase" — a four- or five-word collection that caught on and had a special in-group meaning (e.g., "more bang for the buck," and "that's the bottom line"). The chief executive officer of the organization in question had grown weary of hearing his division managers report on "problems" they were having in achieving their annual operating results. He later declared in a management meeting that he would no longer accept the word *problem* in reports or telephone conversations. As he pointed out, for people with their capabilities and high rates of pay, there were no such things as problems, only "opportunities." When the operations manager of the ship production line called one day to inform the boss that the whole thing had fallen apart and was behind schedule, and he did not have the vaguest notion of what to do about it, his opening remark was, "Sir, I would like to report to you on an insurmountable opportunity."

It seems that there are really two kinds of insurmountable opportunities, those that human nature imposes and those that Parkinson (1962) described in coherent detail dealing with the intricacies of bureaucratic function. However, it should be useful to point out that there are some threads of continuity that run through many change-and-implementation efforts, particularly those that will result in substantial changes in behavior for individuals within the organization.

Means–Ends Confusion

One of these threads of continuity has been well documented in the past — the *means–ends confusion.* A typical means–ends confusion occurs in the training area when one proposes a solution before a problem has been clearly defined. And, since there are few all-around general-purpose solutions that apply equally to all problems, results are rarely what they should be. As a consequence, much effort is expended in attempting to apply a false solution to a problem and upon reporting the failure, simply contending that whatever the innovation or technology was, "it" didn't work. A notable example in contemporary military training is *self-paced instruction.* Many guidance documents currently available stress the importance of adopting self-pacing. Thus, a solution is offered that certainly will not fit all problems. Subsequent to the requirement that self-pacing be implemented, the benefits claimed for it are expected to be documented. Command guidance often follows this syllogism:

> Self-pacing has saved time and money
> in some situations.
> If it were used more widely, it would
> work more often.
> Local commanders should
> self-pace their courses.
> The **success** of all self-pacing efforts
> should be documented.

Perhaps the civilian equivalent of the self-pacing problem is *individualized instruction.* What if the solution imposed does not fit our problem?

Alternatively, one would identify clearly the problem to be solved and then consider the array of possibilities for solving that problem. In training, of course, self-pacing is a reasonable approach to many **but not all** training problems. Rather than require the implementation of a process, the manager should ask for an outcome.

When a senior person tells a subordinate to "self-pace" instead of "improve performance" or "reduce time," he is offering a solution or process. In management terms, he has not placed the responsibility for achieving success on the subordinate. The subordinate is in compliance with the order if he faithfully self-paces. If the expected results do not occur, it is not his fault — he did what was asked.

If the boss says "See what alternatives you can find to cut time from that course," "See if you can improve the performance of that group," he has then asked for a result from the subordinate. If the subordinate cannot produce the results desired — or discover new data — *he* has failed, not the boss.

Senior managers have normally become senior by being promoted within the system. They accumulate experience in this process. Because they were successful (by definition), they often generalize on the basis of successful prior experiences. Thus, it becomes tempting to present solutions and processes to subordinates as commands rather than to issue orders specifying accomplishments. Unfortunately, giving commands in accomplishment language is a learned skill that must be practiced. Giving commands in solution or process terms is a predictable result of prior experience. The difficulty lies in getting the attention of senior managers long enough to explain the difference and allow them to practice.

Jurisdictional Costs

A second important consideration in the application of any technology, particularly when it is being introduced into a large bureaucratic system, is that of the *jurisdictional cost*. Here the term *jurisdictional cost* refers to potential costs or savings that occur in a specific division of the bureaucracy. For example, if Division A of an organization could, by changing its operating procedure, save Division B a large amount of money, it seems only rational that Division A would do so. Though it may on first analysis be rational, it may not make good managerial sense. In the first place, unless the person who controls both budgets — that is, the one who is superior to both the manager of Division A and the manager of Division B — can see the benefit, it is not likely to occur. Why should Manager A expend funds in order to save money for Manager B? What may show up next year is that Manager A spent more money than perhaps was budgeted.

A technology that does not take into account the potential savings or the additional costs may be extremely difficult to implement. A second consideration is that if the technology is going to be implemented and it promises to provide additional benefits through either increased performance, decreased cost, decreased time, or some combination of the above, then somebody must get the benefit. It is much more likely that a technology can be implemented when it is clear in advance who will get to retain and spend the savings. If there is no incentive to the manager in the form of some fraction of the savings being spent or reinvested in that division, the motivation to implement will be considerably less.

Attribution of Success

Another terribly important problem is that of the potential in the innovation for *attribution of success to the current senior manager.* Many managers will not undertake a long-term program that will not show results during their tenure. Since people are often paid and rated on the ability they have to get things done, they have to get something done now so that the results can occur in time to show up on their annual performance evaluation.

Present Cost

Another problem, related to success attribution, is that of understanding and communicating the notion of present cost. One aspect of the present cost is that of the total cost of ownership of the technology for some constant period of time, usually 8 or 10 years. Because planning models that require present cost to be computed do not always take into account the bureaucratic problems of the annual budget, it is often difficult to make correct decisions about a technology because of the front-end investment required. Further, when one invests heavily in the front end of something, it takes a while for the investment to begin to pay off. If that pay-off does not come until after the initiator has departed, it is unlikely that that person would be credited for making a good decision.

Technology Transfer

Traditionally, when an organization decided to procure a new system or piece of hardware, the procurement cycle allowed for the delivery of the hardware and the maintenance and operator's manuals at about the same time. Often these technical manuals were written in such obscure language that the buyer was unable to use them. Then the command making the procurement had to arrange for the translation of the technical manuals into a language that could be understood by users. Thus, the transfer of the technology was made in a very inefficient and expensive manner.

More recently, the Army has developed a new approach to the problem called Skill Performance Aids or Integrated Technical Documentation and Training, in which the vendor is required to provide adequate technical documentation and training on the hardware system prior to the time of the final acceptance procedure. Here the purchaser intends to buy planned performance. The vendor is providing a performance capability, not a machine. Thus, the final judgment is based on the actual operational performance, not solely on the characteristics of the hardware. This procurement method is a major breakthrough. The technology-transfer problem is avoided by requiring the application expertise to be provided by the vendor.

SUMMARY

Implementing any kind of new technology — whether it be an ISD process or a hardware system — can be immensely difficult. Although it may not be difficult to achieve initial installation, achieving the integration and institutionalization of the innovation is not at all certain. There are many instances in the literature in which there has been an effective implementation of an innovation on a project basis, only to find the return to the status quo virtually immediate upon the termination of the project status and the dissipation of the project staff.

This chapter has been concerned with trying to draw insights into the change process in large sociobureaucratic systems. Three case studies in ISD were presented in which certain attributes of relative success and failure could be inferred. The Navy and the Army infantry school have been relatively successful in their implementation efforts, in part because they planned ahead, assigned adequate resources, and held competent people accountable for success. The Army signal school has been relatively unsuccessful in the implementation project, principally because of the lack of priority assigned to the internal effort.

Conditions necessary for successful implementation include financial, human, and physical resources, dedication at high organizational levels, availability of the technology, a sound implementation plan with realistic milestones, proper training in the use of the technology, and maintenance of the staff effort as a high-priority item. Careful attention must be paid to clear problem definition, costs and pay-offs, and attribution of success.

If all of these aspects are given consideration and the implementation effort is carefully planned and carried out with dedication at all levels, chances of success are very good. Institutionalization of innovation can never occur if the innovation is not properly implemented.

REFERENCES

Begland, R. R. *U.S. Army Infantry School instructional systems design implementation plan.* Unpublished manuscript, 1977. (Available from Center for Educational Technology, Florida State University)

Branson, R. K., & Rayner, G. T. *Part I: Evaluation of the Trainer Development Program (TRADEP) at the U.S. Army Infantry School; Part II: Workshop in instructional systems development* (NTIS No. AD-A050 482). Ft. Benning, Ga.: U.S. Army Infantry School, June 1977.

Branson, R. K., Rayner, G. T., Cox, J. L., Furman, J. P., King, F. J., & Hannum, W. H. *Interservice procedures for instructional systems development* (5 vols.) (TRADOC Pam 350-30). Ft. Monroe, Va.: U.S. Army Training and Doctrine Command, August 1975. (NTIS Nos. AD-A019 486–AD-A019 490)

Branson, R. K., Stone, J. H., Hannum, W. H., & Rayner, G. T. *Analysis and assessment of the state-of-the-art in instructional technology (Final report: Task I)*. Ft. Benning, Ga.: U.S. Army Combat Arms Training Board, 1973. (NTIS No. AD-A010 394)

Department of the Army. *Final draft (revised): Staffing guide for U.S. Army service schools* (DA Pam 570-558). Washington, D.C.: Headquarters, Department of the Army, August 1976.

Insgroup, Inc. *A recommended design for a Trainer Development Program (TRADEP)*. Orange, Calif.: Author, December 1973.

Montmerlo, M. D., & Tennyson, M. E. *Instructional systems development: Conceptual analysis and comprehensive bibliography* (NAVTRAEQUIPCENIH-257). Orlando, Fla.: Naval Training Equipment Center, February 1976.

Morgan, R. M., & Chadwick, C. B. (Eds.). *Systems analysis for educational change: The Republic of Korea* (Final Report Contract AID/ea-120). Tallahassee: Department of Educational Research, Florida State University, April 1971. (Available from University of Florida Press, Gainesville)

Parkinson, C. N. *Parkinson's law.* New York: Houghton-Mifflin, 1962.

Roberts, W. K. Training Extension Course: A Manhattan project in educational technology. Part II. *JSAS Catalog of Selected Documents in Psychology, 1976, 6* (Ms. No. 1382).

Roberts, W. K. Implementing instructional technology in Army training: Some obstacles and solutions. In *Proceedings of the 19th Annual Conference of the Military Testing Association.* Washington, D.C.: U.S. Government Printing Office, 1978.

Scanland, F. W. Centralized course development. *Educational Technology,* March 1978, *18* (3), 24–26.

Author Index

Numbers in italics refer to the pages on which the complete references are listed.

Subject Index

209